Romantic Periodicals in the Twenty-First Century

Edinburgh Critical Studies in Romanticism
Series Editors: Ian Duncan and Penny Fielding

Available Titles
A Feminine Enlightenment: British Women Writers and the Philosophy of Progress, 1759–1820
JoEllen DeLucia
Reinventing Liberty: Nation, Commerce and the Historical Novel from Walpole to Scott
Fiona Price
The Politics of Romanticism: The Social Contract and Literature
Zoe Beenstock
Radical Romantics: Prophets, Pirates, and the Space Beyond Nation
Talissa J. Ford
Literature and Medicine in the Nineteenth-Century Periodical Press: Blackwood's Edinburgh Magazine, *1817–1858*
Megan Coyer
Discovering the Footsteps of Time: Geological Travel Writing in Scotland, 1700–1820
Tom Furniss
The Dissolution of Character in Late Romanticism
Jonas Cope
Commemorating Peterloo: Violence, Resilience, and Claim-making during the Romantic Era
Michael Demson and Regina Hewitt
Dialectics of Improvement: Scottish Romanticism, 1786–1831
Gerard Lee McKeever
Literary Manuscript Culture in Romantic Britain
Michelle Levy
Scottish Romanticism and Collective Memory in the British Atlantic
Kenneth McNeil
Romantic Periodicals in the Twenty-First Century: Eleven Case Studies from Blackwood's Edinburgh Magazine
Nicholas Mason and Tom Mole

Forthcoming Titles
Romantic Environmental Sensibility: Nature, Class and Empire
Ve-Yin Tee
Romantic Pasts: History, Fiction and Feeling in Britain and Ireland, 1790–1850
Porscha Fermanis
William Godwin and the Bibliographic Imagination
J. Louise McCray

Visit our website at: www.edinburghuniversitypress.com/series/ECSR

Romantic Periodicals in the Twenty-First Century

Eleven Case Studies from
Blackwood's Edinburgh Magazine

Edited by Nicholas Mason and
Tom Mole

EDINBURGH
University Press

Edinburgh University Press is one of the leading university presses in the UK. We publish academic books and journals in our selected subject areas across the humanities and social sciences, combining cutting-edge scholarship with high editorial and production values to produce academic works of lasting importance. For more information visit our website: edinburghuniversitypress.com

© editorial matter and organisation Nicholas Mason and Tom Mole, 2020, 2022
© the chapters their several authors, 2020, 2022

Edinburgh University Press Ltd
The Tun – Holyrood Road, 12(2f) Jackson's Entry, Edinburgh EH8 8PJ

First published in hardback by Edinburgh University Press 2020

Typeset in 11/14 Adobe Sabon by
IDSUK (DataConnection) Ltd,

A CIP record for this book is available from the British Library

ISBN 978 1 4744 4812 3 (hardback)
ISBN 978 1 4744 4813 0 (paperback)
ISBN 978 1 4744 4814 7 (webready PDF)
ISBN 978 1 4744 4815 4 (epub)

The right of Nicholas Mason and Tom Mole to be identified as the Editor of this work has been asserted in accordance with the Copyright, Designs and Patents Act 1988, and the Copyright and Related Rights Regulations 2003 (SI No. 2498).

Contents

Acknowledgements   vii
Contributors   ix

Introduction   1
Nicholas Mason and Tom Mole

Part I. Book History, Bibliography and Archival Method

1. Rethinking the Periodical Medium in the Digital Archive   17
   Jon Klancher

2. Reading Medicine in *Blackwood's*   33
   Megan Coyer

Part II. Aesthetics, Innovation and Taste

3. 'A Separate and Distinct Tribunal': Libel Law and Reviewing in Early Issues of *Blackwood's*   57
   Tom Mole

4. Performing Personae in *Blackwood's* and Romantic Periodicals   76
   Christine Woody

Part III. Reviewing Politics and the Politics of Reviewing

5. Maga as Medium: Cockneys in Context   97
   Mark Parker

6. 'Some Grand Secreter': Secrecy and Exposure in *Blackwood's*   116
   Mark Schoenfield

7. *Blackwood's* Pastoralism and the Highland Clearances   137
   Alexander Dick

Part IV. Gender, Race and Romantic Periodicals

8. Crashing the *Blackwood's* Boys' Club: Caroline Bowles and Women's Place in Romantic-era Periodicals 161
   Nicholas Mason

9. Mary Prince 'At Home' in *Blackwood's*: Maga's Origins and the End of Slavery 183
   Caroline McCracken-Flesher

Part V. Blackwoodian Genealogies

10. The Politics and Aesthetics of Extraction: Cultural Interventions in *Blackwood's* and the *Imperial* 207
    Kristin Flieger Samuelian

11. The Challenge of Longevity: *Blackwood's* as a Post-Romantic Periodical 227
    Joanne Shattock

Bibliography 244
Index 269

Acknowledgements

As periodicals are collective productions, it seems only fitting that those who study them tend to be especially keen on collaboration. Having first worked together on the 2006 edition *Blackwood's Magazine, 1817–25: Selections from Maga's Infancy*, we welcomed the chance to team up again, albeit this time with a significantly broader group of co-investigators. To these colleagues who enthusiastically accepted our invitation to join forces in this endeavour, we offer our deep gratitude. Your friendship, energy, expertise and forbearance in working with two unusually pernickety editors have made this a collaboration to be remembered.

Our earliest discussions about this project came during the two-day *Blackwood's* bicentenary event we organised in July 2017 at the University of Edinburgh's Centre for the History of the Book. This was among the first of what has proven a remarkable series of 'Romantic Bicentennials' facilitated and promoted by Jon Klancher and Jonathan Sachs on behalf of the Keats-Shelley Association of America. Other generous supporters of our 2017 gathering were the Research Society for Victorian Periodicals (thanks, in part, to the advocacy of David Latané and Joanne Shattock), *Studies in Scottish Literature*, the Bibliographical Society (London) and our respective institutions, Brigham Young University (BYU) and the University of Edinburgh.

Among the many individuals who contributed to this volume behind the scenes, some of the most important were the librarians and curators at the National Library of Scotland, who offered ready access and expert insights on the William Blackwood Collection and other holdings in their archives. Special thanks are also due to Penny Fielding, Ian Duncan and Edinburgh University Press's external reviewers for their valuable input and enthusiastic support for our using *Blackwood's* as a focal point for a broader set of arguments about Romantic periodicals.

In later stages, we have especially appreciated the editorial expertise of Scarlett Lindsay and her team at the BYU Faculty Publishing Service and Anya Tchoupakov at the University of Edinburgh, all paragons of reliability, attention to detail and good humour. Ersev Ersoy and her colleagues at Edinburgh University Press have also proven unfailingly helpful, flexible and supportive.

Finally, we are grateful to our families for their sustaining love and support, which no published acknowledgement can sufficiently recognise. Consider this yet another devoted, if perhaps futile, attempt to make you all avid readers of *Blackwood's* and other Romantic periodicals.

Contributors

Megan Coyer is Senior Lecturer in English Literature within the School of Critical Studies at the University of Glasgow, where she is Deputy Director of the Medical Humanities Research Centre. She is the author of *Literature and Medicine in the Nineteenth-Century Periodical Press: Blackwood's Edinburgh Magazine, 1817–1858* (2017) and co-editor of *Scottish Medicine and Literary Culture, 1726–1832* (2014).

Alexander Dick is Associate Professor in the Department of English Language and Literatures at the University of British Columbia. He is the author of *Romanticism and the Gold Standard: Money, Literature, and Economic Debate in Britain 1790–1830* (2013) and numerous articles on eighteenth- and nineteenth-century literature, philosophy and political economy.

Jon Klancher is Professor of Literary and Cultural Studies at Carnegie Mellon University. He is the author of *Transfiguring the Arts and Sciences: Knowledge and Cultural Institutions in the Romantic Age* (2013), *The Making of English Reading Audiences 1790–1832* (1987), and a range of essays on book and periodical histories. He is currently at work on a study of the rhetoric of 'scale' in scientific and literary history, and on a series of linked essays about periodicals and media history, 1700–1900.

Nicholas Mason is Professor of English at Brigham Young University. He served as the general editor and a volume editor for *Blackwood's Magazine 1817–25: Selections from Maga's Infancy* (2006). He has also written on *Blackwood's* and Romantic-era periodicals in various articles and in the book *Literary Advertising and the Shaping of British Romanticism* (2012).

Caroline McCracken-Flesher is Professor of English at the University of Wyoming. She has published widely on Scottish literature, including *Possible Scotlands: Walter Scott and the Story of Tomorrow* (2005) and *The Doctor Dissected: A Cultural Autopsy of the Burke and Hare Murders* (2012).

Tom Mole is Professor of English Literature and Book History, and Director of the Centre for the History of the Book at the University of Edinburgh. He edited one volume of *Blackwood's Magazine 1817–25: Selections from Maga's Infancy* (2006). His book *What the Victorians Made of Romanticism* (2017) won the Saltire Society Research Book of 2018 and the Dorothy Lee Prize, and was commended for the DeLong Prize.

Mark Parker is Professor of English at James Madison University. His publications include *Literary Magazines and British Romanticism* (2001) and a two-volume scholarly edition of Maga's *Noctes Ambrosianae* for *Blackwood's Magazine, 1817–25: Selections from Maga's Infancy* (2006).

Kristin Flieger Samuelian is Associate Professor of English at George Mason University. She is the author of *Royal Romances: Sex, Scandal, and Monarchy in Print, 1780–1821* (2010) as well as articles in *ELH*, *Studies in Romanticism* and other journals and anthologies. Her current book project, 'The Moving Body and the English Romantic Imaginary', is under contract with Routledge.

Mark Schoenfield, co-winner of the Colby Prize for *British Periodicals and Romantic Identity* (2009), is Professor of English at Vanderbilt University. In addition to working on periodicals, he writes on law and literature during the Romantic era.

Joanne Shattock is Emeritus Professor of Victorian Literature at the University of Leicester. Her research focuses on the nineteenth-century periodical press, and on Victorian women writers. Her recent publications include *Journalism and the Periodical Press in Nineteenth-Century Britain* (2017). She is the general editor, with Elisabeth Jay, of a twenty-five-volume edition of the *Selected Works of Margaret Oliphant* (2011–16).

Christine Woody received her doctorate in English Literature from the University of Pennsylvania and is Assistant Professor at Widener University. Her recent work on Romantic print culture can be found in *Essays in Romanticism* (2018) and the *Keats-Shelley Journal* (2017).

Introduction

Nicholas Mason and Tom Mole

Using and Abusing Romantic Periodicals

In introducing the 'Romantic Age' volume of his four-part encyclopaedia of *British Literary Magazines* (1983–6), Alvin Sullivan, himself a specialist in British modernism, remarked that 'every artistic movement has some advocate in print, but the Romantic movement was embraced by more journals, reviews, and miscellanies than any other'.[1] To no small degree, the phenomenon Sullivan identifies was a product of Romanticism's emerging at an especially vibrant moment in British media history. The half-century between the outbreak of the French Revolution and the coronation of Queen Victoria witnessed the arrival of still-iconic dailies like *The Times* (1785–) and *The Guardian* (1821–); the twin 'monarch-makers in poetry and prose', as Byron dubbed them, the *Edinburgh Review* (1802–1929) and the *Quarterly Review* (1809–1962);[2] and *Blackwood's Edinburgh Magazine* (*BEM*, 1817–1980), the upstart literary, cultural and political miscellany that not only inspired countless nineteenth-century imitators but created a blueprint still found in highbrow magazines like *The New Yorker* and *The Spectator*.

Rather than standing idly by as this new wave of dailies, monthlies and quarterlies shaped nineteenth-century tastes, eminent authors including Mary Robinson, Walter Scott, Robert Southey, Lord Byron, Letitia Landon and Felicia Hemans frequently took to the periodical press both to publish their writing and to critique that of others. Writers best known as poets, novelists or essayists would compose several of the age's most prescient reviews, including Scott's of *Emma* and *Frankenstein*, Leigh Hunt's of Keats's *Poems* of 1817 and William Hazlitt's of *The Excursion*.³ Meanwhile, many texts that later became canonical, ranging from 'Ode on a Grecian Urn' to *Confessions of an English Opium Eater* to 'Casabianca', were originally addressed to readers of literary magazines.⁴ Some leading authors in the period even set about founding their own periodicals, including Samuel Taylor Coleridge (*The Watchman* [1796] and *The Friend* [1809–10]), James Hogg (*The Spy* [1810–11]), Hunt (*The Examiner* [1808–81]) and Byron and Percy Shelley (*The Liberal*, with Hunt [1822–3]).

Writing for literary periodicals, or being written about in them, fuelled what Lucy Newlyn has identified as an acute 'anxiety of reception' among the era's writers. 'The demonization of reviewers by authors – and particularly by poets', she notes, 'was in some cases well founded; but paranoia was so widespread as to appear almost indiscriminate.'⁵ A fed-up Byron, for instance, once pointedly instructed his publisher, John Murray, to 'send me *no periodical works* whatsoever'.⁶ Similarly vexed, Coleridge devoted his third chapter of *Biographia Literaria* to railing against reviewers who had subjected him to 'so merciless and long-continued a cannonading'.⁷ Meanwhile, Coleridge's fellow Lake Poets, Southey and Wordsworth, took such umbrage over *Blackwood's* jests at their expense that, despite the magazine's sharing their conservative values and widely lauding them elsewhere, both flatly rejected entreaties to contribute to it.⁸ So thin-skinned, in fact, was Wordsworth, that his sister-in-law Sara Hutchinson reported in July 1819, 'We females have a great curiosity to see the Reviews &c of Wm's poems &c in *Blackwood's Magazine*; but as Wm will not suffer it to come into the house with his knowledge *we must smuggle it*.'⁹

Avoid literary periodicals as he might, though, Wordsworth regularly heeded his critics when revising. After several reviewers mocked his depiction of the 'little muddy pond' in 'The Thorn', he converted a passage where the narrator 'measured it from side to side: / 'Tis three feet long, and two feet wide' into a more 'poetical' description of the pond's being 'of compass small, and bare / To thirsty suns and parching air'.¹⁰ Similar cases of the anxiety of reception can be observed in Keats's withholding 'Isabella; or, The Pot of Basil' over fears it represented 'what I should call were I a reviewer "A weak-sided Poem"' and Hunt scrubbing the second edition of *The Story of Rimini* to remove the 'jaunty', 'newfangled' coinages (e.g., 'clipsome', 'quoit-like', 'passion-plighted') that *Blackwood's* and others had found so ridiculous.¹¹

Towards a Subfield of Romantic Periodical Studies

Yet, however large periodicals may have loomed in the consciousnesses of the era's writers and readers, they have never occupied more than a marginal place in the academic study of the Romantic period. While the *Edinburgh*, the *Quarterly* and, especially, *Blackwood's* have long attracted coteries of enthusiasts, it was only relatively recently that Romantic periodicals began to be treated as an object of study in their own right. During the 1960s and 1970s, John O. Hayden and Donald H. Reiman laid important groundwork for understanding the age's reviewing culture.¹² In many respects, though, the standard-bearer for fully utilising the era's periodical riches was Jon Klancher's *The Making of English Reading Audiences: 1790–1832* (1987), which its author revisits in this collection's lead chapter. Klancher's deep dive into a cross-section of Romantic periodicals allowed him to offer the most sophisticated analysis to date of such phenomena as 'mass experience' and the 'public sphere' in late eighteenth- and early nineteenth-century England.¹³ Thirteen years later, Mark Parker's equally path-breaking book, *Literary Magazines and British Romanticism* (2000), unabashedly anointed the magazine 'the preeminent literary form of the 1820s and 1830s in Britain' and supported this assertion with insightful readings of 'runs' of *Blackwood's*, *Fraser's*, the *London* and the *New Monthly Magazine*.¹⁴ In the wake of Klancher's and Parker's pioneering work, essay collections on the *Edinburgh Review* and *Blackwood's* and important monographs by David Higgins (2005), Mark Schoenfield (2009), William Christie (2009), Karen Fang (2010), Richard Cronin (2010), David Stewart (2011), Kim Wheatley (2013) and Megan Coyer (2017) have done much to reveal the richness and diversity of the age's periodicals.¹⁵

Partly because of such studies, today's specialists in the Romantic period will likely be able to list the era's leading literary periodicals and, if pressed, recall the basics of especially notorious hatchet-jobs like Jeffrey's eviscerations of Wordsworth in the *Edinburgh* or Croker's 'mansplaining' to Barbauld in the *Quarterly*. Yet, the era's landmark periodicals remain largely an afterthought in most major classroom anthologies and scholarly monographs. The general slowness among Romanticists to develop their own distinctive approaches to periodical studies is all the more puzzling in light of the ongoing boom in periodicals research in adjacent literary periods. Even before the recent windfall of digitised content, Victorianists had built a robust infrastructure for studying their era's periodicals. Upon completing the monumental *Wellesley Index of Victorian Periodicals* in 1968, its lead contributors used the momentum from that undertaking to launch the Research Society for Victorian Periodicals and its house publication, *Victorian Periodicals Newsletter* (renamed *Victorian Periodicals Review* in 1978).[16] Fifty years later, RSVP and VPR remain major presences in Victorian Studies, offering prominent platforms for scholarship in the field and, thanks to bequests from founding members, generous research awards for periodical scholars at all career stages.

While no match for the industrious Victorianists, Romanticists' next-door neighbours on the other side – specialists in eighteenth-century literature and culture – have also made significant efforts in this area – and arguably while working with less promising materials. Classic essays from *The Spectator*, *Tatler* and *Rambler* enjoy a place in the eighteenth-century literary canon unmatched by their Romantic-era counterparts and, correspondingly, have attracted considerably more scholarly attention than comparable essays by the likes of Cobbett, Hazlitt, Hunt and Lamb. Moreover, in both print and the classroom, scholars of the eighteenth century have typically laid much greater emphasis on their era's having invented the modern book review than Romanticists have on theirs transforming it into a distinctive branch of the literary arts.[17]

These efforts by scholars in neighbouring historical periods risk squeezing Romantic periodicals from both sides and marginalising or altogether eliding them from the historical narrative. One seeming indicator of this risk is the new *Routledge Handbook to Nineteenth-Century British Periodicals and Newspapers* (2016). In their introduction to this otherwise impressive reference companion, the editors defend their decision to take the entire century rather than just the Victorian period as their subject by arguing that, 'while the idea of Romantic and Victorian periodization helps to define academic fields of inquiry . . ., newspaper and periodicals scholarship has rightly become more attentive to the nineteenth century as a whole'.[18] This fails to explain, however, why not a single specialist in the Romantic period is to be found among the volume's thirty-two contributors. Nor does it account for the tendency throughout the volume to give short shrift to the century's first three decades. As a case in point, William Gifford, the *Quarterly*'s equally feared and revered editor from its 1809 founding until 1824, gets but a single mention in this nearly-500-page collection, and that for his earlier contributions to the *Anti-Jacobin Review*. His successor, John Gibson Lockhart, who prior to his 28-year editorship at the *Quarterly* (1825–53) had helped launch *Blackwood's* and penned many of its landmark essays, reviews and satires, also receives only one mention, as do William Jerdan (the 'discoverer' of Letitia Landon and widely courted editor of the *Literary Gazette*), John Hunt (the co-founder of *The Examiner* and driving force behind several other progressive journals), John Wilson (*Blackwood's* legendary 'Christopher North') and several other titans of Romantic-era periodicals.

The *Routledge Handbook* is far from unusual, though, in purporting to cover the entire century while, in fact, disproportionately emphasising its final seven decades. The thousand-page *Dictionary of Nineteenth-Century Journalism* (2009) was overseen by a seventeen-person editorial board that included just one Romanticist. Cambridge University Press's new collection, *Journalism and the Periodical Press in Nineteenth-Century Britain* (2017), offers a similar ratio, with a sole Romanticist among its twenty-three contributors. Most recently, Edinburgh University Press's ambitious five-part series, 'History of Women's Periodical Culture in Britain', partitions Romanticism between volumes on 'The Long Eighteenth Century' and 'The Victorian Period', rendering it the only period of modern literary history undeserving of a stand-alone volume.[19]

This growing vogue for 'long' literary periods – a trend often justified less by rigorous and reasoned intellectual debate than by the collapsing of book series and consolidation of faculty lines – is one key context for this collection's attempt to begin restaking the Romantic period's claim as a distinct and unusually dynamic moment in the history of British literary periodicals. Another incitement, this one more welcome, is an exciting series of cultural, theoretical and methodological developments that have revolutionised humanistic studies. The project of creating a more inclusive canon that began with recovering women authors has now extended to writers of diverse ethnic, racial and economic backgrounds, yielding an account of the Romantic period that is socially deeper, geographically broader and more racially representative. This emphasis on greater inclusivity has also sparked efforts to reframe the Romantic period as more than just a golden age for poetry. Accordingly, Romanticists have revisited a broad range of marginalised forms and genres, including drama, non-fiction prose, and album, manuscript and occasional verses. An invigorated subfield of Romantic periodical studies might therefore benefit from and contribute to these theoretical and historiographical developments, as the era's serials were crucial vehicles for foregrounding women's writing and non-fiction prose, mediating European literature for British audiences and shaping domestic understandings of the nation's place in a wider world.

Perhaps the greatest impetus, however, for integrating Romantic-era periodicals more systematically into our research and teaching is the emergence of digital tools that afford twenty-first-century scholars unprecedented access to historical newspapers, magazines and journals. Full-text databases, many of them free, now enable anyone with a basic Internet connection to explore a wealth of periodicals previously available only to those with the time and resources to visit major research libraries. Along with the rapid expansion of digitised texts, advances in optical character recognition (OCR) and search functionality have transformed the types of questions we can answer via periodical research. As Klancher recounts elsewhere in this volume, until recently, those interested in using periodicals were restricted to scrolling through microfilm, browsing bound volumes shelved in the library's stacks or requesting specific titles archived in special collections. In contrast, scholars today routinely begin with keyword searches that yield results from extensive historical spans and hundreds of periodicals at once.

Fully capitalising on this archival windfall will require reconceptualising the basic methods of literary research, retraining ourselves and our students to devise projects that are at once more ambitious in their historical and conceptual reach and more sophisticated in their use of archival evidence. To date, many of the boldest efforts in this regard have taken the form of 'distant' or computer-assisted readings. Pioneers in this area, such as Franco Moretti, Stephen Ramsay, Matthew Jockers, Ted Underwood and Andrew Piper, have modelled how quantitative, statistical and computational surveys of thousands of literary texts might offer compelling new perspectives on literary history. Although largely excluded from such projects to date, literary periodicals would seem an ideal corpus for distant reading, as structured searches might reveal patterns previously hidden from the individual scholar who will never be able to read, let alone remember, more than a fraction of an era's periodical literature over the course of a career. Modern digital tools consequently allow us not only to find new answers for old scholarly questions but, even more excitingly, to ask questions we might never before have entertained.[20]

Blackwood's: Exceptional, but Representative

Without its emphasis on quantitative data and computational method, this collection shares distant reading's interest in modelling how a deeper, more sustained engagement with the newly remediated print archive can yield fresh insights into and, in some cases, revised narratives surrounding literary and cultural history. Aiming to emphasise the distinctiveness of Romantic serials as a whole while nevertheless maintaining a shared focus, we tasked eleven established scholars of early nineteenth-century periodicals (including ourselves) to provide case studies of how a single literary monthly, *Blackwood's Edinburgh Magazine*, supplies a trove of informed, engaging and sometimes jaw-droppingly-rendered perspectives on diverse topics currently at the forefront of studies of the Romantic period. With *Blackwood's* as our common object of study, contributors were encouraged to emphasise features of the magazine that speak to broader patterns in the era's periodicals. The chapters to follow should therefore be read both as finished scholarly products and exploratory shafts sunk into a largely uncharted mine that, if successful, will hopefully inspire future probes both of *Blackwood's* and the broader archive of Romantic literary periodicals.

Besides the editors' long-time fascination with *Blackwood's*, we have made it this collection's unifying focus because it is at once exceptional and not altogether unrepresentative of Romantic literary periodicals as a whole. The oft-told tale of *Blackwood's* arrival on the literary scene generally begins in April 1817, when the ambitious Edinburgh publisher William Blackwood launched the *Edinburgh*

Monthly Magazine with the intent of burnishing his brand, checking the influence of the politically progressive *Edinburgh Review* and offering intellectually minded conservatives an alternative to the frequently stultifying *Quarterly Review*. Before the second issue had gone to press, however, tensions flared up between the publisher and his editors, James Cleghorn and Thomas Pringle, over Blackwood's regular interference and his complaints that the magazine was neither as lively nor as Tory as he had envisioned. By June the relationship had become sufficiently acrimonious that all parties agreed to part ways after six issues.[21]

Accordingly, in October 1817, Blackwood took firmer control of the magazine, installing himself as editor-in-chief, rechristening it *Blackwood's Edinburgh Magazine* and hiring John Wilson and John Gibson Lockhart – two young, Tory, and Oxford-educated Scots determined on avoiding the legal careers for which they had trained – as his lead writers and de facto co-editors. Rather than consigning the magazine's forerunner to oblivion, however, the publisher released the first instalment of *Blackwood's* as 'no. 7'. This decision has ever since left researchers unsure whether the six issues of the *Edinburgh Monthly Magazine* belong to the *Blackwood's* corpus. And, more recently, it has resulted in full-text databases occasionally archiving the magazine's entire run under its short-lived original title rather than the revised title it would retain until it ceased operations in 1980.

The October 1817 debut issue of William Blackwood's rechristened monthly left no question about its principals' intent to establish an entirely new breed of literary magazine. As its opening salvo, Wilson anonymously decimated his fellow 'Lake Poet' Coleridge, thundering, 'We cannot see in what the state of literature would have been different, had he been cut off in childhood, or had he never been born.'[22] The cudgel then passed to Lockhart, who donned the mask of 'Z.' in the first of what would prove a series of Blackwoodian muggings of the 'Cockney School of Poetry'. Fully in character from the start, 'Z.' casts the Cockneys' 'chief Doctor and Professor', Leigh Hunt, as 'a man certainly of some talents' but 'of extravagant pretensions both in wit, poetry, and politics, and withal of exquisitely bad taste, and extremely vulgar modes of thinking and manners'.[23] Yet the article that provoked by far the greatest outcry was the issue-ending 'Translation of an Ancient Chaldee Manuscript'. Collaboratively penned by Hogg, Wilson and Lockhart, this biblically styled 'translation' of a manuscript said to have lately been discovered 'in the great Library of Paris', conspicuously and mercilessly parodied the appearances, reputations and intellects of key members of Edinburgh's Whig establishment.[24] Within days of this 'blasphemous' and 'libellous' lampoon's release, the publisher was deluged by letters of commendation and complaint, the latter often insinuating potential legal action. His subsequent decision to issue a second printing that replaced the 'Chaldee Manuscript' with gentler satirical fare – albeit still focused on liberal figures and causes – only further incited nationwide interest in and debate over the rebranded Scottish monthly.

Far from doubt-ridden over his magazine's new course, William Blackwood allegedly rushed home with a copy and, bursting through the door, declared to his wife in a broad Scottish accent, 'There's ma Maga-zine!'[25] This anecdote quickly led to *Blackwood's* being nicknamed 'Maga', an appellation used ever since interchangeably with its given title in both popular and scholarly discourse. Embracing both the Maga nickname and the notoriety attending the 'Cockney' and 'Chaldee' controversies, *Blackwood's* developed a penchant for self-mythologising that included comically outsized claims about its circulation and influence. Readers of the March 1818 issue, for instance, were told how, when the release date for each new number of *Blackwood's* drew nigh, 'one breathless hush expectant reigns from shore to shore'.[26] On the occasion of its third anniversary, the magazine crowed, 'Our sale is prodigious – and we are absolutely coining money.'[27] This blustering house style routinely veered into boisterous, and sometimes bullying, excess. Especially in the rightfully famous *Noctes Ambrosianae* – the simultaneously boozy and brilliant fictionalised dialogues set in Edinburgh's Ambrose's Tavern – the magazine's regulars showcased both their vast learning, wit and taste and their habitual gastronomic and rhetorical overindulgence.

The spectacle of this boisterous pugnacity has tended to overshadow the ground-breaking fiction, verse and criticism and learned political, social and scientific commentary that kept *Blackwood's* at the forefront of British periodicals for decades to come. Often lost in the sound-bites over its supposedly 'killing Keats' or, as Macvey Napier charged in 1818, contaminating Britain with 'unquestionably the vilest production that ever disfigured and soiled the annals of literature' is Maga's spirited defense of Wordsworth in response to Jeffrey's ongoing attacks in the *Edinburgh Review*, commissioning of the first serious essay on *Frankenstein*, pioneering efforts in serialised fiction and 'tales of terror', and broadminded championing of women writers and the best new voices in Continental and American literature.[28]

Between these genuine accomplishments and the magazine's more nefarious early crusades, the first twenty volumes (or ten years) of *Blackwood's* offer an ideal, if admittedly circumscribed, laboratory for exploring the range of uses twenty-first-century scholars might make of Romantic-era periodicals. To highlight such varied approaches, we have organised this volume's eleven chapters into five sections. Part I, 'Book History, Bibliography and Archival Method', begins with Klancher's aforementioned retrospective on the researching and writing of *The Making of English Reading Audiences*, which ends with a series of astute insights into what scholars have gained and lost in browsing and searching periodicals in digital databases rather than their original print formats. Klancher's chapter is followed by a second largely methodological and retrospective essay in which, having recently published her new monograph on *Literature and Medicine in the Nineteenth-Century Periodical Press*, Megan Coyer provides something of a masterclass for scholars of early nineteenth-century science and medicine on navigating the vast archive of medical discourse in *Blackwood's* and other Romantic-era periodicals.

Part II, 'Aesthetics, Innovation and Taste', includes a pair of essays employing J. L. Austin's concept of performative utterances to analyse periodical writing. Tom Mole examines the role libel law played in shaping *Blackwood's* conception of book reviewing and the kind of cultural authority it and its imitators aspired to exercise. Christine Woody then considers the performance of identity in Maga and the conditions in which a performed identity could be accepted by the readership.

Part III, 'Reviewing Politics and the Politics of Reviewing', begins with Mark Parker revisiting the Cockney School attacks in the context of their satirical inheritance and the medium of the literary magazine. Mark Schoenfield then analyses discourses of secrecy and exposure in Maga, examining how the construction of a secret world that was nonetheless glimpsed by readers in the know was central to its audience-shaping rhetoric. Alex Dick concludes this section with a chapter that shows how the discourse of 'pastoralism' allowed

Blackwood's to process the traumatic events of the Highland Clearances into literary conventions.

Part IV, 'Gender, Race and Romantic Periodicals', opens with Nicholas Mason's analysis of how William Blackwood's avid recruitment of Caroline Bowles – including encouraging her to submit uproarious satires like the Cockney-baiting 'Letter from a Washerwoman' – undercuts traditional narratives about the opportunities and genres available to women writers in *Blackwood's* and Romantic periodicals more generally. While similarly interested in the gender politics of the era's periodicals, Caroline McCracken-Flesher's chapter on Maga's pivotal role in the debates attending the 1831 publication of *The History of Mary Prince, a West Indian Slave* also interrogates how magazines functioned as a key proving ground for late-Romantic theories of race, empire and 'proper' feminine domesticity.

In Part V, 'Blackwoodian Genealogies', Kristin Flieger Samuelian compares the use of extraction – the selection, excerpting and repurposing of passages from other texts – as a mode of exercising cultural authority in *Blackwood's* and the evangelical *Imperial Magazine*. Joanne Shattock then concludes the volume by using a wide-angle lens to assess how *Blackwood's* met the challenge of longevity by repeatedly reinventing itself over the course of the Victorian age. This final chapter therefore not only models the insights to be gained through the diachronic study of a particular serial but also subtly reinforces the need, given the rapidly morphing audiences, formats and economics of nineteenth-century periodicals, for Romanticists to develop the tools, methodologies and theories needed for taking full advantage of their period's still largely unexplored archive of ground-breaking literary periodicals.

Notes

1. Sullivan, 'Preface', p. viii.
2. *Lord Byron's Letters and Journals*, vol. 3, p. 209.
3. [Scott], review of *Emma* and review of *Frankenstein*; [Hunt], review of *Poems*; [Hazlitt], review of *The Excursion*.
4. [Keats], 'On a Grecian Urn'; [De Quincey], 'Confessions of an English Opium-Eater'; [Hemans], 'Casabianca'.

5. Newlyn, *Reading, Writing, and Romanticism*, p. 35.
6. *Lord Byron's Letters and Journals*, vol. 8, p. 219.
7. *Biographia Literaria*, p. 50.
8. For Southey's aversion to *Blackwood's*, see pages 167–72 below; for Wordsworth's, see Mason, *Blackwood's Magazine 1817–25*, vol. 1, pp. 69–70.
9. Hutchinson to Thomas Monkhouse, 25 July 1819, in *Letters*, p. 157.
10. Wordsworth, 'The Thorn', in *Lyrical Ballads*, p. 78.
11. John Keats to Richard Woodhouse, 21–22 September 1819, in Gittings (ed.), *Letters*, p. 298.
12. See especially Hayden's *The Romantic Reviewers, 1802–1824* and Reiman's nine-volume *The Romantics Reviewed*.
13. Klancher, *The Making*.
14. Parker, *Literary Magazines*, p. 1.
15. Important essay collections include Wheatley (ed.), *Romantic Periodicals*; Demata and Wu (eds), *British Romanticism*; Finkelstein (ed.), *Print Culture*; Morrison and Roberts, *Romanticism*; and the special issue of *Romanticism* (vol. 23, October 2017) that Morrison edited on the occasion of *Blackwood's* two-hundredth anniversary.
16. Distad, 'Origins and History'.
17. Powell's essay, 'New Directions in Eighteenth-Century Periodical Studies', suggests both the degree to which eighteenth-century scholars have outpaced Romanticists in their attention to literary periodicals and how they, too, envy the relatively advanced state of Victorian periodical studies.
18. King et al., *Routledge Handbook*, p. 3.
19. That Romanticists can be equally susceptible to the boundary-eliding logic of the 'long eighteenth century' is evident in Denise Gigante's important anthology *The Great Age of the English Essay* (2008), which moves from *The Tatler* (founded in 1709) to *The London Magazine* (founded in 1820) without acknowledging a period break.
20. It bears noting that the initial widespread enthusiasm for big-data methods that attended the release of Moretti's *Distant Reading* (2013) and its equally acclaimed forerunner, *Graphs, Maps, Trees* (2007), may be ebbing. Prominent critiques of distant reading include Brennan's polemic on 'The Digital-Humanities Bust', Da's interrogation of the general utility and statistical integrity of computational literary analysis ('The Computational Case') and Allington, Brouillette and Golumbia's surmises about the links between the celebration of digital humanities research and 'the neoliberal takeover of the university' ('Neoliberal Tools').
21. At various points, Blackwood, Hogg and its original editors, Pringle and Cleghorn, claimed credit for first proposing the *Edinburgh*

Monthly Magazine (*EMM*). For more detailed accounts of the founding of the *EMM* and *BEM*, see Oliphant, *Annals*, vol. 1; ch. 2 of Tredrey, *The House of Blackwood*; Finkelstein's introduction to *Print Culture*; and Mason's general introduction in the first volume of *Blackwood's Magazine*.
22. [Wilson], 'Observations', p. 6.
23. [Lockhart], 'On the Cockney School', No. I, p. 38.
24. [Hogg et al.], 'Translation', p. 89.
25. Tredrey, *House of Blackwood*, p. 51.
26. [Hamilton], 'To the Publisher'.
27. Wilson, 'An Hour's', p. 80.
28. Napier, *Hypocrisy Unveiled*, pp. 5–6. Annotated versions of many of the most original and impactful texts from Maga's first nine years can be found in Mason et al. (eds), *Blackwood's Magazine*. Volume 1 features verse, volume 2 prose fiction and non-fiction, volumes 3 and 4 the first twenty-three 'Noctes', and volumes 5 and 6 selected literary criticism. For a selection of 'Tales of Terror' from early *Blackwood's*, see Morrison and Baldick's Oxford World's Classics edition.

Part I

Book History, Bibliography and Archival Method

Chapter 1

Rethinking the Periodical Medium in the Digital Archive

Jon Klancher

When we go online today, we are invited to 'browse' and to 'search' as we gain access to millions of documents long available only in print archives or rare book rooms. Our field's major databases, from *Eighteenth Century Collections Online* (ECCO) to *Google Books*, were designed largely to retrieve books and make them electronically navigable. Periodicals are a distinctive case, however. In this essay I will examine the special conditions of doing periodical research online, where the original print medium turns out to have quite a different relation to digital processes than do books, and where the digital archive both improves on and in some ways proves inferior to the all-print archive of the past. In what follows, I will attend to the powers of digital search while raising questions about browsing and other approaches to investigating a vast array of print resources like periodicals. More broadly I will ask: what does the digital moment tell us about the medium of the periodical that wasn't as visible when we relied on print collections?

Over the past 20 years, the literary magazine from *Blackwood's* in 1817 to *Fraser's Magazine* in 1830 has been more intensively studied than any other kind of periodical from the Romantic age.[1] I will therefore use *Blackwood's* as a touchstone for a discussion of methods for researching periodicals old and new. At the same time, I aim to raise wider questions about the periodical medium that require a broader exploration of digital databases and formats beyond the scope of the literary magazine. To that end, I will compare my experiences working in the print archive on a range of periodical genres – as I did when researching *The Making of English Reading Audiences* (1987) – with working in the digital archive now.[2]

We speak of the digital's great capacity for search, but the ability to browse is at least as important to periodical study. Thumbing through a periodical – finding pages and articles in any order – is not incidental to its uniqueness and cultural importance. In the larger print libraries, substantial runs of journals like *Blackwood's* were often shelved within their circulating collections, like the one at UCLA where I began my research for *The Making of English Reading Audiences*. At a time when few scholars were reading Romantic periodicals, this ease of access allowed me to browse widely in different kinds of serials and form comparative judgements on their formats, rhetorics and possible readerships. It's a good question whether we can perform similarly productive browsing in the periodicals archive online. As bound volumes of early periodicals are increasingly stored away and thereby made unavailable for browsing, we have to rely more on databases that have only hit-and-miss browsing capabilities in their current state. Likewise, searches are subject to special conditions within given databases and with the time-sensitive periodical medium that distinguish them from searches we might perform with books.

What we encounter in the databases does, however, instruct us about the history of the periodical medium. When, subsequent to the release of serial issues, publishers of periodicals edited six months' or a year's worth of weekly, monthly or quarterly numbers into bound volumes – an established practice by 1700 – they set a pattern that persists into the digital archive: our databases reproduce those bound volumes rather than the circulating single issues readers first encountered. Digitised periodicals also make it clearer what was lost by turning issues into volumes, such as wrappers and pages of advertising or other paratexts. We might well ask, as I will at the end of this essay, whether it is possible to recover surviving single issues to be studied by scholars, and how we might use them to restore digitally the periodical's full existence as a medium in history. Here, the differing scales of the original issue, the bound volume and the digital archive will intersect as a problem of preserving cultural memory in Romantic-age periodicals in both their historical and current mediatic modes.

Earlier promises of a seamless universal library of digital texts have not materialised to date. We have instead, as Anthony Grafton predicted a decade ago, 'a patchwork of different interfaces and databases'.[3] Those specifically dedicated to periodicals, like ProQuest's

British Periodicals, offer more immediate access to journals than those designed for books, and they encourage more journal-focused searches. There is an equally important difference between what I will call 'volume-centred' databases and those that are 'article-centred'. With the first, we encounter digital surrogates for the same bound volumes we studied in the print archive, such as those periodicals included in *ECCO, HathiTrust Digital Library* and *Google Books*. But some databases have been built by extracting individual articles from bound volumes and arranging them to approximate single issues, such as *British Periodicals* and EBSCO's *American Antiquarian Society Historical Periodicals*. The difference between these types is far more than technical, since it speaks to the peculiar character of periodicals as a medium. Neither part of a book nor simply a stack of articles, the periodical issue is a collection in which texts and visual elements produce a whole that is more than the sum of its parts. This surplus is integral to the medium and it is what the databases have difficulty representing in digital form, even while they afford us a substantially greater range of periodicals to study as a corpus.

Corpus in the Print Archive and the Digital

When I began researching *The Making of English Reading Audiences* in 1977, there had been little post-war interest in the Romantic-era periodical (nor was there a field called 'history of the book' nor talk of 'print culture').[4] Thus, one purpose of the book was to provide a cultural map of the territory, drawing on early periodical studies like Walter Graham's of the 1930s and more recent cultural histories by E. P. Thompson, Raymond Williams and Jürgen Habermas.[5] But the largest requirement for my project was an ample, diverse and accessible collection of journals. My initial corpus was made up primarily of UCLA's open-shelf collection of over thirty periodicals published from 1790 to 1832, along with titles I studied at the Clark and Huntington libraries and, at a later stage of revision, the British Library (then housed within the British Museum). With a working corpus of some fifty periodical titles altogether, I enjoyed extensive browsing capacity, both among and within those volumes, giving me uninterrupted access to the primary works. I ultimately drew upon my research in this print corpus between 1977 and 1985 to make the case that the periodical was a print medium with unique capacities to organise audiences and develop both durable and changing relationships with readers.

While it was necessary then, my effort to span the Romantic age as a whole also came at a cost, as Robert Morrison and Daniel Sanjiv Roberts have more recently noticed in calling my perspective an 'aerial view of the field' that could tend to make a periodical appear more unified than in practice it was.[6] Thus, *The Making of English Reading Audiences* has been criticised for neglecting the 'run', or sequence of issues and volumes within a single title, such as *Blackwood's* from 1817 to 1825, an era in the magazine's history very different from its career after 1825 (when it became less evidently literary and 'Romantic').[7] When *Blackwood's* scholars focus on the 'Romantic literary magazine', for instance, the magazine's changes over time have become important for grasping the magazine's intricate complexity in relation to Romantic literary culture of the late Regency and early 1820s. The closer-up the study, the more the 'run' can matter as a key category of analysis.

Yet the need to attend closely to the 'run' should also be compatible today with an effort to embrace a wider span of periodical designs and formats across the Romantic age. The newly expanded corpus available in the digital archive alone suggests this direction for research. A single database today can offer at least three or four times the number of Romantic-age print titles I was able to consult around 1980. *British Periodicals* includes 491 journals published between 1680 and 1940, of which 136 appeared sometime during the Romantic age; a good many more can be located on *HathiTrust* or *Google Books*. Another dedicated database, Adam Matthew's *Eighteenth Century Journals*, provides an array of rarer pre-1800 journals, especially those written by or for women. It goes well beyond the scope of periodical titles one can find on the leading eighteenth-century database ECCO, and its extensive runs of the *Lady's Magazine* (1770–1818) and other such journals often extend through the Romantic age.[8] Taken together, the corpus provided by the six databases I have studied for this essay far surpasses what one could find before in any number of print archives.

Navigating such archives, print or digital, has always required bibliographical controls. For print research, that has meant using indexes and 'finding lists' from the original *Poole's Index to Periodical Literature* (1882) to the more recent *Wellesley Index of Victorian Periodicals*

(1966–89). Perhaps the most useful bibliographical control for my early project proved to be William Ward's *Finding List of Serials in the British Isles, 1789–1832* (1953), a work that gives the titles, formats and archive locations of over 4,000 newspapers and periodicals.[9] In 1977, it gave me an initial map of Britain's print universe, and it was the only finding list that accounted for some of the rarer, short-lived periodicals I came across in the print collections. The digital counterpart of these earlier print indexes is *C19: The Nineteenth Century Index* (ProQuest). This spacious database has bundled the older indexes into a searchable union catalogue that also includes the Nineteenth-Century Short Title List. But it's no longer clear that such indexes, print or digital, are still necessary. Where the print indexes once stood separately from the archive to portray its article contents, the databases build such bibliographical controls into their interfaces. Search terms can outperform any print index, while metadata – to the extent we can rely on it – can describe articles, volumes or publications; perhaps only identifying authorship still requires *C19* or the *Wellesley Index*. Even granting that true 'bibliographical control' will never be achieved over so vast a domain as periodicals, the databases significantly increase its reach.

Moving between digital databases is not like migrating between print archives. Despite important differences in the way libraries work and foster access to print, such as whether they allow open-stacks browsing or instead keep volumes in a rare book room, a set of *Blackwood's* will largely read the same way in all of them.[10] Not so with databases, which require one to learn distinct browse and search protocols for each. This is especially the case when one moves between a volume-centred database like *HathiTrust* to article-based ones like *AAS Historical Periodicals* and *British Periodicals*. The latter method breaks weekly, monthly and quarterly numbers out of their bound volumes and arranges their articles in separate files. This approach follows the methods of database design by dividing volumes into the smallest possible units, processing them as articles, front or back matter, or recurring features like *Blackwood's* 'Register – Meteorological Conditions'. As digitised by the American Antiquarian Society, *AAS Historical Periodicals* serves up each issue in an orderly sequence from contents page and front matter to final page and back matter (excluding, of course, the wrappers and advertising, which were sheared off in making the original bound volumes from which these issues come). The result is a precise digital version of each set of articles for each issue.[11]

But when *British Periodicals* pioneered the article-centred approach in 2006, ProQuest used UMI microfilms rather than its own digitising as a basis for reconstructing issues and articles. Perhaps taking database design principles a step too far, ProQuest effectively disordered each issue by putting only articles first, then an odd jumble of both front and back-matter last. The result is that one encounters not even the simulacrum of a periodical issue, but rather a list of articles and a miscellaneous assortment of other pages, most likely because ProQuest was relying on the model of the modern technical or medical-scientific journal. This is a highly problematic strategy for a humanities journal, however, as almost any thorough study of the periodical as a medium will want to pay close attention to just the kinds of front and back matter that *British Periodicals* relegates to afterthoughts.

Browse: Volume, Article, Page

More than any other print format popularised since 1700, the periodical asks us to browse. Finding lists and indexes can lead us to articles, but the more characteristic pleasure – and path of discovery – is browsing in order to come across the article, the passage, the illustration or the visually striking page. When I began *The Making of English Reading Audiences*, I hunted less often for articles than for textual passages that might stand out on a range of topics; based on my training in close reading and an informal rhetorical education I'd learned from reading classical philological works in the vein of Erich Auerbach's *Literary Language and Its Public in the Late Middle Ages* (1965), I was looking for characteristic rhetorics that might be mapped onto contrasting Romantic-period styles like De Quincey's and Hazlitt's or Burke's and Godwin's. Soon, the project began to refocus on the ways the periodical medium could be used to form readerships, but analysing passages within articles remained a key textual method. Since I could not close read the tens of thousands of pages in those periodical volumes page by page, such intuitive open-access browsing was essential to being able to navigate so wide a swathe of texts. The chances to browse that way today in the print archive are rapidly dwindling as collections are moved offsite (or, in the worst cases, indiscriminately sold off or destroyed as libraries transform book space into digital work spaces). Thus, the question of browsing turns more decisively to how we handle the medium as it appears in the digital archive.

Thirty years ago, scholars rarely questioned the bound-volume form of the periodical or thought to ask how original single issues were turned into volumes in the first place. Today, such questions are impossible to ignore. Just as the advent of the digital has made us look with new eyes at all books, so one's eye for digitised periodicals opens wider at what Sean Latham and Robert Scholes have called 'a hole in the archive'. Their 2006 *PMLA* article 'The Rise of Periodical Studies' defined this 'hole' as the wealth of historical and commercial information that was lost when wrappers and advertising pages were shorn off single issues in order to construct bound volumes.[12] Scholes and Latham found the most dramatic cases of that destruction in American magazines published after 1890, yet it also occurred in lesser but significant proportions throughout the eighteenth century and Romantic period. About 25 per cent of the letterpress in the *Spectator*'s single issues, printed on folio half-sheets, was devoted to advertisements when it circulated in London coffee houses; none of those advertisements survived into the first bound octavo volumes that began to appear in January 1712. Yet they testified to the theatrical, bookish and everyday commercial exchanges of London life.[13] Similar alterations took place across the span of eighteenth- and nineteenth-century periodicals. A rough estimate of such deletions from journals like the *Gentleman's Magazine* or *Blackwood's* would be 6–10 per cent each issue. We will not know more about these questions until we can retrieve more single issues from the uncatalogued depths of the print archive. But our awareness of this absence means we have to grasp the digitised periodical as a remediation not of the original circulating issues, but of their subsequent restructuring into volumes by their own producers or subscribers. Scholars have not recognised the full significance of this process or exactly how it took place, but it has arguably had a cascade of consequences for subsequent literary and print history. The resulting volumes were not like pamphlets bundled and bound by their owners; rather they were planned into the design, the editing and sometimes the writing of periodical production itself.[14]

Even in the same periodical, variations in the bound volume's composition can have larger effects on the digitised journals. Scholars of *Blackwood's* will have noticed the odd disparity between those print volumes that show a monthly contents page at the head of each issue, as it appeared in the original number, and those volumes that show all six contents pages *before* the volume's first article begins. There is no consistency about this pattern in various sets of Maga across a great many print archives; but when it shows up again in volume-centred databases like *HathiTrust*, the difference is magnified. Having all six contents pages at the volume's front now functions like a full-volume guide – a search engine for articles – rather than serving only as a single-issue guide for a digitised volume that has no random access. The variance in these renderings of *Blackwood's* helps us see also that the eighteenth- and nineteenth-century process of binding single issues – where the periodicity of weekly, monthly and quarterly formats was most apparent – was never fully secure.

The codex having dominated the serial in this way can have unexpected effects upon digitisation. As James Mussell, the leading scholar of digitised Victorian periodicals, points out, the sequence of page images in a database

> endorses the codex form of the bound volume (and the decisions made by various librarians and archivists as to what should be preserved and in what shape) rather than any of the other possible states in which periodicals were issued and read. . . . It asserts the *page* as the periodical's constituent unit and restricts its users to turning them one by one [my emphasis].[15]

As users of *ECCO* or *Early English Books Online* know, the database can make the slow, mechanical turning of pages an expense of spirit. Both article-centred and some volume-centred databases can mitigate this obstacle by permitting direct access to articles or a more mobile scrolling of PDFs. But both kinds of database still fundamentally alter the original medium of the periodical by restricting (or negating) random access. Loss of such access is true of any digitised book, of course, but it is more disabling for the browse-worthy periodical. Any wide search for excerptable passages, like the one I conducted for *The Making of English Reading Audiences*, would be diminished or curtailed at the start. The limits on the browsing function for the digitised periodical also throw more emphasis on compensating for diminished access by way of 'search'.

Meanwhile, as Andrew Stauffer quips, the digital has raised our attention to bibliographical detail to the point where 'we see pages, everywhere'.[16] The new centrality of the page can almost seem to displace the article as the constituent unit of the periodical – a significant change in how we pay attention to what periodicals do. Articles have long been the target of periodicals research; they belong to the category of essays, sermons, poems, short stories, reviews and other texts we most readily seek as intelligible complete texts. These are discursive categories – 'genres' if you will – but not really mediatic categories. Digitised pages can often show us the material and design dimensions of the printed pages that we formerly used only as windows onto the text. They can also make us feel we are getting much *closer* to the page, even while we're in fact more fully distanced from holding the print volume in our hands. Here, print and digital media might be said to enact different sensations of closeness or distance that affect their uses, but the digital capacity for close-up inspection on page or image viewers strongly favours the page and is likely to encourage more visual thinking about the periodical medium than did the print volumes themselves. As digitisation slowly shifts from the earlier black-and-white images of microfilm or Google digitising to increasingly common colour page-images, the textures and weathering of the page, combined with visual magnification aids, can render a new complexity to the periodical's makeup that was far easier to miss in the all-print archive.

The visual dimension of periodicals becomes all the more important as we move into grasping such print artefacts as part of a wider media history. If researched today, my book would undoubtedly be more alert to visual materials and the journals that exploited them. Browsing in the print archive reveals rich engravings and other illustrations that made *La Belle Assemblée*, the *Lady's Magazine*, the *Lady's Monthly Museum* and other such magazines far more than assemblages of text. A journal like the Whig satirical magazine *The Scourge* (1811–16) really cannot be understood at all unless we can view the richly hued George Cruikshank plates that fold out from each print issue. But these remain folded up and hardly visible in volume-centred databases like *HathiTrust* or *Google Books*. Despite their other disadvantages, article-centred databases like *British Periodicals* can make such plates accessible in high-resolution grayscale. Students of Romantic-era bibliomania, for instance, will find Cruikshank's caricature of the Society of Antiquaries in the June 1812 issue of *The Scourge*, where we see Thomas Frognall Dibdin clutching his own copy of *The Bibliomania, or Book Madness: A Bibliographical Romance*. This issue appeared in the same summer as the great Roxburghe auction that gave *The Bibliomania* its lasting example of fantastic book prices and bibliomaniacal frenzy.[17] Despite other limitations, an article-centred database like *British Periodicals*, with its capacity for zooming in on pages, illustrations and typefaces, can become indispensable to research projects and programmes intent on understanding the nature of the periodical medium.

So far, I have been pointing to the double-sidedness of the digital archive for periodical research. While it vastly increases our access to eighteenth- and nineteenth-century journals and facilitates building new research corpuses, it also seriously compromises our ability to browse or explore these periodicals by way of random access. One simply cannot 'browse' an 850-page volume of *Blackwood's* online or through a PDF in any useful sense of the word. Instead, we need to use 'search' terms that include words, strings or article titles to find our way through such a volume or across volumes. For such reasons, as the next section will explore, the 'search' function has to assume more of the burden in the study of periodicals online.

Powers and Limits of 'Search'

'Search' is the most highly vaunted new power of the digital archive, enabling us to learn from thousands or millions of documents in the way we formerly learned from dozens or hundreds. Models of 'distant reading' are based on this vastly larger scale of study of printed materials, and it can produce serious (if still controversial) results from its bold initiative to study codex genres like the novel as a mass-publication genre in history. Yet the periodical, as students of the medium like Mark Parker have shown, is genre-sensitive in a very different way. Its shifting modes of attention and reflection make it a powerful means of locating a medley of genres as they combine poetry, fiction and non-fiction prose in varying ways over shorter rather than longer periods of time.[18] This difference from book-oriented searching does not make 'search' less important but does make the searches we do necessarily more responsive to the periodical form and its temporal rhythms.

An excellent case in point is Mark Schoenfield's recent search of the databases to locate the rise of the term *autobiography* in Romantic-age journals, which shows the strengths of a database dedicated to British journals, with its pre-constructed corpus of journals, rather than one designed for books. By using the dedicated database *British Periodicals*, he located 'a sharp rise in the availability of "autobiography" as a term in the 1820s'.[19] First appearing in the 1790s, the word began to multiply rapidly after 1817: 'yearly references climb to 110 articles in 1827, with more than 500 articles using the term throughout the 1820s and double that in the 1830s'. He contrasts the spread of the new word with the older, less modernising term *memoirs*, which registered in far higher numbers of articles in the 1790s (4,000) and the 1820s (10,000).[20] Though Schoenfield cross-checked his search results 'against versions in Google Books',[21] he could not have performed the primary search on a book-designed database like *Google Books* or *HathiTrust*. The latter requires that one choose a periodical first, then search it for the pertinent terms; Schoenfield was seeking a broader cross-periodicals result instead. His absorbing essay and its data show how searches in dedicated periodical databases produce valuable results, even while the *British Periodicals* corpus, as he correctly notes, 'offers a representative, not definitive, sampling of periodical writing'.[22]

No other kind of database could have executed Schoenfield's kind of search, which favours a dedicated focus on periodicals and a set of article results. For instance, *HathiTrust* cannot separate periodicals from other print genres and requires a volume-by-volume search, as does *Google Books*, while *Eighteenth Century Journals* cannot separate weekly or monthly journals from the many newspapers in its database. This is why obtaining search results cannot be separated from the specific kind of architecture that a given database uses. Many researchers who work with these databases will also want to download chosen articles or even (my own preference) full volumes for extended use. But only some PDFs can be fully searched. Those developed from a microfilm-based collection, such as *British Periodicals*, cannot be searched in PDF form (though they are searchable through the archive's interface). I have found this to be a severe and unexpected limitation of the ProQuest product, especially compared to the fully searchable PDFs available from *Google Books* or *HathiTrust*.

All such databases deploy a common search basis (optical character recognition; OCR), but even here they differ in what part of that underlying text they make available to study. *ECCO* and *British Periodicals* do not provide plain-text transcripts from their underlying OCR, while

Eighteenth Century Journals gives us the most fully curated, accurate transcriptions of any database I have worked with. *HathiTrust* and *Google Books* transcripts tend to require considerably more correcting and cleaning up before they can be of any further use. Once again, the question is whether we want to study the content and style of a text – for which databases offering good transcripts are useful – or as a medium, in which case the transcript is of less importance than page images. For these and other reasons, large-scale text mining seems to me less promising for the periodical, a moment-to-moment medium, than it may be for millions of books. Still, a well-defined search of a significant run – say, of the *Bee, or Weekly Literary Intelligencer* from 1790 to 1794 or *Blackwood's* from 1817 to 1825 – might produce interesting results when paired with Voyant Tools, a user-friendly and freely available program. Voyant can measure word frequency or perform basic topic-modelling from transcriptions taken from databases with effective OCR. Yet data mining is also problematic because we are measuring the *actual* medium that has been digitised – the bound volumes, not the original single issues – and the results will necessarily blend what was preserved from those issues and what was added to make the bound volumes a somewhat different entity (such as volume title pages, indexes or 'visual embellishments' inserted to complete a volume).

On the whole, the 'search' function in digitised periodicals must bear the burden of compensating for curtailed browsing capacity on the one hand, and of remaining less useful over longer time spans compared to something feasible like the 15-year extent of Schoenfield's essay, on the other. But search capacity is also the most likely dimension of the digital archive to change and improve over time. The newest major periodicals database, *Eighteenth Century Journals*, provides a 'thumbnails' function – small page images for navigating – missing from other periodicals databases, and the result is to improve browsing to one extent and searching to another. Critical assessment of these databases by scholars may help future versions improve even more.

Rethinking the Periodical Medium

I want to conclude with two points about future scholarship in the Romantic-era periodical. First, it was a key assumption of my earlier work that Romantic periodicals faced an entirely different historical situation than Victorian journals, both in their sense of audience and in their material modes of publication. Thirty years of subsequent work by many hands, as far as I can see, has not changed that perception about the historical and textual differences between the periods stretching from 1790 to 1832 and 1832 to 1914. Hence, it is still misleading today when new works of 'nineteenth-century' periodical scholarship actually begin, more often than not, at 1832 or 1837.[23] As articulated throughout the collection at hand, the distinctiveness of Romantic periodicals still needs to be fully registered on the wider scholarly landscape; and today that case needs to be made for the digital archive as much as for the print libraries, if not more.

Second, it is likewise important to observe through the digital medium what we did not fully realise before it existed. In the print archive, we could use the browsable bound volumes in our hands to project and describe vivid scenarios of periodical circulation among users in the Romantic age, as if those volumes offered us direct access to the cultural past and its literary magazines, critical quarterlies or weekly political journals. Yet the same volumes can no longer be an open window of this kind in the digital archive, which has altered our relation to them by way of their digital surrogates. Instead, they appear to us as one of the two forms that actual periodical production and reading took in the eighteenth and nineteenth centuries – as single circulating issues and as bound volumes. In fact, single issues were designed to be bound up in volumes since the late seventeenth century (including volume-style pagination in each issue) and the two forms of the periodical medium were always, as I have argued elsewhere, parts of an overall print-media design.

To grasp these issues and others, it is first essential to protect the bound volumes in the print archive from potential destruction (as has too often happened already) when they are considered obsolete in light of the existence of digital copies. Preserving and keeping available the print volumes is indispensable to knowing the medium and how it worked, educating us about the mediation of the periodical since its first circulating issues to what is now their third textual dimension in the digital archive.

Our inability to 'browse' the digitised bound volumes in the ways we still can in the print archive also means we should pay new kinds of critical attention to the periodical artefacts now online: how were they made, what was added to volumes even as parts of the issues were being torn away? Meanwhile, many periodical scholars have run into single issues in the print libraries largely by happenstance. They are rarely catalogued with accuracy and remain a great difficulty for archivists to know what do to with. Even before one can imagine digitising such issues as an important addition to the current digital archive, they must be found (to the extent they still survive) and made available to scholars to study. For the future of periodicals research, it could be very useful to form a network of scholars interested in these issues who would work with archivists to locate and catalogue the single copies in the print archive. We know that once found, such issues can potentially be digitised in the currently feasible ways, such as online page images and downloadable PDFs. The best model for such an initiative is the remarkable *Modernist Journals Project*, which for two decades has been digitising single issues of American commercial, political and 'little' magazines from multi-year runs of twenty-two periodicals and one-year runs of another twenty-four.[24] This project aims to redress for at least one historical period a problem common to periodicals research for all eras since 1700 – in this instance, how, by the early twentieth century, up to 50% of pages in American commercial magazines were discarded when serial issues were converted into bound volumes. It can be stunning to compare a full issue of a journal like *Scribner's Magazine* in 1910 with its badly diminished counterpart in the digitised volume version in *Google Books*.

To be sure, Romantic and eighteenth-century scholars would almost certainly find far fewer surviving single issues from their eras than American modernists have for theirs, both because of the winnowing of old 'ephemera' and the remarkable periodical explosion of the later nineteenth century. Yet even without complete runs of such artefacts at our disposal, studying single issues may well give us a new media education about the bound volumes we're now seeing online in such great numbers. How were the single issues built and fastened? What happened to an issue when it was prepared for binding? Exactly what kind of cultural information was lost in the process? What was added to these altered issues in order to form volumes (such as title pages, indexes, engravings and other matter)? How variable was this process? Did the issues bound into Volume 2 of *Blackwood's* in 1817–1818 have the same composition as those bound into Volume 18 in 1825? (From the issues and volumes I have examined, the answer is no.) How did other journals compare to *Blackwood's* on these matters, and how did weekly journals differ from monthly magazines in this process of conversion?

Granted the things we could learn by recovering and studying these issues, it then seems possible to imagine digitising single issues not only as PDFs, where we are still limited to page-by-page reading, but as fully browsable surrogates, perhaps using three-dimensional rendering software or other digital tools that would make an issue truly interactive online. With a more delicate kind of digitising for single issues than has ever been done with bound volumes in the past, our grasp of periodicals as a medium would be closer to the way users handled them in the past than the databases show us now.

Acknowledgement

I want to thank Tom Mole and Nick Mason for their generous editorial help with working out the issues in this essay.

Notes

1. Such studies include Parker, *Literary Magazines*; Schoenfield, *British Periodicals*; Higgins, *Romantic Genius*; Stewart, *Romantic Magazines*.
2. Klancher, *The Making*.
3. Grafton, *Worlds Made of Words*, p. 309.
4. I have discussed the gestation of this book in fuller detail in 'Configuring Romanticism', pp. 373–9. In the 1970s, Romanticists referred to periodicals almost exclusively as a source of literary reviews, as is attested by two still-useful collections: Hayden, *The Romantic Reviewers* and Reiman, *The Romantics Reviewed*.
5. Graham, *English Literary Periodicals*; Altick, *The English Common Reader*; Thompson, *The Making of the English Working Class*; Williams, *The Long Revolution*; Habermas, *The Structural Transformation*.
6. Morrison and Roberts, '"A character so various"', p. 9.
7. Parker, *Literary Magazines*, p. 10. Jon Mee makes a related point for my study of the Edinburgh *Bee, or Literary Weekly Intelligencer* in chapter 1. See 'The Buzz about the *Bee*', pp. 63–74.
8. In conjunction with *Eighteenth Century Journals*, see also the University of Kent's useful approach to recovering this magazine: www.kent.ac.uk/

english/ladys-magazine. I want to thank Jennie Batchelor for advising me on this journal (personal communication to the author, 15 June 2019).
9. For an important discussion of 'bibliographical control' in periodicals, see Mussell, *The Nineteenth-Century Press*, pp. 44–67. William S. Ward's *Index and Finding List of Serials Published in the British Isles 1789–1832* is not included in *C19*. Were it to be properly digitised today, Ward's *Finding List* would still be a leading resource for the period, but thus far it is only accessible online in the form of a PDF.
10. See also Grafton: 'Every library embodies a perspective of its own. Their contents, the way in which manuscripts and books are catalogued and arranged on shelves, and their gaps – all tell stories to those who can listen, about writers, readers, and collectors, and the historical worlds they inhabited' (*Worlds Made of Words*, p. 291).
11. That said, it has a more limited range of British journals (while it is prolific in its coverage of American periodicals).
12. Latham and Scholes, 'The Rise of Periodical Studies', p. 520.
13. Donald F. Bond revealed the extent of advertising in the original *Spectator* issues in a few pages of his introduction to *The Spectator*, but then, like all editors before him, used the octavo bound volumes without the advertising as his copy-text for this four-volume edition.
14. For a study of the relation between single issues and bound volumes as a 'media design' governing all periodicals between 1700 and 1900, see Klancher, 'What Happened to the Periodical?'.
15. Mussell, 'Digitization', p. 20.
16. Stauffer, 'My *Old Sweethearts*', p. 218.
17. See *The Scourge, or, Monthly Expositor of Imposture and Folly* 3 (June 1812), frontispiece in original issue, file no. 21 in the June 1812 issue in *British Periodicals*.
18. Parker, 'Repurposing and the Literary Magazine'.
19. Schoenfield, 'Periodical Auto-Biography', p. 95.
20. Ibid. p. 95.
21. Ibid. p. 101.
22. Ibid. p. 101.
23. Among other examples, the 'nineteenth century' begins for all intents and purposes at 1832 in King et al. (eds), *Routledge Handbook* and Easley et al. (eds), *Researching the Nineteenth-Century Periodical Press*.
24. See http://modjourn.org. For a fuller account of the project and its impact on American modernism scholarship, see Scholes and Wulfman, *Modernism in the Magazines*, pp. 196–222.

Chapter 2

Reading Medicine in *Blackwood's*

Megan Coyer

The purpose of this chapter is to act as an illustrative guide for studying medical content in Romantic-era literary magazines, taking *Blackwood's* as a case study, highlighting some possible approaches and attending to the possibilities offered by digital resources. In doing so, I build upon my experience researching my 2017 monograph, *Literature and Medicine in the Nineteenth-Century Periodical Press: Blackwood's Edinburgh Magazine, 1817–1858*. In this book, I argue that *Blackwood's* distinctive Romantic ideology and innovative form shaped its medical contents, contributing to the formation of a humanistic and often self-consciously 'literary' popular medical culture. Revisiting this study several years later, this chapter provides a supplemental, primarily methodological commentary on researching medical discourse in Romantic-era periodicals. One might adapt the methods discussed to study other types of content, such as, for example, scientific, legal or theological subject matter.

Projects such as the online index *Science in the Nineteenth-Century Periodical* (1999–2007) have highlighted the omnipresence of science and medicine in general periodicals of the nineteenth century. However, in my research I have regularly found myself examining the medical contents of key literary periodicals, including not only *Blackwood's*, but also, for example, the *Edinburgh Review*, the *Scots Magazine* and the *Edinburgh Magazine and Literary Miscellany*, which, despite their richness, have never been systematically studied by historians of medicine or scholars within the field of Literature and Medicine with methodological attentiveness to the magazine context.

Since Jon Klancher's and Mark Parker's seminal works on Romantic periodicals, critics have paid more careful attention to the journals and magazines of the era as complex texts worthy of independent investigation, rather than as archives to mine in support of other arguments.[1] Periodicals certainly remain valuable archives of popular culture through which one can study the circulation of medical and scientific ideas. As Sally Shuttleworth has modelled in *Charlotte Brontë and Victorian Psychology* (1996), for instance, studying *Blackwood's* might shed light on the Brontës' exposure to ideas relating to altered states of consciousness and phrenology, given the magazine was 'the young Brontës' favourite reading material'.[2] However, my own research has been primarily concerned with reading medical content in relation to its contextual appearance within the magazine, making the magazine itself the primary object of study. This approach brings with it certain challenges, not least that *Blackwood's* did not often publish articles that one can readily categorise as 'medical'.

An epistolary exchange between the publisher, William Blackwood, and the surgeon and prolific Blackwoodian contributor, David Macbeth Moir (1798–1851), aptly illustrates this point. In one of his regular private critiques of Maga, Moir wrote to Blackwood in January 1826, 'Who is this physician that you have got to prate on Contagion and Nugae Literariae? He writes well enough, but why not wash his hands of the Shop? We'll give him a little soap for the sake of metre.'[3] The February 1826 articles Moir references – 'The Quarterly Review of Dr Macmichael on Contagion and the Plague' and 'Nugae Literariae. No I' – were both by Dr Robert Gooch (1784–1830), an English physician and friend of the poet Robert Southey.[4] Gooch's 'Protestant Sisters of Charity', which had appeared in the December 1825 issue, received similar censure from Moir for smelling 'a vast deal too much of the Shop'.[5] In contrast, when Dr Charles Badham (1780–1845), newly minted Professor of the Practice of Medicine at the University of Glasgow, published 'Lines written at Warwick Castle' in the April 1829 issue, Moir quipped to Blackwood, 'Well done Badham. I rejoice to see an M.D. at poetry', alluding, of course, to his own long-time status as Maga's leading 'medical poet', 'Delta'.[6]

Moir's comments highlight one of the core issues in studying the medical contents of *Blackwood's*. While he praises Badham for his extra-professional pursuits, he criticises Gooch's articles for being too purely medical in subject matter. As one might conclude from Moir singling out these contributions, such articles were relatively rare in *Blackwood's* at this time. One explanation for this rarity is that *Blackwood's* was launched during a period when the boundaries between general and professional periodicals were solidifying and medical content could be viewed as less suitable for general periodicals.[7] The *Edinburgh Review* notably stated in 1806 that 'MEDICAL subjects ought in general, we think, to be left to the Medical Journals'.[8] While *Blackwood's* short-lived precursor, the *Edinburgh Monthly Magazine*, followed the model of the London-based *Monthly Magazine* in including a 'Medical Report of Edinburgh', this feature only lasted until February 1818. It incited the derision of a contributor to Archibald Constable's *Edinburgh Magazine and Literary Miscellany* in November 1817, who declares in a published letter to the editor:

> MR EDITOR, I SHOULD very willingly comply with your request to contribute a periodical report upon the diseases prevalent in Edinburgh . . . if I could satisfy myself that such a report would be either useful or fit for a Magazine, which is intended for general readers.[9]

Medical news was also reported in the *Edinburgh Monthly Magazine* and subsequently in *Blackwood's* via the 'Literary and Scientific Intelligence' column.[10] For example, in October 1817 the column contains a recipe for treating 'the bite of a mad dog . . . proved by the first medical men of the age', while Laennec's invention of the stethoscope in France is discussed in October 1818 and September 1820.[11] This column only ran, though, from April 1817 to January 1821.

However valuable such reports can be, studying the medical contents of *Blackwood's* requires moving beyond articles explicitly categorised as 'medical'. As Geoffrey Cantor and Sally Shuttleworth contend in relation to scientific culture more broadly, '[i]f we are to understand how scientific ideas were woven into the texture of nineteenth-century cultural life, then we need to examine how scientific language and concepts permeated the entire range of periodical content, from glancing asides to elaborate fictional conceits'.[12] What Ian Duncan terms *Blackwood's* 'innovative mixture of literary forms and discourses' means that, rather than medical content decreasing with the development of the 'self-consciously literary magazine', it is instead dispersed throughout its contents.[13]

Accordingly, in my research, while considering how *Blackwood's* ideology and form shaped its medical contents, I have also attended to how medical representations and language throughout its contents shaped the magazine's fictionalised world and self-positioning in the literary marketplace. In the first section below, I outline some of the archival and bibliographical methods I have utilised, with the hope that other scholars and students studying medical or similarly subject-specific content in literary periodicals might find utility in applying, adapting or building upon these methods. The second section provides a fuller worked example, focusing upon an article not addressed in my monograph: John Wilson's review of Dr William Kitchiner's *The Traveller's Oracle; or, maxims maxims for locomotion: containing precepts for promoting the pleasures, and hints for preserving the health of travellers* (1827). This example is intended to demonstrate the need to apply a range of methodological approaches to even a single article if one is to attend fully to the dialogic magazine context.

Archival and Bibliographical Methods

In an attempt to track medical discourse in miscellanies like *Blackwood's*, how does one find relevant articles? Identifying essays that primarily address medical topics, such as 'The Medical Schools of Dublin and Edinburgh' (January 1819) or 'Beck and Dunlop on Medical Jurisprudence' (March 1825), can be done with a fair degree of ease by browsing tables of contents and end-of-volume indices in *Blackwood's* and by utilising indices such as Strout's *A Bibliography of Articles in Blackwood's Magazine, 1817–1825* (1959) and the *Wellesley Index to Victorian Periodicals*. E. M. Palmegiano's bibliography, *Health and British Magazines in the Nineteenth Century* (1998), which lists articles relating to health and medicine in a range of British periodicals, including *Blackwood's* between 1824 and 1900, is also a helpful resource for medical content. However, Palmegiano's work also highlights the difficulties of identifying medical (or any subject-specific) material from titles alone. Her work, which excludes poetry and fiction, is based upon her survey of titles indexed in the *Wellesley Index* and *Poole's Index*. For the period up to 1832, she lists just six articles from *Blackwood's*. The list includes Gooch's 'Protestant Sisters of Charity' and 'The Quarterly Review of Dr Macmichael on Contagion and the Plague', along with two reviews of medical texts by John Wilson, 'Health and Longevity' (1828) and 'Anatomy of

Drunkenness' (1828), an article on speech impairment from 1825, and an article on the Poor Laws and their provision for the ill in 1828.[14] Notable omissions in Palmegiano's survey include Wilson's 'Clark on Climate' (1830) (a review of a treatise on consumption) and 'The Traveller's Oracle' (1827) (discussed below), which she likely deemed non-medical based on their titles.[15] A key takeaway, then, is that simply surveying titles often leads to missing relevant content.

The stand-alone index to the first fifty volumes of *Blackwood's*, published by Blackwood in 1855, does enable identification of a limited amount of embedded medical content. The entry on 'medicine', for example, cites content within five articles, none of which is likely to be identified via a survey of titles.[16] However, this index, like the end-of-volume indices in *Blackwood's*, is extremely hit-and-miss for embedded material, limiting its usefulness. The *Science in the Nineteenth-Century Periodical* project sought to remedy this problem with their *SciPer* database. This valuable index provides annotations and searchable keyword classifications for scientific and medical content throughout the range of a periodical's contents. For example, *SciPer* notes that a review of cookery books in the December 1817 issue of *Blackwood's* contains commentary on 'remedies for consumption, wind, and "the Gripes"'.[17] Unfortunately, the database only covers the six published issues of the *Edinburgh Monthly Magazine* and the first six issues of *Blackwood's* (October 1817 to March 1818).

Identifying embedded medical content in subsequent issues of Maga therefore requires keyword searching of databases like ProQuest's *British Periodicals* collection, which since 2008 has included full texts of *Blackwood's* from April 1817 to June 1902. However, the list of 682 hits that result, for example, from searching for uses of 'medicine' between 1817 and 1832 is daunting, even when one eliminates duplicate results (where the same article appears in the list of results twice).[18] Part of what makes it difficult to navigate is that the list of search results decontextualises the articles from their original placement in the magazine, and, as Patrick Leary notes, assessing a text via the digital interface of a 'search engine distorts the original context in ways that can, in turn, distort the meaning of those search results'.[19] The list of results will also inevitably include a large number of irrelevant items, while at the same time excluding potentially more relevant articles. John Mussell explains that searching for topics such as 'medicine' is generally problematic, since

> the assumption that underpins search is that if a particular search term appears in an article, then that article is likely to be about that search term. This works well for named entities (people, places, events, objects, etc.), especially when terms are sufficiently distinct, but less well for concepts, themes or topics.[20]

Conversely, an article with medical content may not contain the keyword 'medicine', but rather, for example, 'medical', 'physician', 'surgeon', 'disease' or 'contagion', necessitating further searching. This is not to downplay the utility of the keyword search, particularly when one is able to construct a more focused search. Still, when researching medical discourse in Romantic periodicals, more strategic approaches are necessary, and after initial survey work, further bibliographical work can be guided by modes of exegesis. The three primary approaches to studying medical content in literary miscellanies I would like to highlight might be classed into three categories: discourse and ideology, genre, and authorship.

Discourse and ideology

When one identifies an article addressing medical subject matter, an important initial question to consider is how to interpret it in relation to its periodical's wider ideological self-positioning and within relevant strands of discourse across a larger run of the magazine or journal. However, to build the necessary bibliography of contextual material, one must understand the political and historical significance of any given medical debate. Gooch's February 1826 *Blackwood's* article 'Contagion and the Plague', which implicitly expands upon his own recent *Quarterly Review* essay on William Macmichael's *The Progress of Opinion on the Subject of Contagion* (1825), provides one relevant example. The articles defend contagion theory – the theory that 'the bodies of the sick give out a noxious material, which excites [diseases] in the bodies of the healthy' – against the epidemic theory of disease causation for the plague. The epidemic theory linked the disease to environmental factors like 'marsh exhalations' that are 'so diffused as to affect many persons in the same place at the same time'.[21] The political nature of this debate is well documented, as 'anti-contagionism' was widely associated with liberal politics and the promotion of commercial interests.[22] As Philip Connell explains, anti-contagionism at this time was closely associated with the work of Charles Maclean, 'a political pamphleteer and long-standing employee of the East India Company', who argued against the contagious theory of disease causation as part of a wider attack on the quarantine laws.[23] More specifically, though, Gooch's articles in *Blackwood's* and the devoutly Tory *Quarterly Review* respond to the physician Thomas Southwood Smith's 1825 anti-contagionist articles in the Benthamite *Westminster Review*, which criticised quarantine laws as inimical to commercial progress. As such, one could read Gooch's *Blackwood's* article as an extension of the magazine's larger ideological opposition to liberal politics and free trade, prevalent throughout its range of contents but more pronounced from 1826 onwards.[24]

From here, one might seek out other articles in *Blackwood's* addressing the contagion debate to consider if Gooch's critique forms part of a strand of medical discourse on this topic. Such a query would allow for more strategic keyword searching and browsing. For example, Gooch contributed 'Nugae Literariae. No. I' to the same February 1826 number, which contains an extract on 'The Plague' in support of contagion theory. Searching for 'contagion' also leads to the earlier series, 'The Medical Report of Edinburgh' (with three of the four reports leading the list of search results based on 'relevance'), a series which addresses contagion theory in relation to continued and intermittent fever. And, intriguingly, the January 1823 spoof 'Vox Populi' contains an invented 'extract' supposedly taken from the *Edinburgh Medical and Surgical Journal* advising readers that reading *Blackwood's* is a mental stimulant capable of preventing the 'contagion spreading' in '*Delirium Constitutionale, D. Taxator, D. Nobilitas, D. Agraria, D. Infidelitas*, and the other species of this tantalizing disease'.[25]

Jessica Roberts's recent article 'Radical Contagion and Healthy Literature in *Blackwood's*' addresses this strand of medical discourse in the magazine. She specifically argues that *Blackwood's* exploited 'an existing cultural anxiety about literal disease in its discussion of metaphorical contagion', tracing this conservative rhetorical tradition back to Edmund Burke's pathologising of the French Revolution.[26] Roberts reads a range of political articles in *Blackwood's* as drawing upon the language of contagion to stress rhetorically the threat of radical 'disease' spreading through the lower classes in Britain. At the same time, she argues that *Blackwood's* represents itself in its literary criticism as 'a remedy for this radical disease' by striving 'to maintain the health of its readership by identifying salutary literature for its readers and the lower orders'.[27] Read alongside my own analysis of Gooch's 'Contagion and the Plague', Roberts's impressive study further evidences both the value of searching beyond explicitly 'medical' articles and the importance of considering what impact a periodical's broader affinities and ideologies may have had on its medical discourse.

Genre

In working to offer models and methods for future researchers of *Blackwood's* and Romantic periodicals more broadly, the second approach to studying medical content I would like to highlight is genre. By genre, I refer here to the genre of particular articles, but one must also attend to how a given periodical's generic norms might shape subject-specific content. One of Maga's key innovations was the generic hybridity of its contents, and one can examine how its contributors experimented with particular genres of medical writing and the type of medical subject matter typical to British monthlies in the first decades of the nineteenth century. As briefly noted above and discussed at length in my book, the *Edinburgh Monthly Magazine* and the early issues of *Blackwood's* included the type of non-fiction medical writing typical of British monthlies at this time, such as city-specific medical reports and historical and modern medical case histories with sufficient popular appeal.[28]

Yet, as Tim Killick has illustrated, *Blackwood's* contributors regularly experimented with the 'potent source material' and the 'tone and structure' of these medical case studies, one outgrowth of which was the magazine's 'tales of terror'.[29] Through the 1820s and 1830s, Maga's trademark 'tales of terror' routinely engaged with medical subject matter.[30] For example, two medical men who contributed to the magazine, John Howison (1797–1859) and Robert Macnish (1802–37), experimented with medical narrators assuming the characteristic first-person voice of these hair-raising tales. This trend culminated with the more overt hybridisation of the 'tale of terror' and medical case studies in Samuel Warren's *Passages from the Diary of a Late Physician*, serialised in *Blackwood's* from 1830 to 1837.[31]

This diachronic approach (examining generic development across time) can be complemented by synchronic comparisons with medical writing published in other contemporaneous periodicals. Warren's series, in particular, inspired a range of imitations and parodies.[32] Additional genres of interest within Romantic-era magazines include confessional patient narratives, biographies and obituaries of prominent physicians, medical news, popular medical advice, and reviews of medical texts.

Authorship

A third approach to studying medical content in literary magazines – authorship – primarily involves identifying medical contributors and considering how articles by these writers relate to their wider medical and literary writings and careers. The *Wellesley Index* and periodical-specific studies like Strout's enable identification of contributions by medical practitioners who wrote literary or scientific articles on the side. Especially helpful is the *Wellesley*'s practice of listing any known occupation next to a contributor's name (e.g., 'Dunlop, William, 1792–1848, M.D., army officer'). While Strout's bibliography lacks such detail, his list of 'Articles in *Blackwood's Magazine* arranged by author' includes the title of 'Dr' where relevant. Since, of course, this title was not exclusively reserved for medical doctors, further biographical research is necessary to discern any medical connections. Moreover, not all physicians and surgeons are given the title 'Dr' in Strout's list, which means this method will not reliably identify all medical contributors to the early volumes of *Blackwood's*.

Cataloguing contributions by specific medical men can often facilitate connections one might otherwise have neglected. For example, David Macbeth Moir, who regularly published sentimental verses in Maga under sign of 'Delta', also contributed the anonymous 1821 articles 'Why are Professional Men Indifferent Poets?' and 'On the Vulgar Prejudices Against Literature'. Analysis of these two articles, which I might have overlooked if I had not identified them as written by a surgeon, proved crucial to my book's treatment of how *Blackwood's* constructed an idealised notion of literary medical men as 'men of feeling' as part of its broader critique of the trends towards increasing professionalism and a utilitarian emphasis on science over natural feeling.[33] Recognising Moir's authorship of these articles also led me to a range of valuable contextual materials, including his extant correspondence, medical writings, and documents suggesting his work's wider reception. These archival texts evidence how, in spite of an unfavourable cultural climate for medical men with literary pretensions, Moir came to exemplify the compatibility of literature and medicine as kindred arts.[34] As such, this approach enabled me to consider the relationship between literary and medical cultures at this time, both within and beyond the pages of *Blackwood's*. A key general point, then, is that in working to analyse any article within a magazine or journal, attending to authorship can enable one to identify further materials of interest within and beyond a given periodical and also help to contextualise the article within a wider culture.

'The Traveller's Oracle': John Wilson and the Medico-Literary Review

Having suggested various methods for researching medical content in Romantic-era periodicals, I will devote the second half of this essay to highlighting the important and wide-ranging insights to be gleaned through several approaches discussed above. Here I will model, in part, what Linda Hughes has termed thinking 'sideways', which 'includes analysis across genres; texts opening out onto each other dialogically in and out of periodicals; sequential rather than "data mining" approaches to reading periodicals; and spatio-temporal convergences in print culture'.[35] In the specific case of Romantic-era *Blackwood's*, the importance of attending to the dialogical relationship across time between texts within the magazine itself is amplified. With its innovative experimental form, which blurred the boundaries between fact and fiction, the magazine encouraged a dizzying range of associations to be made between articles, particularly through the *Noctes Ambrosianae* series. As Parker suggests, the 'dynamic relation among contributions informs and creates meaning'.[36] This fact makes studying *Blackwood's* particularly challenging, as the modern scholar or student is unlikely to have time to read the magazine sequentially in full. However, it also makes it of particular value to the field of Literature and Medicine, since one is able to see a dynamic relationship between medical and literary content (categorisations that are often difficult to make). The fuller example I have selected to illustrate my methodological approach, a reading of Wilson's October 1827 *Blackwood's* review of Dr William Kitchiner's *The Traveller's Oracle* within the dialogic magazine context, explores this relationship. Applying all three approaches to studying medical content discussed above to this article, I argue that Wilson's essay on Kitchiner may be read as a hybrid 'medico-literary' review, contributing both to the fictional world of *Blackwood*'s and the magazine's ideological self-positioning in the literary marketplace.

I first discovered Wilson's review of Kitchiner when surveying reviews of medical texts in *Blackwood's* (a genre-centred bibliographical approach). Comparing how different journals and literary magazines responded to a particular text can reveal how commentary might be shaped by a periodical's political ideologies or stylistic conventions. A keyword search of *British Periodicals* located seven other contemporary reviews of Kitchiner's work, and a survey of these reviews revealed something rather curious. None of the other reviews treats Kitchiner's book as a medical text. Yet *Blackwood's* devotes significant attention to medical aspects of the text, commenting upon Kitchiner's recommendation against sudden transitions from sedentary life to active travel, his suggested treatment for a cold, the negative effects of night air and damp sheets, his flawed reasoning relating to the health benefits of living in the country, the danger of hydrophobia, and his understanding of exercise as a bodily stimulant. In contrast, reviewers outside of *Blackwood's* frequently refer to Kitchiner as 'the doctor' but generally focus on non-medical aspects of the text. For example, the *New Monthly Magazine* covers his recommendations for keeping the Sabbath when travelling, punctually writing to friends, items one should carry, and adopting the language and customs of the area where one is travelling.[37] The *London Magazine*, after deriding Kitchiner's work as 'mere rubbish collected from every source, and thrown together in a mass for the sake of making a book', proceeds to only consider extracts from the second volume, 'Comprising the Horse and Carriage Keeper's Oracle', which was not written by Kitchiner but 'By John Jervis, an Old Coachman'.[38]

Whether or not *The Traveller's Oracle* is indeed a medical work is debatable, necessitating research into the author and text itself. William Kitchiner (1778–1827) styled himself 'M.D.' on his title pages and claimed to have graduated from the University of Glasgow. As Tom Bridge and Colin Cooper English indicate, while the university archives contain no record of him as a student, 'it is just possible that he was a medical student at the University of Glasgow, and left without gaining a degree before records began in 1802'.[39] Regardless, during his lifetime he regularly published as an MD, and his letters to his publisher, Archibald Constable, are peppered with medical advice, including warnings against 'tampering with us Doctors!!'[40] His large inheritance enabled a hobby-horsical publishing career, rendering actually practising medicine unnecessary, and he became famous as the author of *The Cook's Oracle* (1817) and the eccentric host of dinners for the 'committee of taste' at his London residence.[41] Regardless of the topic, Kitchiner offered the perspective of a physician, a tendency that led William Jerdan, the influential editor of the *Literary Gazette*, to remark,

> his medicating was book-making, and his book-making medicating! . . . His medical ('Peptic') precepts and gastronomic practices were wonderfully combined, insomuch that it was not always easy to tell, in partaking of what was set before you, whether you might be swallowing a meal or a prescription at his hospitable, or, as the case might be, his hospital board.[42]

In the case of *The Traveller's Oracle*, the opening 'General Observations on Travelling' contains much of the medical commentary discussed by Wilson, but sections on 'Aperient Medicine', 'Cholera Morbus', 'Peristaltic Persuaders' and 'Travelling Medicine Chests' appear alongside sections on 'How to get a well-fitting Shoe' and 'For Personal Defense', all interspersed with 'Seven Songs, For One, Two and Three Voices'.

Wilson's review adds to a long tradition of references to Kitchiner within *Blackwood's*. After lamenting that 'Dr Kitchiner should have died before our numerous avocations had allowed us an opportunity of dining with him', the review alludes to a tumultuous relationship with the magazine:

> The Doctor had, we know, a dread of Us, – not altogether unallayed by delight, – and on the Dinner to Us, which he had meditated for nearly a quarter of a century, he knew and felt must have hung his reputation with posterity – his posthumous fame.[43]

A full-text keyword search of *British Periodicals* for 'Kitchiner' (as well as a frequent misspelling, 'Kitchener') within *Blackwood's* in the lead-up to this review clarifies, in particular, his posited 'dread of Us'. Perhaps the most significant hit is 'The Leg of Mutton School of Prose. No. I. The Cook's Oracle' from December 1821, a bantering review that presaged a satirical poem in the February 1822 number dedicated to 'Dr Kitchener, to console him for the roasting he met with when you put him on the spit' and further riffing on the doctor in 'Noctes X' of July 1823. In this latter piece, Odoherty outs himself as the author of 'The Cook's Oracle' review, explaining to Christopher North that he cut up the book because he 'had a most excellent Cookery-book written, founded on the principles practised in the 99th mess, and was going to treat with Longman's folks about it, when Kitchener came out, and pre-occupied the market'.[44]

To understand the significance of this discursive strand in relation to the wider ideology of the magazine, one must more closely examine the politics of the 1821 review of *The Cook's Oracle*. In the review, Dr Kitchener's 'strong powers of digestion' are said to disqualify him as man of taste, since 'strength in the digestive organs is never found united to delicacy of perception in the palatal ones; or, in other words, that nicety of taste is found to be uniformly connected with delicacy of stomach'. As such, 'to that exquisite and transcendental "*gout*" which marks the most complicated dishes of a master', Kitchiner is 'an utter stranger'.[45] Noting the politics at play here, Brian Rejack has rightly observed that 'Kitchiner wants to align gastronomic sophistication with middle-class ideals of moderation and productivity, while the *Blackwood's* model holds on to the more exclusive aristocratic notion'. In doing so, he argues, the magazine 'combats what it perceives as an attempt at audience formation through principles of taste (the *beau monde* of the kitchen), precisely by posing its own community of tasteful readers in opposition to the Leg of Mutton School'.[46]

Returning to Kitchiner six years later, Wilson's review of *The Traveller's Oracle* likewise critiques his promotion of 'middle-class ideals of moderation', but takes a characteristically Blackwoodian self-contradictory approach to Kitchiner. The review takes the doctor's advice for preserving the health of travellers as an opportunity to facetiously construct the ideal contributor and subscriber to *Blackwood's* as manifesting a robust, masculine healthfulness – 'a sound

Tory Church and King stomach and constitution' – which makes Kitchiner's overzealous instructions and warnings laughable.⁴⁷ For example, while Kitchiner suggests 'a broth diet, a warm room, a tea-spoonful of Epsom salts, [and] early roosting' for an incipient cold, Wilson's review asks: 'What say you, dear subscriber or contributor, to half-a-dozen tumblers of hot toddy? Your share of a brown jug to the same amount?'⁴⁸ From here, Wilson launches into a list of alternative cures, recalling the decadent fare of the *Noctes*, including 'small-bearded oysters, all redolent of the salt-sea foam, and worthy, as they stud the Ambrosial brodd, to be licked off all at once by the lambent tongue of Neptune'. He continues:

> And if you contrive to carry a cold about you next day, you deserve to be sent to Coventry by all sensible people – and may, if you choose, begin taking, with Tims, a tea-spoonful of Epsom salts in a half-pint of warm water every half hour, till it moves your bowels twice or thrice – but if you do, be your sex, politics, or religion what they may, never shall you be suffered again to contribute even a bit of Balaam to this Magazine.⁴⁹

While Kitchiner urges travellers to moderate their eating and drinking to prevent 'violent irritation and fatal inflammation', Wilson writes that 'these are complaints to which no writer in this Magazine is subject. Should any of us be so attacked, he has only to compose for himself an Opening Article'.⁵⁰

Returning to the question of why the *Blackwood's* review stands out as more 'medical' compared to other contemporary reviews of *The Traveller's Oracle*, one can see that medical content is foregrounded in the *Blackwood's* review of Kitchiner, as it suits Wilson's ideological ends in shaping his reading (and writing) public. Additionally, turning to an author-centred approach, the energetic, associative style of the review, which includes at one point a list of vivid illustrations of poor health in rural areas spanning three pages (inspired by a single sentence from Kitchiner's work), rhetorically illustrates a correlation between physical health and imaginative energy made elsewhere in Wilson's corpus.⁵¹ In 'Salmonia', his August 1828 review of Sir Humphry Davy's *Salmonia: or Days of Fly Fishing, in a series of Conversations; with some account of the Habits of Fishes belonging to the Genus Salmo* (1828), Wilson declares that 'no man should write a book of any kind during severe and dangerous illness; for, under such circumstances, how can it escape being mortally stupid?'[52] He particularly lights into Davy for writing a book on angling while ill, as 'a good book upon Angling can be written . . . only in a state of vigorous health of mind and body – tongue pure, eyes bright, stomach strong, pulse steady, and palate tremblingly alive to the taste of Glenlivet'.[53]

One might read such correlations between physical health and imaginative energy in relation to Wilson's own authorial persona. As Richard Cronin has argued, during his lifetime and posthumously in his Victorian reception, 'Wilson's authorship' was seen 'as a function of his impressive physicality'.[54] Robert Macnish, the Glaswegian surgeon, phrenologist and regular contributor to *Blackwood's*, aptly illustrates this reputation. Writing to Moir in February 1835, he pronounces Wilson's brain to be 'one of vast energy and . . . fiercely stimulated by the circulation', concluding that '[i]f Wilson had been a man of feeble body and small chest his intellectual manifestations would by no means have come up to their present standard'.[55] However, Wilson's construction in his review of Kitchiner of the ideal, physically robust Blackwoodian, with 'sound Tory Church and King stomach and constitution', was clearly linked not only to his own developing persona but also to the particular politics of the magazine.

Rolf Lessenich has read the 'excesses of food and drink' in the *Noctes* as part of 'the magazine's political commitment' to Toryism. He points, for instance, to Timothy Tickler's opposition both to 'the Radical poet Percy Bysshe Shelley's vegetarianism' and 'the Radical physician Thomas Trotter's recommendation of a moderate diet and abstention from alcohol'.[56] Wilson's subsequent review of Dr Thomas John Graham's *Sure Methods of Improving Health, and Prolonging Life, &c.* (1827), entitled 'Health and Longevity', published in the January 1828 number, likewise reflects this dedication to excess. Here, Christopher North compares the sparse diet recommended by Graham, whom he denigrates as an 'Old Woman', with the rich fare relished by those with even 'the most distant chance of admission' to Maga's inner circle.[57] As Lessenich indicates, '[e]ating and drinking to excess had been a traditional cultural practice in Britain', and *Blackwood's* returns to this tradition in the formation of its reading and writing public, with an ability to healthfully consume food and drink in abundance becoming symbolic of an ability to consume the excesses of *Blackwood's* itself.[58] As such, the dramatic characters of Davy's *Salmonia* (who warn against drinking while angling and are accused of over-attentiveness to 'the state of their bowels') are declared 'all alike incapable of enjoying the wit of Blackwood's Magazine'.[59]

As I have argued elsewhere, medical texts are infrequently reviewed in *Blackwood's*, and those that are reviewed appear to be selected, at least in part, for their thematic relevance to developing strands of literary discourse in the magazine. I have suggested using the term 'medico-literary review' to capture this literary cross-referentiality and contribution to the construction of the fictitious world of *Blackwood's*.[60] In this vein, Wilson's review of *The Traveller's Oracle* may be read as part of a trilogy of medico-literary reviews he wrote in the aftermath of the infamous 'Preface' of January 1826.[61]

Pivotal articles such as the 'Preface', which attempt to articulate the overall remit of a miscellany, can usefully inform how one interprets more particularised articles of interest within the magazine context. The 'Preface' celebrated *Blackwood's* revolutionary effect on the reading public in terms that emphasise embodied affect, as '[t]hat long icy chill was shook off their fancies and imaginations, and here, too, in Criticism as in Politics, they began to feel, think, and speak, like free men'.[62] As David Latané has argued, this lead essay for 1826 marked a turning point in the magazine's history, as '[a]fter the "Preface", John Wilson fully absorbs the persona of Christopher North, and . . . Wilson/North becomes the hallmark of Maga'.[63]

I would like to suggest that Wilson's medico-literary reviews of Dr Kitchiner and Dr Graham become an opportunity to playfully emphasise a link between embodied and imaginative liberation, which furthers the Romantic ideology of the 'Preface'. This link is foregrounded in 'Streams', one of a series of lead articles published in the wake of the 'Preface' written in the voice of Christopher North and addressed to the 'feeling and imaginative reader'.[64] Between April and September 1826, in 'Streams' and the subsequent series 'Hints for the Holidays', North detailed his travels to Tweedsmuir, the Lake District and the Highlands. The physicality of the journeys and the landscapes inspires a range of energetic stream of consciousness anecdotes and asides, deemed journeys into the 'ideal lands of the Imagination'.[65] In 'Streams', a ride atop a mail coach 'along the royal road both to Philosophy and Poetry' enables a physical transformation which builds upon the running joke on North's gouty toe: 'Why, our crutch is now altogether unnecessary. Our toe is painless as if made of timber, yet as steel elastic. Gout, who certainly mounted the mail with us in Prince's Street, has fallen off the roof.'[66]

Given Wilson/North's penchant for energetic, imaginative travel writing, it is perhaps unsurprising that Kitchiner's moderate recommendations would soon thereafter become prime targets for the magazine within Wilson's 1827 review of *The Traveller's Oracle*. Kitchiner's warning that 'the number of miles a man may journey in a day' should be regulated by 'a sense of lassitude, which is as unerring in exercise as the sense of satiety is in eating' becomes an opportunity to celebrate physical and mental resilience and liberation from such restrictive practices:

> What [is] more common than to feel oneself very much fatigued – quite done up as it were – and unwilling to stir hand or foot. Up goes a lark in heaven – tira-lira – or suddenly the breezes blow among the clouds, that forthwith all begin campaigning in the sky – or quick as lightning the sunshine in a moment resuscitates a drowned day . . . Where is your sense of lassitude now, nature's unerring guide in exercise? You spring up from the mossy wayside bank, and renewed both in mind and body, 'rejoicing in Nature's joy,' you continue to pass over houseless moors, by small, single, solitary, straw-roofed huts, through villages gathered round Stone-cross, Elm-Grove, or old Monastic Tower, till, unwearied in lith and limb, you see sunset beautifying all the west, and drop in, perhaps, among the hush of the cottar's Saturday night.[67]

Subsequently, in 'Health and Longevity' in the January 1828 issue, a consideration of the importance of regularity in preserving physical health leads to a discussion of North's obedience only to

> the finer impulses and movements of our own spirits. When we feel our Fancy free, we fly away over flowery fields, and disappear from before the ken of our contributors in a shower of sunshine; – when we know that our Intellect is strong, we tackle to philosophical criticism and politics.[68]

As such, the moderation recommended by Dr Kitchiner and Dr Graham becomes an opportunity to construct, in humorous juxtaposition, both the North character and the ideal 'feeling and imaginative reader', who follows in his model.

Blackwood's emphasis on physical bodies, as exemplified in these reviews, was central to its innovative approach to literary criticism. As J. H. Alexander explains, Maga's world was one where 'critical judgments emerge from concrete situations – from living men reading works under particular circumstances and varying in their reactions'.[69] This innovation is what the 'Preface' of 1826 refers to when it declares that in 'Criticism', in particular, *Blackwood's* encourages readers to 'feel, think, and speak, like free men'. David Stewart argues that we should view this concern with physical bodies ironically, with North's signature gouty toe paradoxically emphasising his purely textual existence and functioning as the type of in-joke that creates a sense of intimacy between *Blackwood's* readers and writers.[70] The narrative voice of Wilson's medico-literary reviews certainly exemplifies the *Blackwood's* style of literary criticism, while the medical subject matter becomes a humorous opportunity to further the ironic obsession with the physicality of contributors. However, Wilson's particular critique of the moderation recommended by Dr Kitchiner and Dr Graham is also politicised and is part of what Gavin Budge identifies as a wider Romantic medico-literary concern with reading and writing as embodied processes.[71] For the imaginative liberation of the 'Preface' to be achieved, *Blackwood's* contributors and readers must also reject the restrictive bodily regimes of such 'radical reformer[s]', while actual (rather than imagined) readers enjoy the conceptual slippage between fictional and bodily worlds.[72]

While I first identified Wilson's review 'The Traveller's Oracle' when browsing the magazine for reviews of medical texts, the only way I have been able to construct the above contextual reading, without reading the magazine in its entirety, is by using digital resources effectively. The reading by no means exhausts all potential methodological directions, but rather exemplifies how one can work outwards from a particular article to trace discursive strands in the magazine and consider their ideological significance, while also using genre and authorship as bibliographical and exegetic tools. One could apply similar methods to, for instance, a review of a scientific or legal treatise. In my example above, tracing previous references to Kitchiner in the magazine via keyword searches and attending to Wilson's contributions to *Blackwood's* in the period just before and just after the review was published was particularly valuable, and the *Wellesley Index* contributor search function can quickly identify Wilson's currently established list of articles and collaborations in *Blackwood's*. There is currently an understandable concern regarding the effects of mass digitisation on periodical studies, but any scholar or student who disregards the tools of digital resources is doing themselves and their work a disservice. What is required is what Paul Fyfe has termed 'curatorial intelligence', an ability 'to assess and recontextualize digital objects'.[73] In reading medical (or any similarly subject-specific) content in Romantic literary magazines, I propose discourse and ideology, genre, and authorship as three approaches that can collectively enable such recontextualisation.

Notes

1. Klancher, *The Making*; Parker, *Literary Magazines*.
2. Shuttleworth, *Charlotte Brontë*, pp. 12, 63.
3. Moir, Letter to Blackwood, 26 January 1826.
4. This attribution appears in the *Wellesley Index to Victorian Periodicals* and is confirmed by Gooch's letters to Blackwood dated 18 November 1825 and 2 January 1826.
5. Moir, Letter to Blackwood, 20 November [1825?].
6. Moir, Letter to Blackwood, April 1829.
7. See Porter, 'Lay Medical Knowledge'; Dawson et al., 'Introduction', p. 12; Coyer, *Literature and Medicine*, pp. 21–32, 179. On this trend in relation to the scientific content of *Blackwood's*, see Christie, '*Blackwood's Edinburgh Magazine* in the Scientific Culture'.
8. Jeffrey and Duncan Jr, 'Willan and Others on Vaccination', p. 32.
9. Duncan Jr, 'Report on the Present State of Fever in Edinburgh', p. 347. On this attribution and for further context regarding the 'Medical Report of Edinburgh' series and this response, see Coyer, 'Medical Discourse', pp. 115–16.
10. Strout notes that William Laidlaw 'conducted this department in its early days', but concludes that '[n]o doubt various individuals contributed to the "Intelligence," both literary and scientific, from time to time' (p. 24).
11. 'Literary and Scientific Intelligence' (October 1817), p. 97; 'Literary and Scientific Intelligence' (October 1818), p. 101; 'Literary and Scientific Intelligence' (September 1820), p. 689.
12. Cantor and Shuttleworth, 'Introduction', p. 4.
13. Duncan, *Scott's Shadow*, p. 27; Dawson et al., 'Introduction', p. 12.
14. Palmegiano, *Health and British Magazines*, pp. 60–1.

15. In her Preface, Palmegiano herself notes that 'nineteenth-century papers impede inquiry by ... masking articles' meanings with arbitrary headings inhospitable to index investigators' (*Health and British Magazines*, p. viii).
16. *General Index to Blackwood's Magazine*, p. 329.
17. Available at https://www.sciper.org/browse/BE1-2.html (last accessed 10 September 2018).
18. Using the same search parameters in the *HathiTrust Digital Library* returns 215 results, whereas a *Google Books* search for the keyword 'medicine' within publications titled 'Blackwood's' and published between 1817 and 1832 only returns two results.
19. Leary, 'Googling the Victorians', p. 80.
20. Mussell, 'Beyond the "Great Index"', p. 24.
21. Gooch, 'Plague', p. 219.
22. See Ackerknecht, 'Anticontagionism'.
23. Connell, *Romanticism*, p. 250.
24. For the most thorough examination of *Blackwood's* post-1826 political ideology, see Milne, 'The Politics of *Blackwood's*, 1817–1846'.
25. Mr Starke, 'Vox Populi', p. 128.
26. Roberts, 'Radical Contagion', p. 422.
27. Ibid. pp. 425, 427.
28. Coyer, *Literature and Medicine*, p. 42.
29. Killick, '*Blackwood's* and the Boundary', pp. 170–1.
30. For a collection of these tales and background on their generic development, see Morrison and Baldick, *Tales of Terror*.
31. See Coyer, *Literature and Medicine*, pp. 36–87, 124–71.
32. Ibid. pp. 152–60.
33. Ibid. pp. 95–100.
34. Ibid. pp. 88–123.
35. Hughes, 'SIDEWAYS!', pp. 1–2.
36. Parker, *Literary Magazines*, p. 3.
37. Review of *The Traveller's Oracle*, *New Monthly Magazine*, pp. 300–4.
38. Review of *The Traveller's Oracle*, *London Magazine*, p. 181.
39. Bridge and English, *Dr. William Kitchiner*, p. 43.
40. Kitchiner, Letter to Archibald Constable, 26 March 1822.
41. See McConnell, 'Kitchiner, William (1778–1827)'; Bridge and English, *Dr. William Kitchiner*, pp. 7–20; Schiller, 'Haslam of "Bedlam"'.
42. Jerdan, *Men I Have Known*, pp. 282–3.
43. Wilson, 'The Traveller's Oracle', p. 445.
44. St. Barbe, 'Another Ladleful', p. 160; Maginn, 'Noctes X', p. 101.
45. Lockhart [?], 'The Leg of Mutton', p. 563.
46. Rejack, '"Schooling" of Taste', pp. 731–2.

47. Wilson, 'The Traveller's Oracle', p. 455.
48. Ibid. p. 447. The identity of the narrator is ambiguous. Though the style is similar to other articles by Wilson written under the Christopher North pseudonym, the narrator notes at one point that he is 'a friend of Christopher North' (ibid. p. 455), possibly in humorous reference to the relationship between Wilson the author and his fictitious persona, North. When the article is republished in *The Recreations of Christopher North* (1842), this brief aside is removed (see vol. 3, p. 154).
49. Wilson, 'The Traveller's Oracle', pp. 447–8. 'Brodd' is a Scots word meaning 'plate'.
50. Ibid. p. 455.
51. Ibid. pp. 452–4.
52. Wilson, 'Salmonia', p. 248.
53. Ibid.
54. Cronin, 'John Wilson', p. 206.
55. Macnish, Letter to Moir, 4 February 1835.
56. Lessenich, '"Noctes Ambrosianae"', p. 189. On the Romantic-era politics of eating and drinking, see also Morton, 'Introduction', pp. 1–32.
57. Wilson, 'Health and Longevity', p. 107.
58. Lessenich, '"Noctes Ambrosianae"', p. 189.
59. Wilson, 'Salmonia', p. 252.
60. Coyer, *Literature and Medicine*, pp. 2, 31.
61. The three I refer to here are 'The Traveller's Oracle', 'Health and Longevity', and 'Clark on Climate', the last of which I discuss in *Literature and Medicine*, pp. 2–3. Wilson also reviews Robert Macnish's popular medical work, *The Anatomy of Drunkenness* (1827), in April 1828; however, this review differs in that it does not self-consciously contribute to the fictional world of *Blackwood's*. These attributions are all confirmed in the *Wellesley Index*.
62. Wilson et al., 'Preface', p. xxii.
63. Latané Jr, 'William Maginn', p. 235.
64. Wilson, 'Streams', p. 391.
65. Ibid. p. 384.
66. Ibid. pp. 384, 388.
67. Wilson, 'The Traveller's Oracle', p. 446. 'Lith' is a Scots word meaning 'joint'.
68. Wilson, 'Health and Longevity', p. 109.
69. Alexander, '*Blackwood's*', p. 63.
70. Stewart, *Romantic Magazines*, pp. 138–50.
71. Budge, 'Transatlantic Irritability', pp. 267–92.
72. Wilson, 'Health and Longevity', p. 106.
73. Fyfe, 'Technologies of Serendipity', p. 262.

Part II

Aesthetics, Innovation and Taste

Chapter 3

'A Separate and Distinct Tribunal': Libel Law and Reviewing in Early Issues of *Blackwood's*

Tom Mole

In *English Bards and Scotch Reviewers*, his 1809 satire on contemporary literary culture, Lord Byron wrote that he would 'make [his] own review' in the poem, and become, like the reviewers, 'Self-constituted Judge of Poesy'.[1] In this satirical thrust at the periodical writers who had condemned his earlier book, *Hours of Idleness* (1807), Byron took aim at a weak point in his opponents' rhetorical armour. He suggested that there was no firm basis for the authority that periodical writers claimed for themselves as judges of contemporary literary culture. If their authority lay only in their own assertion of it, then anyone could proclaim himself (but almost never herself) a 'Judge of Poesy', as Byron does here. With heavy sarcasm, Byron elaborates a comparison between Francis Jeffrey, editor of the *Edinburgh Review*, and his near-namesake George Jefferies (1644–89), a notorious hanging judge:

> Health to immortal Jeffrey! once, in name,
> England could boast a judge almost the same:
> In soul so like, so merciful, yet just,
> Some think that Satan has resigned his trust,
> And given the Spirit to the world again,
> To sentence Letters, as he sentenced men.[2]

Like Jefferies returned from the grave, Jeffrey passes judgement. History repeats itself in diminished form: where Jefferies sentenced men to death, Jeffrey sentences books to readerly indifference or contempt. But while the judge's sentences were underwritten by English law, the reviewer's judgements are his alone. And if judges of poetry are 'self-constituted', then Byron – or anyone else – can speak with just as much authority as Jeffrey wields in the pages of the *Edinburgh*.

When *Blackwood's Edinburgh Magazine* was founded eight years later in 1817, its reviewers were acutely sensitive to the line of attack Byron had articulated and others had echoed in the intervening years. They faced the challenge of constituting themselves as judges of literature and the need to pre-empt claims that their authority rested on no solid basis. Seeking to police the literary culture they inhabited, *Blackwood's* reviewers didn't want to express personal opinions that were open to debate so much as to issue rulings that made further debate impertinent. They wanted to pronounce verdicts, not to offer views. Reviewers for other journals faced similar problems, but *Blackwood's* pushed the existing terms of debate to almost parodic extremes, making visible in its heated prose the rhetorical strategies that underwrote its claim to speak with authority.

As Richard Cronin has argued, reviewers in this period were anxiously concerned about their own status as professionals.[3] Being a professional man often involved belonging to a particular linguistic community and speaking with authority within it. Lawyers, doctors and other professionals had their own occupational terminology and rules governing who could speak with authority and in what circumstances. Periodical writers aspired to this kind of professional status and authority and cultivated it in several ways. They also patrolled the boundaries of their profession by scrutinising the language of other professionals who made incursions into the world of periodical writing. As Megan Coyer shows elsewhere in this volume, the surgeon and *Blackwood's* contributor David Macbeth Moir wrote repeatedly to William Blackwood complaining that the contributions of other medical men contained too much 'shop' talk (see p. 34). In Moir's view, doctors writing in the magazine should leave their medical identities behind. Periodical writers could also face similar condescension from other professions. In 1808, for example, the benchers of Lincoln's Inn considered that writers for the press were unfit to be called to the bar.[4] Cultivating a professional identity that would entitle them to pronounce critical verdicts was therefore a priority for the *Blackwood's* reviewers.

The legal profession provided the most obvious examples of professionals who enjoyed status and authority as a result of their mastery of particular linguistic protocols. In early nineteenth-century Edinburgh, the main professional organisations for lawyers were conspicuously thriving and expanding. The Faculty of Law at the

University of Edinburgh had moved to the newly built 'Old College' in 1789; the Society of Writers to the Signet completed its library building on Parliament Square in 1815; and the Faculty of Advocates opened its library in the same building in 1822 before moving to an adjacent building in 1826. These institutions played a key role in professional training, accreditation and discipline.[5] John Gibson Lockhart and John Wilson had both qualified as lawyers (as had their rivals at the *Edinburgh Review*, Francis Jeffrey and Henry Brougham). Several periodical writers combined journalism with legal practice, not least Walter Scott; and even when they gave up legal careers, many of them continued to mix with lawyers through clubs such as Edinburgh's Speculative Society, of which Scott, Jeffrey and Lockhart were all members. As home to the highest courts in Scotland – the High Court of Justiciary and the Court of Session – Edinburgh was a national centre of legal activity. The law was part of the city *Blackwood's* writers inhabited and the social circles in which they moved.

In this essay, I will examine *Blackwood's* interest in one area of law in particular: the law of libel. This interest was shared by other periodicals as well, but I will suggest that *Blackwood's* developed it in a distinctive fashion. There were several reasons for this fascination with libel. In the magazine's early years, those connected with it were repeatedly threatened with libel suits by people attacked in its pages. In November 1817, John Dalyell sued William Blackwood over his appearance as the man whose 'face was like unto the face of an ape' in the infamous 'Chaldee Manuscript' of Maga's October number and won £230 at arbitration.[6] Leigh Hunt threatened legal action over the first of the Cockney School articles in the same issue.[7] In September 1818, Hazlitt retained a lawyer to sue for £2,000 in damages after another Cockney School article. *The Times* reported the dispute, opining that the Maga was 'a book filled with private slander', and William Blackwood settled out of court.[8] In the second instalment of the *Noctes Ambrosianae*, in April 1822, 'Timothy Tickler' observed that there was a 'prosecution mania'. 'Now-a-days, every word is said to be actionable,' he complained. 'You cannot open your mouth, or put pen to paper, without feeling a libel-lawyer.'[9]

Libel cases were part of the business of running the magazine. In 1819, when he was in discussions with William Blackwood about contributing to Maga, Samuel Taylor Coleridge told William Davies (of the firm of Cadell and Davies) that many people in the book trade thought Blackwood had embedded a libel campaign into his business model. Davies reported that Coleridge 'had heard it confidently stated by many persons that, in an early stage of the publication [Blackwood had] determined to bring certain characters into notice'.[10] Knowing that this strategy would provoke libel cases and incur expenses in damages and settlements, Blackwood had apparently ensured that 'a very handsome sum had been subscribed' to bear the cost.[11] Coleridge was reporting hearsay, but the rumour that Maga had a dedicated fund for the costs of libel cases indicates how widely libel was understood to be part of the magazine's stock in trade and one of its distinctive features.

Libel law was also part of the larger political context in which the magazine operated, because libel cases were becoming the government's preferred legal mechanism for regulating the press. The laws on blasphemous and seditious libel were notoriously used as a de facto form of censorship, directed against critics of the government and its policies. Looking back from 1839 and remembering the 'thousand evils' that the *Edinburgh* was founded to oppose, Sydney Smith included among them the fact that 'Libel was punished with the most cruel and vindictive imprisonments.'[12] Periodicals – especially those that were politically opposed to the government – were concerned with libel law because it was the law that was most likely to land them in court. Leigh Hunt and his brother John were a famous example, as they had been imprisoned on charges of libel in 1812 for their attacks on the Prince Regent in *The Examiner*. Following the Peterloo Massacre of 1819, the Blasphemous and Seditious Libels Act, one of the notorious 'Six Acts', increased the penalties for convicted libellers to a maximum sentence of 14 years' transportation. Between 1817 and 1821, there were 131 prosecutions for seditious or blasphemous libel, out of an estimated total of 183 between 1816 and 1834.[13] While *Blackwood's* conservative political views meant that its journalists were unlikely to be charged with blasphemous or seditious libel by the Tory governments of its first 13 years, all periodical writers had good reason to pay attention to debates about the libel laws and their application.

But I suggest that there was another, less obvious reason why *Blackwood's* was concerned with such laws. Libel courts offered a model of authority that Maga's writers tried to adapt to their own purposes.

Contemplating the form of regulation to which they were subject gave them a way to imagine the form of regulation they might exercise. Jon Klancher asserts that while William Pitt's government had relied on 'the state's force against the radical writer's passions . . . , after 1820 [British] culture had to become capable of generating its own principle of protective control'.[14] *Blackwood's* sought to develop that 'principle of protective control' as an independent tribunal for policing culture. Libel courts and book reviews, after all, were engaged in similar projects. Both aimed to regulate public discourse, defining the limits of what was acceptable to say or write in public. They did this via authoritative pronouncements: verdicts and sentences in the case of libel courts, decisive critical judgements in the case of reviews. When they searched for models of the kind of authority they wanted to cultivate, then, the *Blackwood's* reviewers needed to look no farther than the libel cases with which their legal training had familiarised them, and in which their work as writers had sometimes involved them.

In order to understand why libel law interested the *Blackwood's* reviewers, and how they turned the judicial procedures of the libel courts into the rhetorical strategies of their book reviews, we need to grasp the rather complex laws that governed libel cases at the time. William Blackstone elucidated the English law on libel in his *Commentaries on the Laws of England*, originally published in 1765–70 and updated well into the nineteenth century as a standard textbook. Blackstone defined libels as 'malicious defamations of any person . . . made public by either printing, writing, signs, or pictures, in order to provoke him to wrath, or expose him to public hatred, contempt, and ridicule'.[15]

During the early nineteenth century, English law sustained two distinct understandings of libel: one as a civil offence and the other as a criminal offence. The categories of utterance developed by J. L. Austin in his 1962 book *How to Do Things with Words* provide a helpful way to understand the differences between the civil law and criminal law approaches to thinking about libel. In civil law, a libel was understood as what Austin would call a 'constative utterance', that is, it stated something or reported on some state of affairs, either accurately or inaccurately.[16] In criminal law, however, a libel was conceived as what Austin would call a 'performative utterance', that is, the kind of utterance that accomplished something in the act of uttering, such as a promise, vow or bet.[17] This kind of utterance does not report on an existing state of affairs; instead, it brings about a new state of affairs. I will argue below that the kinds of performative utterance scrutinised and deployed in criminal cases of libel were of particular interest to the *Blackwood's* reviewers because they resembled the kinds of performative utterance they hoped to produce in their reviews.[18]

Libel in the Law

In civil law, libel cases were a tort: that is, a case involving a wrong allegedly committed by the defendant against the plaintiff, resulting in some harm to the plaintiff and some liability for damages for the defendant if convicted. Civil libel was usually understood as a subset of property law: libel constituted a form of damage to your reputation, or theft of your good name. Reputation was treated as a kind of property or asset, since its loss could result in loss of earnings. If you published statements accusing a butcher of selling tainted meat, a maid of stealing from her employer or a barrister of appearing drunk in court, then the butcher could seek damages for the loss of earnings when customers spurned his shop, the maid for the loss of earnings when her employer turned her out, and the barrister for the loss of earnings when clients ceased to use his services. Civil cases were particularly concerned with whether the alleged libel was true. If the butcher really were dishonest, the maid a thief or the barrister a drunkard, there would be no case to answer. You could not rob someone of a reputation they were not entitled to in the first place. In civil court, then, the defence could maintain that a published attack was not libellous because it was true. Here, the allegedly libellous utterance was understood, in J. L. Austin's terms, to be constative; it described a pre-existing fact either accurately or inaccurately.[19]

In contrast, Blackstone explained, criminal law defined libel primarily as a breach of the peace. Publishing a libel, it was supposed, risked inciting retribution, possibly in the form of physical violence. Criminal libel was therefore not an offence against the individual libelled but against the community that was disturbed by the fracas it provoked. The law existed not to redress an injury done to one person but to uphold the peace for everyone. As a result, strange though it might seem, in criminal cases it didn't matter to the law whether the allegedly libellous statement was true or not. As Blackstone put it, 'it is immaterial with respect to the essence of a libel, whether the matter of it be true or false; since the provocation, and not the falsity, is the thing to be punished criminally'.[20] The same reasoning applied in Scottish law. According to John Borthwick's 1826 treatise on Scottish defamation law, 'it is the general rule of the law of Scotland that the truth of the imputation, or the *veritas convicii*, shall not be admitted as a justification of the offence' of libel.[21] In certain circumstances, it might actually aggravate the offence if the statement were true. An 1834 parliamentary hearing on potentially reforming libel laws heard remarks from Henry Brougham, who was then Lord Chancellor but had been a founding contributor to the *Edinburgh Review* three decades earlier at the start of his legal and political career. Elucidating the English law of criminal libel, Brougham imagined

> the case of a woman, having had a bastard child in Cornwall, afterwards living with a blameless reputation in Northumberland; a man, who has knowledge of that fact, takes advantage of it to solicit the consent of the woman to an improper connection, and being rejected, revenges himself by the publication of her former disgrace.[22]

In such a case, the published assertion would be true, but it would still be libellous under the existing law, because the test the court applied was whether the alleged libel was published maliciously and was liable to disturb the peace of the community. Here, the libellous utterance was understood to be performative in Austin's terms. Its illocutionary force was realised in the act of publication; to publish a libel was to bring about a state of affairs, not to represent one.

In 1827, the progressive *Examiner* explained the nature of criminal libel for its readers using the device of a letter from a fictitious rustic buffoon called Zachariah Homespun. Zachariah wrote to the magazine in a state of confusion. He had learnt that his son's schoolmaster had been convicted of attempted pederasty while employed at another school. As well as withdrawing his son from school, Zachariah wished to reveal the schoolmaster's criminal past to the parents of the other boys. But as he was about to do so, he met the local lawyer, who advised him that speaking up might well lead to his being indicted for libel. When Zachariah protested that the schoolmaster's conviction was a fact, the lawyer informed him that it made no difference to the law. Plunged into perplexity by this apparently absurd situation, Zachariah wrote to 'Muster 'Zaminer' for advice.[23]

A debate over whether it was morally right that a statement could be true in fact but still legally libellous raged throughout the Romantic period. The Whig leader Charles James Fox's Libel Act of 1792 gave juries the responsibility for deciding if a publication was libellous and, if so, the damages to be paid. Prior to this, judges had often directed juries to bring in a verdict of guilty if they concluded that the offending statement had been published, since the libellous nature of the publication was understood as a matter of law, best adjudicated by the judge.[24] In 1843, the English law changed again, making evidence of the truth of a libel permissible as a defence in criminal cases. This effectively removed the illocutionary dimension from criminal libel, rendering both criminal and civil libels understandable as constative utterances.

The independence of Scottish law having been guaranteed under the 1707 Act of Union, Scotland had its own common-law understanding of libel, which was handled under the more general common law for defamation and slander.[25] It, too, allowed for both criminal prosecutions – handled in the early nineteenth century by the Sheriff Court – and civil actions for damages, handled by civil courts. Civil courts, however, gradually took over almost all actions for defamation in the first decades of the century.[26] As in England, the truth of an alleged defamation was not always legally relevant at the beginning of the nineteenth century, but the truth of the statement became more acceptable as a defence by the middle of the century.[27] Because *Blackwood's* was distributed in England as well as Scotland, actions for libel could be brought in either legal system, either against Blackwood himself, one of his contributors, or the magazine's English distributors John Murray and later Cadell and Davies. Margaret Oliphant reports that when John Hunt called at the offices of the London publishing firm Baldwin, Cradock and Co. demanding to know the identity of the author of the Cockney School articles so that his brother Leigh could bring an action for libel against the writer, the *Blackwood's* contributors were anxious to know whether the case would be brought in London or Edinburgh.[28] (In the event, Hunt seems to have thought better of bringing a case at all.)

To attend to the debates surrounding libel between 1792 and 1843 is to enter into a curious, looking-glass world, in which you could be convicted for stating the truth, even if you could prove the truth of your statement. This world greatly interested periodical writers and readers, but I will suggest that *Blackwood's* developed a distinctive response to it. While other periodicals reported on libel cases and treated the debates over libel laws as a topic for discussion, *Blackwood's* reviewers saw in the discourse and procedures of the libel courts possibilities for constructing their own literary authority.

Libel in the Periodicals: A Case Study from the *Quarterly Review*

Major Romantic periodicals such as the *Edinburgh Review* and the *Quarterly Review* included detailed and repeated discussions of libel law. These discussions could run to great length: the *Edinburgh* carried a 42-page review of Thomas Ludlow Holt's book on the law of libel in 1816, and the *Quarterly* ran a 40-page analysis of Thomas Starkie's *Treatise of the Law of Slander and Libel* in 1827. These articles rehearsed the question of whether it was right that the criminal law took no account of the truth of an alleged libel. In their conclusions, the magazines largely divided along party lines. The conservative *Quarterly* supported the existing law, claiming that libel prosecutions seldom concerned matters of fact, and that when they did, 'the question of truth or falsehood in real effect can seldom any more enter into the inquiry than the colour of the paper or the ink by which they are set forth'.[29] The Whiggish *Edinburgh*, conversely, blasted the existing law, arguing that the truth or falsehood of the statement was always relevant.[30] The *Quarterly*'s article is particularly germane for this essay, because it contains an extended discussion about the use of libel laws to restrict freedom of the press. Although the *Quarterly* article dates from a decade after *Blackwood's* was founded, it sets out a conservative understanding of the relationship between libel laws and the press that *Blackwood's* had already been reacting against for some time.

In its 1827 review of Starkie's *Treatise of the Law of Slander and Libel*, the *Quarterly* produced an extended comparison between the libel courts and the press, evaluating the claims of each to regulate public discourse. The reviewer was Charles Edward Dodd, a barrister who reviewed a number of legal books for the *Quarterly* around this time. He argued that periodicals should restrict themselves to the strictly secondary role of reporting the judgements of the courts 'with all comments that are temperate and useful'. 'Thus far,' Dodd pointed out, 'the press exercises no judicial or censorial functions; it neither passes convictions, nor inflicts sentences.' '[I]t is obviously one thing to *report* decrees,' he concluded, 'and another to *pronounce* them.'[31] In this article, then, the *Quarterly* reviewer understood the connections between the business of the libel courts and that of the periodicals. But he was careful not to represent them as equivalents to one another. On this understanding, the periodicals had an important social role to play in publicising the judgements of the courts, but they did not make judgements of their own. Their authority was secondary to an authority constituted elsewhere.

Dodd acknowledged that the role he reserved for periodical writers was a modest and limited one, and he disavowed any more ambitious aspiration. It was only 'self-styled friends of the press', he claimed, who 'demand[ed] for it an extended empire, and an original jurisdiction of its own'. Even as he rejected this idea, however, Dodd gave it voice in an extended description. On the view attributed to 'self-styled friends of the press', he explained, periodical writing ought

> to constitute of itself a separate and distinct tribunal, not only taking cognizance of, and stigmatizing legal crimes which may escape the vengeance of the law, but, over and above all this, punishing offenders against morals and decency, and even good taste and good manners, whom the ordinary laws consider entirely beyond their controul [*sic*].[32]

Here, then, was a clear articulation of the idea that periodical writing should be understood not as an inferior assistant to the courts, but as their full and equal partner in regulating society. The role of periodicals, on this view, was not simply to amplify and disseminate the judgements of the courts, but to pronounce judgements of their own. By doing so, periodicals could aspire to police areas of culture that the courts could not reach, to become 'a separate and distinct tribunal' with its own jurisdiction and its own distinctive kind of authority. This, I will argue, was the understanding that *Blackwood's* was busy developing in the decade before this review appeared.

This understanding gained strength from the legal opinion that libel laws should not apply to criticism of published works. In the same article, Dodd noted that:

literary criticism, and the free discussion of the merits and defects of authors, ... are ... totally without any legal restraint – and even the weapons of sarcasm and ridicule are perfectly lawful for the purpose of exposing ignorance, bad taste, or false pretension.[33]

He quoted Lord Ellenborough, the Lord Chief Justice, who set out his reasoning for this exemption in full in his judgement on the 1808 libel case of *Carr v. Hood*:

> One writer, in exposing the follies and errors of another, may make use of ridicule, however poignant. Ridicule is often the fittest weapon that can be employed for such a purpose. If the reputation or pecuniary interests of the person ridiculed suffer, it is *damnum absque injuriâ* [a loss without injury]. Where is the liberty of the press, if an action can be maintained on such principles? Perhaps the plaintiff's tour through Scotland is now unsaleable; but is he to be indemnified by receiving a compensation in damages from the person who may have opened the eyes of the public to the bad taste and inanity of his compositions? ... We really must not cramp observations upon authors and their works. They should be liable to criticism, exposure, and even ridicule, if their compositions be ridiculous; otherwise; the first who writes a book on any subject will maintain a monopoly of sentiment and opinion respecting it. This would tend to the perpetuity of error. Reflection on personal character is another thing. Show me an attack on the moral character of this plaintiff, or any attack upon his character unconnected with his authorship, and I shall be as ready as any judge who ever sat here to protect him; but I cannot hear of malice, on account of turning his works into ridicule.[34]

In ridiculing published works, then, the periodicals exercised jurisdiction over an area of culture that the courts could not reach. Periodicals had no authority to punish illegality, but they could castigate bad morals, bad manners, bad writing and bad taste.

The *Quarterly* was careful to distinguish between the work of the courts and that of the reviews. First, it claimed, the courts and the reviews performed different kinds of speech act. The courts pronounced verdicts and passed sentences, while the reviews reported and offered commentary. Second, it suggested, courts and reviews operated in different areas of culture and society. The courts dealt with crimes or torts, while the reviews discussed *mores*. This understanding gave the periodical reviews their own regulatory role in society, while circumscribing their jurisdiction and limiting their power. For Maga's ambitious and often intemperate writers, these constraints threatened to stifle their conception of the magazine as a powerful cultural force capable of delivering authoritative verdicts on writers and their works.

Libel in *Blackwood's Edinburgh Magazine*

When they took the helm of Maga's first incarnation as the *Edinburgh Monthly Magazine*, James Cleghorn and Thomas Pringle were content to remain within the understanding of a magazine's limited role later articulated by Dodd in the *Quarterly*. They reported on libel cases involving other periodicals from as early as August 1817, when the magazine carried a note of the libel case brought by the government against T. J. Wooler and the *Black Dwarf*, observing that 'the defendant pleaded his own cause with considerable force and eloquence'.[35] They were also well aware of the controversy surrounding whether the truth of a libel should be a defence. Reporting on Wooler's conviction, they noted how some jury members had objected to the law constraining them to find a true statement libellous. (Three jurors wished to add a qualification to their decision – 'As truth is declared by the law of the land to be a libel, we three are compelled to find the defendant guilty' – but the judge refused to allow it.[36]) In its first incarnation, then, the magazine operated within accepted understandings of propriety by reporting on libel cases decided in the courts, but shying away either from committing libels or from trying to pass verdicts of its own.

With the launch of *Blackwood's Edinburgh Magazine* in October 1817, however, a new approach to questions around libel began to take shape. Increasingly, the language of the courtroom penetrated the rhetoric of the magazine's reviews, even as its writers became willing to treat libellous statements as just another weapon in the reviewer's arsenal. The language of the law overflowed from reportage to reviewing, to the extent that it significantly shaped the magazine's distinctive rhetorical style. Courtroom metaphors became explicit in literary polemics like 'Letter from Z. to Mr Leigh Hunt' (January 1818) and 'Hazlitt Cross-Questioned' (August 1818). In 'Letter from Z. to Mr Leigh Hunt', Lockhart cast the magazine as a courtroom and himself as an advocate presenting the case against Hunt. 'My October paper was merely an opening of the case,' he wrote, 'I said, as plainly as words could speak it, that the examination of witnesses, and the closing address, would both follow in their season.'[37] In 'Hazlitt Cross-Questioned', Hazlitt is cast in the role of a defendant called to the stand, and the reviewer appears as the prosecuting advocate examining him.[38] *Blackwood's* appropriation of legal rhetoric was especially conspicuous in these articles, where legal forms provided an organising principle. But Maga's reviewers routinely adopted such rhetoric in less systematic ways; they appealed to the jury of public opinion, painted themselves as advocates, prosecutors and judges, and pronounced sentence on poems that had been convicted at their tribunal. With these rhetorical tactics, they imagined the magazine's reviews as exactly the 'separate and distinct tribunal' that the *Quarterly* would later disclaim.

This image of the book review as a courtroom existed alongside other ways of imagining book reviewing and periodical controversy. Reviews were also figured as a kind of assault: in July 1818, Z. imagined Hazlitt being 'stripped to the naked skin, and made to swallow his own vile prescriptions', while, in April 1821, William Maginn would describe Z. in the pages of the magazine as 'wet with the blood of the Cockneys'.[39] And this kind of rhetorical violence sometimes prompted physical violence. John Douglas, a Glasgow writer pilloried in Maga's pages, attacked William Blackwood with a horsewhip in Princes Street in 1817. Blackwood responded by going after his assailant with a cudgel, with John Wilson and James Hogg lending support.[40] This kind of behaviour fitted the self-image of the Maga crew (and Wilson in particular) as hearty, masculine and intemperate.[41] But, for professional men, the legal brief, not the horsewhip, was the preferred tool for dealing with disputes. While *Blackwood's* belligerent style tried to cudgel its foes into submission, its adoption of legal vocabulary helped to cultivate a professional identity for its reviewers.

As that identity took shape, the reviewers shored up their authority to pronounce verdicts of their own. This process took time, and it was accompanied by moments when the magazine appeared to defer to the judgement of the public it served. In July 1818, Z. employed legal language when condemning Leigh Hunt, but imagined the 'public voice' passing the sentence, rather than the reviewer. 'The public voice has lifted up against Hunt,' he claimed, 'and sentence of excommunication from the poets of England has been pronounced, enrolled, and ratified.'[42] Lockhart turned a similar rhetorical strategy against Percy Shelley in January 1819. In his 'Observations on *The Revolt of Islam*', Lockhart associated Shelley with 'the sophistical and phantastical enemies of religion and good order among mankind', who had already been condemned by all right-thinking people.[43] 'Their sentence was pronounced without hesitation, almost without pity,' he wrote, 'for there was nothing in [Shelley's works] to redeem their evil.'[44] In these cases, Maga made a show of deferring to public opinion, reporting sentences that had apparently already been pronounced by the 'public voice'.

But *Blackwood's* display of deference was actually a strategy for cultivating its own authority to speak on behalf of a public, as a judge in a libel court did. The magazine's apparent willingness to defer to public opinion was in fact a rhetorical device for forming public opinion. Wilson, in his October 1819 essay on Coleridge – the third in the series of 'Essays on the Lake School' – accused other reviewers of using the 'wicked arts, by which the superficial mass of readers are so easily swayed in all their judgments' in order to put down Coleridge's reputation.[45] He proposed to re-educate the public, affirming that 'we can never suppose ourselves to be ill employed when we are doing any thing that may serve in any measure to correct the errors of the public judgment'.[46] Lockhart, meanwhile, moved smoothly from reporting the public verdict on Hunt to casting the Cockney School essays as the trial that would produce that verdict. He advised Hunt not to respond until

> the end of the trial, when the proofs had all been produced, when your accuser had closed his mouth, and the impartial jury of your country were about to form their final opinion, whether you were or were not guilty of the things which had been laid to your account.[47]

Blackwood's, then, continually muddied the distinction the *Quarterly* would later draw between reporting verdicts and pronouncing them. It employed a rhetoric of reviewing that sought to establish the magazine as a 'separate and distinct tribunal' policing the limits of public discourse.

Both the law court where libel cases were heard and its metaphorical double, the book review, offered spaces in which to debate competing views about how best to police the boundaries of acceptable public discourse. In both cases, the legitimacy of the verdicts depended on appealing to a shared understanding of propriety. A literary reviewer was not concerned so much with the truth or falsehood of the text under review as with its effect on the community at large. As with the judge and jury in a criminal libel trial, the key point was the effect a statement tended to produce in the public sphere, rather than its truth. While accuracy might be important in a travel guide, for example, what mattered in a volume of poetry was the effect the poems were likely to have on the community of readers.

Judging that effect meant appealing to a set of shared values, a usually unarticulated moral consensus. Libel laws relied on a common understanding of which public statements were acceptable and which were likely to constitute or incite a breach of the peace. Book reviews similarly appealed to an imagined consensus about the kinds of writing that were socially valuable, and those that were a threat. The periodical writers and the libel courts, then, were similarly engaged in the project of regulating public discourse. They both carried out this project in the name of a moral consensus about what kinds of public speech were acceptable and therefore what kind of society was desirable.

The problem Maga faced in carrying out this mission was that its writers lacked the illocutionary authority of the libel courts to pronounce verdicts. In his long *Quarterly* review of Starkie's book on libel law, Dodd tackled this problem head on. 'The sentence of a court carries credit on the face of it; and the individual there pronounced guilty, is believed to be so by the world,' he explained. 'But the unauthorised stigmas of the press are often treated as malicious and idle rumours – at best they create vague suspicion, and distrust, rather than stamp clear guilt on the offender.'[48] *Blackwood's* solution to this problem was to make up for its lack of authority with a style that sought to produce its own authority. The court, having established authority to pronounce verdicts and sentences, had no need of assistance from heightened rhetoric. The *Quarterly* observed that the courts 'award[ed] the calm and dispassionate sentence of the law'.[49] By contrast, the *Quarterly* made clear that a periodical reviewer's authority was inseparable from the rhetorical strategies he employed: he was 'obliged to resort to the language of vehement castigation and censure, with which personal and malignant feeling is almost certain to be mixed up'.[50] Dodd found such heated rhetoric regrettable, but

Blackwood's would adopt it wholeheartedly in pursuit of its programme of social and cultural regulation. Maga's heated style reflects the periodical's efforts to conjure up the kind of authority that the libel courts wielded.

From the beginning of Lockhart and Wilson's involvement with the magazine in October 1817, *Blackwood's* was distinguished among other periodicals by its willingness to engage in a kind of rhetoric that could be understood as libellous. Its October 1817 issue set the tone for what was to come. The Chaldee Manuscript seemed so obviously libellous that it prompted Dalyell's legal action; the long negative review of *Biographia Literaria* led Coleridge to consider suing for libel; and the first of the Cockney School articles established libellous attacks on political opponents as part of the new magazine's stock in trade.[51] Seven months later, in May 1818, Z. responded to Hunt's legal threats by charging that, through his *Examiner*, Hunt himself was guilty of 'the publication of many hundred libels, both of a public and private kind'.[52] Furthermore, he charged, 'you, who have libelled so many men, ought not to have considered yourself sacred from the hand of vengeance'.[53] Maga seemed intent on distinguishing itself from other periodicals by its use of libel as just another tool of reviewing. This understanding rapidly became *Blackwood's* distinctive position, even as it continued to entertain other views in its pages.

When he argued that criticisms of published works could not be libellous even when they ridiculed the work under review, Lord Ellenborough sought to draw a clear line between attacking a work and attacking the character of its author. *Blackwood's* would continually test this boundary.[54] 'What are books that don't express the personal characters of their authors?', its 'editor' rhetorically asked in the first instalment of the *Noctes Ambrosianae* in 1822, 'and who can review books, without reviewing those that wrote them?'[55] If there was no line between the book and the individual who wrote it, then, far from being exempt from libel, book reviews necessarily entailed libels. *Blackwood's* distinctive understanding of book reviewing and literary commentary was that it provided a way of regulating the conduct of individuals within the public sphere, not just a forum for criticising published works.

Maga thus sought to trade on an analogy – usually implicit but sometimes explicit – between the libel courts and the book reviews. Like libel courts, book reviews policed public discourse in the name of a shared understanding of propriety; in doing so, they helped to shape that understanding. Like libel courts, book reviews appealed to an unarticulated consensus about what constituted an acceptable public statement. This appeal was underwritten by a conception of the community that sponsored the consensus and therefore authorised proclamations in support of it. The *Blackwood's* writers showed that they were willing to perpetrate libels, but they also modelled their reviewing to some extent on the languages and practices of the libel courts. They did so because they aspired to be the acknowledged, authorised representatives of a community, charged with enforcing the conventions governing acceptable public speech. They therefore continually gestured towards an authorising group of people among whom certain things could be said and other things could not – or not without incurring the social sanctions of the community, the disapproval of people like us who agree on this sort of thing. There were some things that you could not say and remain a full member of the community. The *Blackwood's* review, like the libel court, aspired to be the place where judgements about those things were pronounced. The community it helped to shape and define came into view at its edges, where the boundaries of acceptable speech were made visible in the verdicts of libel courts and the judgements of book reviews. That community's peaceful functioning was threatened by breaches of decorum, whether they appeared in the form of libellous statements or supposedly immoral poems. The law of libel, with its performative dimension, therefore underwrote the *Blackwood's* writers' claims to exercise an important civic function in the literary sphere.

Notes

1. Byron, *English Bards*, p. 231, lines 60, 62.
2. Ibid. pp. 242–3, lines 438–43.
3. Cronin, *Paper Pellets*, esp. pp. 1–17, 123–53.
4. Woodward, *The Age of Reform*, p. 30.
5. It took some time for periodical writers to evolve their own professional associations. The Chartered Institute of Journalists was founded in 1884 and received its Royal Charter in 1890.
6. 'Translation from an Ancient Chaldee Manuscript', p. 94. See Flynn, 'Beginning *Blackwood's*', pp. 28, 32 and Oliphant, *Annals*, vol. 1, pp. 130–1.

7. Oliphant, *Annals*, vol. 1, pp. 134–5.
8. Wu, *William Hazlitt*, pp. 256–7.
9. [Wilson], 'Noctes II', p. 485.
10. Davies, Letter to Blackwood, 6 April 1819.
11. Ibid.
12. Smith, *The Works*, vol. 1, p. vi.
13. Woodward, *The Age of Reform*, p. 31.
14. Klancher, *The Making*, p. 61. Klancher refers in this passage to 'English culture's interests', but the context makes clear that comparable concerns operated in the Scottish context.
15. Blackstone, *Commentaries*, vol. 4, p. 150.
16. Austin, *How to Do Things*, pp. 3–5.
17. Ibid. pp. 6–7.
18. I seek here to build on the analysis of performative discourse in *Blackwood's* offered by Christine Woody in this volume, as well as on my own previous work. See Mole, '"We Solemnly"', pp. 353–62.
19. Austin, *How to Do Things*, p. 3.
20. Blackstone, *Commentaries*, vol. 4, p. 150. Blackstone acknowledges that prosecutions for libel are rare where the substance of the libel is acknowledged to be true by the plaintiff, and that the truth of a libel may extenuate the offence, even in the criminal law (p. 151).
21. Borthwick, *A Treatise*, p. 256.
22. As reported by 'A Constant Reader', 'Libel Law', p. 562.
23. 'Zachariah Homespun', 'Law of Libel', p. 2.
24. The key section of Fox's Libel Act (32 Geo. III, c. 60) is reprinted in Aspinall and Smith, *English Historical Documents 1783–1832*, pp. 363–4.
25. A comprehensive overview of the history of Scottish law in this area is provided by Blackie, 'Defamation', pp. 633–708.
26. Blackie, 'Defamation', pp. 684–5.
27. Ibid. p. 693.
28. Oliphant, *Annals*, vol. 1, p. 134.
29. [Dodd], 'Starkie on the Law', p. 581.
30. Review of *The Law of Libel*, pp. 102–44.
31. [Dodd], 'Starkie on the Law,' p. 586; italics in original.
32. Ibid. p. 586.
33. Ibid. p. 574.
34. Quoted in ibid., pp. 574–5.
35. 'Register. – British Chronicle', p. 543.
36. Ibid. pp. 543–4.
37. [Lockhart], 'Letter from Z. to Mr. Leigh Hunt', p. 414.
38. [Wilson], 'Hazlitt Cross-Questioned', pp. 550–2.

39. [Lockhart], 'On the Cockney School of Poetry, No. III', p. 456; [Maginn], 'Hymn to Christopher North', p. 62.
40. Gibbon, *The Life of George Combe*, vol. 1, p. 112, cited in Morrison, 'William Blackwood', p. 23.
41. Mark Schoenfield examines in detail how Maga 'organizes issues of aesthetics through metaphors of violence, and confronts violence within a paradigm of aesthetics' in 'The Taste for Violence', p. 187.
42. [Lockhart], 'On the Cockney School of Poetry, No. III', p. 454.
43. [Lockhart], 'Observations on *The Revolt of Islam*', p. 475. For a discussion of the attribution of this review, see Mole (ed.), *Selected Criticism*, p. 243.
44. [Lockhart], 'Observations on *The Revolt of Islam*', p. 475.
45. [Wilson], 'Essays on the Lake School', p. 3.
46. Ibid. p. 3.
47. [Lockhart], 'Letter from Z. to Mr. Leigh Hunt', p. 414.
48. [Dodd], 'Starkie on the Law', p. 589.
49. Ibid. p. 588.
50. Ibid. p. 588.
51. Coleridge wrote to Henry Crabb Robinson on 4 December 1817 about the possibility of 'bringing to legal Justice the Publisher of the atrocious Calumny' (*Collected Letters*, vol. 4, p. 786).
52. [Lockhart], 'Letter from Z. to Leigh Hunt', p. 197.
53. Ibid. p. 200.
54. For a discussion of this aspect of the magazine, see Mole, '*Blackwood's* "Personalities"', pp. 89–99.
55. [Lockhart], 'Noctes I', p. *362.

Chapter 4

Performing Personae in *Blackwood's* and Romantic Periodicals

Christine Woody

Peter Murphy's reading of the dangerous disjuncture between texts and realities in *Blackwood's*, 'Impersonation and Authorship in Romantic Britain', remains one of the most succinct and often-quoted descriptions of the problems of magazine personae at the end of the Romantic period. He argues that the deadly duel between John Scott, the editor of the *London Magazine*, and Jonathan Christie, the second of John Gibson Lockhart, was 'an assertion of coherence' between 'two worlds': the worlds of public identity and of discourse.[1] It was an assertion, he argues, that grew out of *Blackwood's* 'nearly obsessive interest in the interaction, attachment and slippage between authors (published names) and persons (bodies indicated by names)'.[2] As Kim Wheatley has insisted, *Blackwood's* did not invent this focus on the private and personal, but 'intensif[ied] the virulence inherited from the *Edinburgh* and the *Quarterly*' and went 'a step further than the quarterlies in embracing the practice of character assassination'.[3] *Blackwood's* interesting tension between authors and persons is not an aberration, but a natural outgrowth of Romantic periodical culture.

The need that Murphy notes – the need to reconcile authors (as published names) and persons (as bodies indicated by names) – participates in what I will term the 'authenticity' approach to periodical literature. This approach seeks to distil from the chaotic space of the periodical the productions of known authors. The study of Romantic periodicals is much indebted to this approach for its legitimacy: periodicals like *Blackwood's* owe their original claim on our attention to their ability to draw in and trade on the great names of the Romantic period. Looking back at Mark Parker's seminal treatment in *Literary*

Magazines and British Romanticism, the names of Hazlitt, Carlyle and 'Elia' (Charles Lamb) serve as anchors and justifications for his insistence on the value of this new area of literary investigation. This emphasis on the contributor's name is a useful – and at times necessary – means of engaging with, and determining a path through, the complex textual object of the periodical.

Names are not merely incorporated but produced by *Blackwood's* and its imitators; from Maga to the *London Magazine* to *Fraser's Magazine*, a complex social world can be traced. Maga famously fabricated, borrowed and even hijacked the names of different writers and public figures. In examining the breadth of contributor names, Murphy elaborates an ever-shifting taxonomy. He uses the term 'pseudo-person' to describe a contributor whose name is a pseudonym and who is created and used 'almost exclusively' by a single person.[4] Elsewhere on the continuum, we find 'pseudonym[s] on [the] way to being pseudo-person[s]' as well as the 'simple' pseudonyms and even entirely fictional characters (for example, he cites 'Winnifred Jenkins, a character from *Humphry Clinker* who appears as a contributor to the magazine').[5] The centrality of unreliable acts of naming to *Blackwood's* culture of publication rebounds against our impulse to use verifiable names to chart a course through Maga. To do so would obscure the complexity of the magazine's use of personae and would artificially divorce an author like James Hogg from the periodical, even while its monthly issues were still invoking his name and involving his reputation. The named, authenticated authorship pathway, as it were, does not allow us to engage with the magazine's use of personae on its own terms. While it has been essential to advance arguments about the work of certain contributors, this approach struggles to capture the logic of the medium itself.

This chapter will seek to add another method of analysis to the periodical scholar's arsenal. It will focus on the system that structures and gives meaning to individual periodical personae. In this sense, it is a diachronic analysis of the growth of personae, a mapping of the horizon of meanings that they take on over the course of their publishing lives. In order to animate this method, I will draw on the speech act theory of J. L. Austin, mobilising his definitions of felicity and infelicity to explain the way that individual personae function within the pages of a periodical. By replacing the language of authenticity with the language of felicity, I will be able to read those inauthentic but characteristic performances which a periodical like *Blackwood's* confabulates about its contributors.

Periodical Performativity

Blackwood's key contribution to periodical writing lies in its ability to stretch to its limits the performative work of magazine publication. By deploying contributor names, stolen identities and highly developed personae in a complex but consistent manner, Maga highlights the performative quality of publication. Performativity, as I am using it in this chapter, refers to the category of utterances that do not describe a state of affairs, but actually accomplish an action. These are utterances that have the force of action rather than the passivity of information transfer. In this usage I am borrowing from J. L. Austin, who identified this class of 'speech acts' in his series of lectures, *How to Do Things with Words*, delivered at Harvard University in 1955. Austin's lectures elaborate a theory of performative utterances, tracing it through a complex and ultimately unravelling taxonomy of classes of speech and speech acts. The involuted nature of the taxonomy, as well as its shifting vocabulary – Austin described himself as being 'bogged down' and eventually shifted to a new terminology of 'illocutionary forces' – has made his theory difficult to apply.[6] His further move to bracket all literary texts from consideration in his analysis has sat uncomfortably with literary scholars, drawing responses from Derrida and de Man.[7]

The persona-filled pages of *Blackwood's*, however, offer an important cause to return to Austin, in part because they are bedevilled by the same problems that Austin himself confronted. Constructing a systematic taxonomy of different personae and personalities in Maga inevitably bogs down. Furthermore, the line between literary and non-literary language is one that is crossed and recrossed by the magazine format. What Austin offers in his concept of the speech act is a way to look at individual elements of the magazine as performances embedded in both a temporal unfolding and a context that helps to shape their meaning. Austin's theory is still exemplary in its ability to capture how we use language performatively in social contexts, and what *Blackwood's* inaugurated for British reading audiences was the habit of reading about a pseudo-fictional social context not merely in the self-contained pages of a novel, but in a periodical text that bleeds out into the real world. Austin's theory is one that is willing to talk seriously about types of speech that might otherwise be considered 'nonsense' – and it is well-positioned, I believe, to unpack the famous nonsense of Maga.

The classic example of a speech act for Austin is the marriage ceremony. During this ceremony, words are said ('I do') that constitute an action beyond their descriptive meaning. They are a performative utterance, by which, when performed correctly, the people involved become married. According to Austin, utterances of this nature cannot be true or false, only felicitous or infelicitous. A performative utterance that is not performed correctly is not 'void or without effect', but rather is an action begun but not successfully 'implemented' or 'consummated'.[8] As such, his theory recognises the role of utterances that fail or misfire within a larger system of meaning. Austin itemises the conditions of 'felicity' in the following manner:

(A. 1) There must exist an accepted conventional procedure having a certain conventional effect, that procedure to include the uttering of certain words by certain persons in certain circumstances, and further,

(A. 2) the particular persons and circumstances in a given case must be appropriate for the invocation of the particular procedure invoked.

(B. 1) The procedure must be executed by all participants both correctly and

(B. 2) completely.

(Γ. 1) Where, as often, the procedure is designed for use by persons having certain thoughts or feelings, or for the inauguration of certain consequential conduct on the part of any participant, then a person participating in and so invoking the procedure must in fact have those thoughts or feelings, and the participants must intend so to conduct themselves, and further

(Γ. 2) must actually so conduct themselves subsequently.[9]

As the above breakdown suggests, a speech act is made felicitous both by the conditions under which it occurs (A), the forms through which it is completed (B) and the subsequent reactions or events that reconfirm that it did in fact take place (Γ). To return to the marriage example, if the words are spoken and all forms of the marriage ceremony are observed but there is no marriage licence issued, the act becomes infelicitous due to inappropriate circumstances (A. 2). In another case, all legal forms might be correctly observed, but the marriage is being conducted for purposes other than the accepted intent – a marriage conducted to prevent deportation, for instance. In such a situation, according to Austin, the speech act itself is not false; rather, it is infelicitous due to a failure of intent (Γ. 1). The felicity of a speech act can vary widely based on social conventions. Thus, in some countries, the fact that both participants are of the same sex will render the marriage infelicitous under condition (A. 1); in others, it will not.

Periodicals like *Blackwood's*, insofar as they cultivate a community of editorial and authorial personae, are performative in Austin's sense. They, too, establish a horizon of expectations in their readers and include performances that will be read as felicitous or infelicitous as a result. This is most clear when we contemplate Maga's most striking textual feature: the *Noctes Ambrosianae*. In this series of dialogues, *Blackwood's* presents to its audience a behind-the-scenes look at the production of the magazine. Authors, real people and magazine personae hobnob in the social setting of Ambrose's Tavern, eating, drinking, arguing and planning articles for the periodical. In so consistently and frequently representing the social space from which the magazine is said to proceed, *Blackwood's* conjures a world of imagined interactions and conventions. The kinds of social agreements described by Austin in his list of performative utterances – betting and swearing, for instance – are a standard feature of the narrative space of the *Noctes*. Debates over contemporary literature, spats between contributors and an endless flow of gossip, high jinks and nonsense illuminate the backstage of the periodical. This is not merely performance in the sense of a stage set, but performativity in the sense of speech that constitutes an action. When 'Mr Blackwood' requests and is promised an 'Article on the State of the Highlands of Scotland' from an actual 'Highland Chieftain' appearing in 'Noctes VI', for instance, this exchange has the effect of projecting the future article, offering it as the thoughts and opinions of the Chieftain that the readership has just met.[10] Much like the speech act 'I promise', it is a performative sentence that announces a future action that may be followed through or not. We might state the conditions of felicity for this act as follows:

(A. 1) We expect in the *Noctes Ambrosianae* to encounter characters who contribute to the magazine, and

(A. 2) these characters and the articles they publish in Blackwood's should both be in line with the magazine's political and aesthetic missions.

(B. 1) Articles should be requested by the editor or publisher or proposed to them by the contributor and

(B. 2) should be promised, accepted, refused or rejected.

(Γ. 1) The tone of the exchange and of the imagined article should match the tone of the *Noctes* and

(Γ. 2) the article in question should appear, if the tone were serious, and should not, if the tone were satirical.

Mr Blackwood's exchange with the Highland Chieftain offers a clear instance of performative language in action. The reader is invited to consider the appropriateness of the rough Highland Chieftain as sociological commentator for the Tory, Edinburgh-based journal. Yet the article is merely requested and promised; rather than pointing to a specific article already in the journal, the exchange references a future article, leaving the speech act hanging. For dedicated *Blackwood's* readers, deciding how to parse the seriousness of the exchange is part of the pleasure. The savvy reader will likely assess the Chieftain as an unlikely contributor, and the failure of the article to appear in subsequent numbers confirms this reading of the exchange as a satirical comment on local authority. In evaluating this performative, one is able to account for the non-appearance of the article as an important part of the joke, one that extends beyond the individual number of the *Noctes* into a wider sense of the periodical's logic.

It is essential, in this example, that the performative has to do with the production of the periodical. Romantic periodical personae routinely produce diegetic commentaries on their own acts of creation. That is to say that not merely do these personae appear and interact in the magazines, but they perform as the personae of writers. Discussing their own writing is a central focus of their work; by writing about writing, they perform their own labour rather than simply doing it. This pattern appears not just in *Blackwood's*, but in periodicals that imitate its logic. In the *London Magazine*, Charles Lamb's 'Elia', for example, celebrates his newfound control over his time after retiring from his work as a clerk in 'The Superannuated Man': 'I walk, read or scribble (as now) just when the fit seizes me. I no longer hunt after pleasure; I let it come to me.'[11] This emphasis on the constraints of time and money that produce periodical writing is a key feature of periodical personae. It provides a refrain that unites periodical personae across political and geographic lines. While Maga's *Noctes* relate the requesting and promising of various articles, the *London*'s 'Janus Weathercock' spends precious column inches in his 'Sentimentalities on the Fine Arts' procrastinating by describing his clothes and writing rituals.[12] Richard Cronin explains this phenomenon in terms of the very real pressures of periodical hackwork: 'The magazine article about writing a magazine article quickly established itself as a favorite sub-genre, especially with writers who needed to produce copy but found themselves without materials.'[13]

Despite these very pragmatic motivations, this phenomenon has wider implications: it establishes performative utterances about periodical production as one of the baselines and hallmarks of magazine personae. Because of this emphasis on periodical personae as writers, the biggest test of felicity or infelicity in the performances of a given persona is the reader's desire to incorporate a given text into the canon of texts 'written' or sentiments 'uttered' by this persona. Periodicals fictionalise the authentication process, emphasising felicitous performance over veracity. Austin argues that an overemphasis on the veracity of statements in linguistic and philosophical analysis has obscured the great number of so-called statements that were 'strictly nonsense' when considered as constative (or descriptive) statements. An 'unfortunate dogmatism, that a statement (of fact) ought to be "verifiable" . . . led to the view that many "statements" are only what may be called pseudo-statements' because they are not verifiable in any reliable sense.[14] For Austin, the classificatory move that would represent a statement of an 'ethical proposition', for instance, as a 'pseudo-statement' came from a discomfort on the part of philosophers and linguists with 'the amount of nonsense that we are prepared to admit we talk'.[15] This choice of the word 'nonsense' to describe the mistaking of a performative utterance for a descriptive one seems particularly appropriate to unlocking the brand of writing that we find in *Blackwood's*. There is without a doubt a great deal of nonsense printed in the periodical, but it is nonsense that marks out the unique style of writing made possible by pseudonymous periodicals like *Blackwood's*.

In the example of the Highland Chieftain's article, the question of felicity centred around the consistency of the article's content with the political line of *Blackwood's* and the tonal effect of the article's non-appearance in subsequent numbers. These conditions of felicity were determined not by a set of laws, as in the case of Austin's marriage example, but by the reader's familiarity with the conventions of the magazine, the comic tone of the *Noctes* and the possible outcomes for articles that are proposed within these short dialogues. In this sense, this type of periodical speech act functions less like a marriage contract and more like Austin's performatives of feeling. In a performative of feeling (Austin's examples include 'I am sorry' or 'I thank you'), there is no strict legal condition of felicity. Instead, one must look to contextual clues to evaluate the felicity of the utterance based on an imagined internal state: As Austin explains, 'when someone says "I welcome you" . . . we may say "I wonder if he really did welcome him?"'[16] This need to verify the performative utterance based on social conventions opens up a more flexible set of criteria of felicity than found in the legal instance of the marriage. The evaluation of an apology, for instance, depends on more than the correct usage of the formula 'I apologise'; cultural conventions may deem that the introduction of a conditional clause ('*if* my actions hurt you') renders this performative infelicitous.

The process of determining felicity in emotional performances provides a fitting model of how readers respond to performances by a periodical persona. In both cases, context is key: a reader's previous acquaintance with the persona is a strong determinant of the conditions of felicity that will be evaluated. Readers will have to consider their experience with the persona thus far, instinctively comparing the new performance with previous iterations. They may reject a performance as an unhappy iteration if it deviates too far from expected attributes; readers are empowered to decline to read or incorporate a given performance into their sense of the persona.

Alternatively, readers may accept gradual shifts and changes in the persona, revising their sense of the character in light of new performances. When encountering, for instance, a speech by 'Byron' in the *Noctes Ambrosianae* in which he declares his ultimate intention to render Don Juan 'one of the gravest and most devout Tories in the world', readers must determine if this speech should be assimilated to their reading of the poem itself.[17] In this case, any reasonably savvy reader of these *Noctes* in July 1822 would have been aware of Byron's presence in Italy and of his 'Unholy Alliance' with Percy

Shelley – who drowned that very month – and 'Cockney' poet Leigh Hunt.[18] By looking at this external material, the reader would recognise the infelicity of this Byronic pronouncement and engage with it as the bit of nonsense that it is.

In turning from the celebrity author (Byron) to the periodical persona, the horizon of information is narrower: Christopher North is strongly yoked to the pages of Maga, for instance, and therefore the reader must make determinations of felicity and infelicity based solely on prior encounters with the Christopher North persona. In mobilising felicity as a metric for discussing the construction of persona in periodicals like Maga, I want to propose that different personae exist on a spectrum of breadth or flexibility. For some personae, a narrow horizon of felicity is defined; a few distinct conditions of felicity exist, and as long as they are fulfilled, the performance will be felicitous. For other personae, a wider horizon exists – often, these personae are more complex, more changeable and more attractive, but they are also more prone to deformation over a longer period of time. In the remainder of this chapter, I will explore three case studies that spotlight different points on this spectrum.

The Narrow Periodical Persona: Christopher North

'Christopher North' is a persona with few conditions of felicity. He is descended from previous editor-figures such as 'Sylvanus Urban, Gent.', who had 'edited' the *Gentleman's Magazine* since its founding in 1731. As such, North is very strongly associated with his function in the periodical in which he appears. His physical characteristics – his age, his limp – are conventionalised by his role as the elder statesman of the magazine and are displayed consistently and almost formulaically in his different appearances in the *Noctes*. His social roles – editor of Maga and confirmed bachelor – tend to circumscribe him to the club-like space of Ambrose's Tavern. As David Stewart has observed of his limp, 'North's foot had become something of a stylistic trait: any writer could "do" North ... and to do North meant mimicking this attention to physical details.'[19] This narrow set of traits might leave North open to a great deal of manipulation: With so much emphasis on his body, what comes out of his mouth is potentially flexible. Yet what is unspoken in the context of Stewart's observation is that by 'any writer' here he means any writer in *Blackwood's*. Beyond the limp and the role of editor, the place of publication is what defines the North persona. Insomuch as North's entire identity is rooted in his role as editor of *Blackwood's*, performances of the persona that appeared in some other magazine would be deemed infelicitous. Furthermore, when North ventures outside the quasi-professional space of Ambrose's, Maga makes a point to draw attention to the uncharacteristic action. During a visit to a farmhouse in Girnaway on the occasion of the King's visit to Scotland, North's person is remarked upon with as much astonishment as the King's: the rustic 'Gudeman' is amazed to discover North to be 'a loupin', livin', flesh and bluid man, with real rudiments and a wooden crutch, just as gien out in that ance-a-month peerioddical'.[20] The contradictory characterisation – North's crutch and his love of loupin' (jumping) run at cross-purposes – underlines the unreality of the character when separated from his professional space. North belongs primarily to the pages of *Blackwood's* and destabilises when moved too far from his professional milieu. By confining him primarily to his role in the *Noctes*, *Blackwood's* ensures that he remains a relatively stable, if narrow, persona during his active periodical career.

The Wider Periodical Persona: The English Opium-Eater

Turning now from the relatively narrow bounds of the Christopher North persona, I will consider the case of Thomas De Quincey's 'English Opium-Eater', which exemplifies a somewhat wider construction of the conditions of felicity. The persona was inaugurated with his 'Confessions of an English Opium-Eater' in the September and October 1821 issues of the *London Magazine*. This text was signed only X.Y.Z., less a pseudonym than a general sign for anonymity in the period.[21] In contrast to the North persona, which is programmatically constructed in terms of physical and occupational characteristics from its inception, the Opium-Eater grows organically out of the success of this initial narrative. This is an important contingency to acknowledge and helps account for the breadth and flexibility of this persona.

Both the *London Magazine* version of the 'Confessions' and its 1822 republication as a stand-alone book emphasised the Opium-Eater's drug use and dream visions as central aspects of his persona.

Despite reviewers' attacks on his scholarly credentials and private morality, De Quincey went on to contribute under the signature of 'The English Opium-Eater' to several periodicals. His later appearances in the *London Magazine* include the 'Letters to a Young Man whose Education has been Neglected', which played off the (disputed) scholarly status of the Opium-Eater persona to provide reflections on the state of contemporary authorship and publishing.[22] William Maginn (most famous as one of *Blackwood's* early contributors) outed De Quincey as the author of the *Confessions* in an 1824 *John Bull Magazine* article 'The Humbugs of the Age. No 1'. Rife with personalities, the article probed the disjuncture between the real life of the author and the Opium-Eater, highlighting De Quincey's transgressions and quirks: the illegitimacy of his first child, his pretentious assumption of the noble particle, his unsubstantiated status as a scholar and his uneasy friendship with the Lake Poets. In this article, the *John Bull Magazine* revealed the author behind the Opium-Eater, but rather than destroying the Opium-Eater as a persona, this article had the effect of policing its coherence – and, of course, increasing its fame.[23] Despite the exposure, the Opium-Eater persona persisted, authoring 'Sketches of Life and Manners from the Autobiography of an English Opium-Eater' in *Tait's Edinburgh Magazine*. Here, he provided less a continuation of the life-narrative from the original *Confessions* than a use of that persona to offer his audience what he called 'the flower of all my reading, thinking, and scheming for twenty odd years'.[24] In this iteration, the Opium-Eater's retrospective pose, along with his hallmark descriptive and linguistic excess, are emphasised as the key features of the persona.

Over the course of these various performances, then, the key criteria of felicity for writing by the 'English Opium-Eater' gradually shifted. In the initial 'Confessions', De Quincey highlighted his opium use as the centrepiece of the character and narrative. However, as he redeployed the persona in subsequent publications, he increasingly emphasised the character's scholarly achievements and his rich powers of description. By the time John Wilson wrote the Opium-Eater into the *Noctes Ambrosianae*, the persona was chiefly rendered through pedantic literary criticism and long, florid passages of description:

ENGLISH OPIUM-EATER: The Periodical Literature of the Age is infinitely superior to all its other philosophical criticism – for example, the charlatanerie of the Schlegels, *et id genus omne,* is as certain – Mr Hogg, pardon me for imitating your illustrative imagery, or attempting to imitate what all the world allows to be inimitable – as that the hotch-potch which you are now swallowing, in spite of heat that seems breathed from the torrid zone –

SHEPHERD: It's no hotch-potch – this platefu's cocky-leeky.

ENGLISH OPIUM-EATER: As that cocky-leeky which, though hot as purgatory, (the company will pardon me for yielding to the influence of the *genius loci,*) your mouth is, and for a quarter of an hour has been, vortex-like engulfing, transcends, in all that is best in animal and vegetable matter, – worthy indeed of Scotland's manly Shepherd – the *soup maigre,* that, attenuated almost to invisibility, drenches the odiously-guttural gullet of some monkey Frenchman of the old school, by the incomprehensible interposition of Providence saved at the era of the Revolution from the guillotine.[25]

This is a comical exaggeration of the Opium-Eater persona, and a remarkable example of how even a non-authorised and somewhat infelicitous performance of the persona might reinforce rather than dilute it.[26] Certainly, the descriptive excesses of the speech – and the vision of the Shepherd's vortex-like mouth – recall the language of the famous opium visions, but the Opium-Eater's disgust for Schlegel feels out of place with his position as a celebrator of German literature. This near-miss of a performance renders the Opium-Eater recognisable even as it reaffirms the limits of his persona. Although infelicitous as a performance of the Opium-Eater, it enters into productive dialogue with his shifting characterisation.

In a case study such as this one, the persona develops more organically over time, as De Quincey gradually shifts the emphasis among the different elements of the persona. Unlike the relative rigidity of Maga's Christopher North, the Opium-Eater proves a relatively adaptable persona, as De Quincey seeks to trade on the notoriety of his *Confessions* even while continuing to evolve as a writer. By reusing not just the signature but stylistic elements, De Quincey produces felicitous performances of the persona across different periodicals. In my final section, I will turn to consider a persona that moves far beyond the governing hand of its original creator in order to probe the limits of how the conditions of felicity for a given persona can mutate across different periodicals and performances.

The Hijacked Persona: James Hogg and the 'Ettrick Shepherd'

James Hogg's 'Ettrick Shepherd' has been held up as a signal case of the abusive potential of periodical personae. Initially introduced by Hogg to accompany his volumes of poetry, the Shepherd has been characterised by Douglas Mack as 'a beguiling fictionalized representation and distortion of certain aspects of Hogg's personality'.[27] Yet over time, the Shepherd persona is forced to knit together vast contradictions. In what Mark Schoenfield has called an act of 'butchery', the Ettrick Shepherd was co-opted by John Gibson Lockhart and John Wilson in the *Noctes Ambrosianae*, serving as both 'ventriloquist and dummy' for his different authors.[28] In some numbers, he is reduced to 'a rural philosopher-clown', where elsewhere he appears as the custodian of shared culture in his local tales. For the majority of Hogg's original readers, understanding the Ettrick Shepherd as a persona required reconciling these differing performances to a single horizon of meaning.

Because Hogg moves between different periodical and book publications, venue alone cannot define a felicitous performance the way it does for Christopher North. Instead, we find a shifting set of characteristics that limn the character, mutating more quickly and more complexly than the Opium-Eater's. Thus, in the instance of *The Mountain Bard* of 1807, Hogg names himself the Ettrick Shepherd, adopting the standard pose of the late eighteenth-century rustic poet. The 'Memoir' of his life emphasises his lower social standing, natural piety and late arrival at literacy. He is, after all, a 'shepherd' who commits the Psalms of David to heart as a child and can barely read at eighteen years of age.[29] His dedication to Walter Scott and acknowledgement of his subscribers, moreover, place him in the position of seeking patronage. Coupled with his Scots speech, these attributes form the core of the Ettrick Shepherd persona.

Hogg was a savvy user of personae in his own right, long before his involvement with *Blackwood's*. In his 1810–11 single-author periodical *The Spy*, he moved between different personae with ease, writing as both a canny metropolitan character and the more familiar rustic. The embedded character of John Miller in *The Spy* incarnates the sort of ignorance and rustic genius that would later be attached by *Blackwood's* to Hogg himself. Hogg's 'Spy' persona describes John Miller as 'the son of a poor school-master in a remote corner of the country; a good English and Latin scholar; yet uses the broadest dialect of the district, in his common conversation'.[30] Hogg consistently held this characterisation at a distance, as part, but not all, of his poetic identity. Hogg's work on the famous Chaldee Manuscript and in the relaunch of *Blackwood's* similarly plays outside of the Shepherd persona. Put simply, the Shepherd persona was not one that Hogg felt the need to occupy consistently.

As a result, when John Gibson Lockhart and his collaborators began to write the Shepherd into the *Noctes* in December 1822, the Shepherd was not Hogg's primary writing persona and was amenable to a shift of emphasis. In this number, the Shepherd is strongly associated with his Scottish identity; his first speeches are devoted to the celebration of the Scottish countryside:

> Oh! nothing like that magnificent country – nothing in all the North; and anybody may see it, for there are most noble roads through woods extremely valuable and important to the country, being now almost the only remains of the Caledonian Forests.[31]

From Scottish patriot and tour guide, however, the Shepherd quickly slips into new characteristics that will mark his persona in Maga. In place of his bardic role in Hogg's poetry, he becomes more of a comic rustic, announcing 'I canna sing yet, Captain: just bear wi' me till I've had another tumbler or twa'.[32] The Shepherd of the *Noctes* is a tippler, and his overindulgence couples with increasing representations of gluttony to become a key characteristic of felicity.

The Shepherd proved a popular and reliable persona in the early *Noctes*. In what J. H. Alexander has termed its first series ('Noctes' I–XVIII and XX), co-authors John Gibson Lockhart, John Wilson and William Maginn hit upon the inclusion of the Shepherd in their sixth instalment after having experimented with the depiction of Byron, the King, the aforementioned Highland Chieftain and Gudeman. It is the latter two that seem most relevant, as the Shepherd is consistently made the representative of Scottish rusticity. The Ettrick Shepherd quickly became a feature: billed alternately and seemingly indiscriminately as 'Shepherd' and 'Hogg', he features in over half of the initial series and in 96 per cent of the instalments produced by John Wilson during the 1820s.[33] Yet his characterisation is not static. With additional iterations, a more strident Tory politics is added to the drinking and gluttony. Later performances of the persona slip into the role of a kind of Tory *id*, with the Shepherd indulging in behaviours and expressing views that would be inappropriate in the more gentlemanly contributor. In the *Noctes* of April 1830, for instance, the Shepherd gobbles his meal indiscriminately, with a gusto that prevents him from even tasting it:

> SHEPHERD: Hae I eaten anither dish o' hotch-potch, think ye, sirs, without bein' aware o't?
> TICKLER: No, James – North changed the fare upon you, and you have devoured, in a fit of absence, about half-a-bushel of peas.
> SHEPHERD: I'm glad it was na carrots – for they aye gie me a sair belly.[34]

The Shepherd's ravenous indulgence leads him to risk compromising his health by accidentally consuming the carrots he finds unwholesome. Between bites, the Shepherd entertains his friends with the tale of a drunken, half-clothed escape from a bull, revelling in low comedy and farce.[35] The Shepherd's role in doing or saying things that would be ungentlemanly in others takes on a distinctly political cast in the *Noctes* of April 1824, when he glibly pronounces that he

> hate[s] slavery as an abstract idea – but it's a necessary evil, and I canna believe a' thae stories about cruelty. There's nae fun or amusement in whipping women to death – and as for a skeln [blow] or twa, what's the harm? – Hand me ower the rum and the sugar, sir.[36]

Here, the juxtaposition of his lip service to justice with his greedy consumption of rum and sugar taps into what Timothy Morton has called the 'blood sugar topos', an abolitionist claim that these products were tainted with the blood of abused slaves, underscoring the Shepherd's role as a figure who will do and say those things that the more upstanding Blackwoodian daren't.[37]

Examining the classification of these performances outlined in Table 5.1, a mutation can be traced in the attributes that are associated with felicitous performances of the Shepherd. Just as for Austin the context for an emotional performative may mutate according to social conventions, here, the evolving social world of the *Noctes* gradually transforms the contexts in which readers encounter the Shepherd. By

Table 5.1 Shifting conditions of felicity for the Ettrick Shepherd

Conditions of felicity	Hogg, *The Mountain Bard* (1807)	Maginn et al., 'Noctes VI' (1822)	Wilson, 'Noctes XIV' (1824)
Is a poet/connection to song	✓	✓	
Works/has worked as a shepherd	✓	✓	✓
Humility topos/in need of patronage	✓		
Pious/'deserving poor'	✓		
Delayed literacy/'unlettered'	✓	✓	✓
Scots speaker	✓	✓	✓
A *Blackwood*'s contributor		✓	✓
Drinks to excess		✓	✓
Overt Tory politics			✓

maintaining a baseline of characteristics (namely, his use of Scots, pastoral occupation and rustic semi-literacy), the *Noctes* performances of the Shepherd are able to remain felicitous, even as they shift emphasis away from the Shepherd's poetic identity and onto a new identity as Tory clown. Over the course of the 1820s, the *Noctes* exert a growing control over the persona of the Shepherd: in part because of their frequency of publication, in part because of their greater readership and perhaps most because they seem to present the 'real' Shepherd – Hogg as he 'really is' behind closed doors.

It is telling that by the late 1820s, Hogg attempts to wrest the Ettrick Shepherd back from the *Noctes Ambrosianae*. First in the *Edinburgh Literary Journal* (1828–9) and again in *Fraser's Magazine* (1833), Hogg attempted to produce his own *Noctes*.[38] This move makes sense in terms of the parameters of felicity that we have identified for the Ettrick Shepherd persona. Despite Hogg's steady rate of book publication – his books during the Shepherd's run in the *Noctes* include *The Three Perils of Man* (1822), *The Three Perils of Woman* (1823) and of course *The Private Memoirs and Confessions of a Justified Sinner* (1824) – he had not matched the rate of recurrence nor the circulation of the Shepherd in the *Noctes*. Writing in this persona in a periodical venue, and in particular a *Noctes* imitation, shows a clear need to render a more felicitous performance.

Hogg's attempt to recalibrate the Shepherd's periodical persona is not felicitous. Hogg's first *Noctes* imitations are the two *Noctes Bengerianae* published in the *Edinburgh Literary Journal* on 27 December 1828 and 21 March 1829. In form, these *Noctes* are rather different from the *Blackwood's* version: at only three pages of double-column text, they are markedly shorter than those in Maga. Moreover, they inconsistently deploy the dialogue form, sometimes including paragraphs from a central narratorial voice (the Shepherd's). In content, too, they depart from the Maga model, with the Shepherd being repositioned at the centre of the story. For instance, in the 27 December 1828 number, while the Shepherd dips into Scots in his dialogue, his narratorial voice is firmly situated in contemporary English. Finally, in a move that echoes the inclusion of John Miller in *The Spy*, lower, more rustic characters like Wat Nicol are introduced to occupy the lowest point on the social scale. While in this *Noctes* Hogg displays an impressive ability to imitate the personae and literary styles of Byron, De Quincey and Hazlitt, his performance does not accord with the expected characteristics of the Ettrick Shepherd, and the speedy discontinuation of the series speaks eloquently to the readerly reception it must have received. He loses control of the Shepherd decisively here; for the readers of *Blackwood's*, it is Lockhart and Wilson's Shepherd who will remain canonical.

Conclusion

The above exploration of North, the Opium Eater and the Ettrick Shepherd maps the extent to which one can use the kind of criteria of felicitous performance identified by Austin as a frame through which to examine the various deployments of a given persona in different periodicals and occasionally by different hands. Performances of a given persona serve to outline a set of conventions or parameters by which they are defined – for instance, the Opium-Eater's florid style and opium use, or the Shepherd's poetic aspirations and use of Scots. Subsequent performances may expand or revise the conventions of the persona, but if they differ too greatly, readers will deem them infelicitous. While subtle, gradual persona mutation can take place through multiple felicitous performances; iterations of a persona that stray too far afield function less as threats to the 'authentic' performance of the persona than as limits by which the requirements for a felicitous performance can be understood.

Blackwood's Edinburgh Magazine, with its endless play with the names and identities of individuals both real and fictional, public and private, proves an essential site for the elaboration of a practice of persona that flouts all expectations of authenticity. Part of the achievement of Maga – and part of the pleasure of reading it – lies in the instability and unreliability of the personae produced. Readers are invited to enter into the play, forming their own impressions of the felicity and success of different performances. Rather than a reception model in which one must doggedly uncover the (perhaps unrecoverable) truth of authorship, *Blackwood's* invites readers to be their own judges, to decide whether a Byron who plans to make Don Juan grow up into a Tory is a felicitous fiction. By invoking Austin's concept of felicity, we can begin to conceive of the importance of repetition and reiteration to Romantic magazine writing in *Blackwood's* and its imitators. Approaches that map the parameters and social worlds that emerge from a series of seemingly ephemeral Romantic texts offer a new opportunity to capture the flexibility and limits of this kind of periodical writing. By taking Maga on its own performative terms, persona-based analysis can offer new avenues of assembling and representing the experimental genius of the late-Romantic magazine.

Notes

1. Murphy, 'Impersonation', p. 625.
2. Ibid. p. 626.
3. Wheatley, *Romantic Feuds*, p. 85.
4. Murphy, 'Impersonation', p. 632.
5. Ibid. p. 633.
6. Austin, *How to Do Things*, p. 149.
7. See overview in Miller, *Speech Acts*.
8. Austin, *How to Do Things*, p. 16.
9. Ibid. pp. 14–15. Formatting in the original.
10. [Wilson?], 'Noctes V', p. 372.
11. Lamb, *Works*, p. 196.
12. [Wainewright], 'Sentimentalities', p. 286.

13. Cronin, *Paper Pellets*, p. 92.
14. Austin, *How to Do Things*, p. 2.
15. Ibid.
16. Ibid. p. 79.
17. [Maginn], 'Noctes IV', p. 104.
18. Marchand, *Byron*, p. 385.
19. Stewart, *Romantic Magazines*, p. 141.
20. [Maginn?], 'Noctes VI', pp. 386–7.
21. In fact, the Gale British Periodicals database returns over 150 hits with 'X.Y.Z.' in the author field prior to 1820.
22. The scholarly persona is not quite stable, and swings between defences of the sort of periodical work in which De Quincey himself was engaged and more conventional admonishments against the flood of new books. The letter of January 1823, for instance, is devoted to a refutation of Coleridge's claim in the *Biographia Literaria* that authorship is a profession to be avoided. Meanwhile, the letter of March 1823 contains more conservative (even cliché) criticism of the 'enormous "gluttonism" for books' of the contemporary reader (De Quincey, *Works*, vol. 3, p. 65).
23. [Maginn], 'Humbugs of the Age', p. 21.
24. De Quincey, *Works*, vol. 10, p. xiii.
25. [Wilson], 'Noctes XLVIII', p. 666.
26. In this respect, the *Noctes* version of the Opium-Eater shares a satirical function with Thomas Grattan's De Quincey parody, also in *BEM*, 'The Confessions of an English Glutton'.
27. Hogg, *The Shepherd's Calendar*, p. xiii.
28. Schoenfield, 'Butchering', p. 208.
29. Hogg, *The Mountain Bard*, pp. v, viii.
30. Hogg, *The Spy*, p. 119.
31. [Maginn?], 'Noctes VI', p. 697.
32. Ibid. p. 697.
33. Alexander, *The Tavern Sages*, p. viii. In the first series ('Noctes' I–XVIII and XX), the Shepherd appears in numbers VI, VII, VIII, IX, XII, XIV, XV, XVII, XVIII and XX. During the 1820s, he appears in all but one of Wilson's *Noctes* (XIX, XXI–LXVII).
34. [Wilson], 'Noctes XLVIII', p. 663.
35. Ibid. p. 674.
36. [Lockhart], 'Noctes XIV', p. 372.
37. Morton, *The Poetics of Spice*, p. 175.
38. Hogg, '*Noctes Bengerianae*', December 1828 and March 1829; 'Shepherd's Noctes', July 1833.

Part III

Reviewing Politics and the Politics of Reviewing

Chapter 5

Maga as Medium: Cockneys in Context

Mark Parker

In 'The Periodical Press', his survey of the lively market for reviews and magazines for the *Edinburgh Review* of May 1823, William Hazlitt clearly sets forth the new requirements for periodical success. The *London Magazine*, he notes, has declined since its 1820 inauguration because it lacks coherence. 'The articles seem thrown into the letter-box,' writes Hazlitt, 'all is in a confused, unconcocted state, like the materials of a rich plum-pudding before it has been well boiled.'[1] Hazlitt's characteristic gusto here – employing not one but two metaphors for the new expectations readers bring to literary magazines – suggests the scope of the transformation in this sector of the publishing world. His tasty analogy implies that what has been so carefully 'concocted' should be savoured and that such confections cannot be reduced to their individual ingredients. Articles might arrive piecemeal, but, in a successful magazine, they emerge in a rich state, informed by ongoing concerns from earlier numbers and ultimately inflecting the work that surrounds them.[2] The literary magazine is no longer a container that delivers individual articles but a medium that suffuses these contributions and is in turn suffused by them.

The present chapter undertakes to examine the Cockney School attacks within their most immediate context: the pages of *Blackwood's Edinburgh Magazine*. It argues that the medium of the magazine itself is more fundamental to understanding this campaign than either politics or class animus, although these are deeply implicated. *Blackwood's*, over time, developed a series of rules of reading for its implied audience, a set of protocols that governs the interpretation of the Cockney School series as well as the occasional references to Hunt, Keats and Hazlitt elsewhere. Read against other contributions to the magazine and in terms of the individual numbers in which they emerge, the attacks on Hunt and Keats take on meaning less narrowly political than critical and institutional. Each article smacks of the medium itself.

Towards a New Medium

The October 1817 number, which features the inaugural Cockney School essay, marks a decided shift of course for William Blackwood's magazine. A month earlier, the publisher had fired the magazine's first two editors, Cleghorn and Pringle, after six lacklustre numbers and had given their de facto replacements, John Gibson Lockhart, John Wilson and James Hogg, licence to create the spectacle that would soon bring his magazine prominence and notoriety. Over the next 100 numbers, these and other core writers would give *Blackwood's* a coherent shape by creating an unusual textual dynamic that blended dialogism, self-consciousness, contradiction, performative rhetoric, hoaxing and pseudonyms. They would shape the magazine into what William Maginn, another of the *Blackwood's* principals, would call 'a classical work'.[3] Over this run of 100 numbers, the literary miscellany, often a grab bag of articles of varied interest, became Maga, as the *Blackwood's* regulars termed it, and *Blackwood's* took on a consistency that approached that of a genre.

This formation did not emerge at once: during the first year we can still see the residue of the older formation of *Blackwood's*, as well as the more general contours of the traditional literary miscellany. While a small, productive crew of writers – Lockhart, Wilson and later Maginn – shaped *Blackwood's*, it remained a work of many hands. But, for the purposes of exposition, two elements can provide a rough approximation of the scope and innovative method of this magazine.

One of these tendencies coalesces in April 1822, with the formal emergence of the *Noctes Ambrosianae*. This series, the purported transcript of conversations at fictional dinners and drinking parties of *Blackwood's* contributors and selected guests, concentrates essential features of the magazine. The exchanges combine freedom of enquiry with an often outrageous freedom of expression, producing dialogues in which the principals contradict themselves, argue for effect, launch scurrilous personal attacks and rely on puns, song and excessive drinking to shirk responsibility for their claims. This vitality of exchange mimics the distinctive effect of the larger magazine, the dialogism among articles and contributors which gives unusual coherence to *Blackwood's*. Just as Lockhart, Maginn or Wilson, by turns writing anonymously and pseudonymously, could take up opposite sides of a question in a series of articles, so do the speakers in the *Noctes* revel in contradicting their earlier claims. They do not so much render final critical judgement, as did many of their rivals in the magazine and review trade, as make the case – or, more exactly, the cases – to be made.

While the *Noctes* distil the magazine's distinctive features, they also reflect a strictly defined genre – Menippean satire – in which exaggeration and ridicule become a mode of intellectual enquiry. Essentially dialogical, Menippean satire takes the form of a conversation, colloquy or, in its most classical form, a symposium. In its raucous encounters, laughter becomes a way of scrutinising and debunking ideas and ideologues, who are often overwhelmed by outlandish versions of their own rhetoric or jargon. The humour is fearless, unsparing and nimble, creating, as Mikhail Bahktin puts it, 'a zone of crude contact', a world 'utterly familiarized' in which 'the subject moves with extreme and fantastic freedom'.[4] The relentless embodiment of ideas in Menippean satire, which puts cranks, bigots and pedants of all types – philosophical, literary and political – to the test, becomes the convivial physicality of Ambrose's Tavern.

Articles in *Blackwood's* had emulated the form of Menippean satire long before the appearance of the *Noctes*. The magazine's dialogic play of anonymous and pseudonymous voices does not settle into a definitive statement on a writer or literary work. The result is less indecision than the emergence of an innovative critical method. Instead of the *ex cathedra* feel of other periodicals, *Blackwood's* develops a critical programme that is more faithful to the complexities and uncertainties of reading and of literary evaluation.

The second strand of the magazine's discursive formation is ideological. While Maga's Tory politics are evident to any reader, its programme exceeds simple partisan division. *Blackwood's*, at least in its early years, projects and carries out a capacious programme of counter-Enlightenment resistance. This element of Maga recurs throughout, but it can be most easily traced in the special emphasis given by publisher William Blackwood and John Gibson Lockhart to Friedrich Schlegel, one of the central figures in the Continental reaction to Enlightenment.

Blackwood's interest in Schlegel preceded the publication of his magazine. He commissioned a translation of Schlegel's *Lectures on the History of Literature, Ancient and Modern*, sending Lockhart to Germany in the early autumn of 1817 for the purpose of carrying it out. Lockhart completed the work quickly, the volume emerging from Blackwood's and Co. in 1818, and he eventually reviewed the book himself for *Blackwood's Magazine* in August of the same year. Nor was Lockhart shy about recycling parts of the translation: in *Peter's Letters to his Kinsfolk*, his anonymous and scandalously gossipy account of Edinburgh society published in 1819, some of Lockhart's characters make speeches directly lifted from Schlegel.[5]

During the first four years of Lockhart's tenure with the magazine, he consistently applied a Schlegelian measure to literature as well as to culture more generally. A quick look at the opening pages of *Lectures on the History of Literature* clarifies the basis of Lockhart's attraction. Schlegel grounds his argument in a sociological observation: 'Our men of letters formed, till of late, a body altogether cut off from the rest of the world, and quite as distinct from the society of the higher orders as these were from the mass of the people.'[6] This isolation, which separates men of letters from vernacular traditions in language and culture, is disastrous for national literature as well as for national character. Schlegel insists upon the value of a new intellectual, one alienated neither from 'courtly society' nor from the 'common people',[7] who would display

> The learning of the philosopher – the acuteness and promptitude of the man of business – the earnestness and enthusiasm of the solitary artist – that lightness and flexibility of mental impression, and every fleeting delicacy which we can only find, and learn to find, in the intercourse of society.[8]

A literary magazine such as *Blackwood's* was calculated to provide this recombination of 'literature and active life'.[9]

Accordingly, this new intellectual, in Schlegel's estimation, would define literature broadly as

> first, the art of poetry, and the kindred art of narration, or history; next, all those higher exertions of pure reason and intellect which have human

life, and man himself, for their object, and which have influence upon both; and, last of all, eloquence and wit, whenever these do not escape in the fleeting vehicle of oral communication, but remain displayed in the more substantial and lasting form of written productions.[10]

Such breadth, and in particular the inclusion of such 'fleeting vehicle[s]' as 'eloquence and wit', affords a liberating scope for Lockhart as well as other *Blackwood's* writers. Compared to the more traditionally elitist literary purview of the *Quarterly* and *Edinburgh*, Schlegel's programme authorises the engaging and smart forays of *Blackwood's* writers into more downscale and disreputable scenes. Popular spectacles such as boxing or public executions, as well as less canonical literary genres such as the Gothic, become elements of a vibrant cultural revival.

But perhaps the most attractive feature of Schlegel's thought for Lockhart was its intense nationalism. For Schlegel, the interconnectedness of reason and language, or as he puts it, 'mind and language',[11] requires the maintenance of a national literature:

> there is nothing so necessary to the whole improvement, or rather to the whole intellectual existence of a nation, as the possession of a plentiful store of those great national recollections and associations, which are lost in a great measure during the dark ages of infant society, but which it forms the great object of the poetical art to perpetuate and adorn. Such national recollections, the noblest inheritance which a people can possess, bestow an advantage which no other riches can supply; for when a people are exalted in their feelings and enobled in their own estimation, by the consciousness that they have been illustrious in ages that are gone by, – that these recollections have come down to them from a remote and a heroic ancestry, – in a word, that they have *a national poetry* of their own, we are willing to acknowledge that their pride is reasonable[.][12]

Schlegel's programme essentially connects organicism and nationalism through the action of literature. Those who contribute to this national literature – or even codify it – leave a legacy greater than the 'conqueror and legislator'.[13]

When Lockhart, with characteristically Blackwoodian cheek, reviewed his own translation in August 1818, he did not fail to stress the central tenets of Schlegel's thought. But he deftly tuned the book to the English literary scene as well as to his own sense of what shape the counter-Enlightenment should take. Schlegel builds his opposition to Enlightenment principles on a careful chain of reasoning about human nature, which stresses an organic relation of mind and language. He dismisses Kant's overvaluation of reason, recommending that '*enlightened* judgment must watch over those mighty energies of reason and of fancy' (emphasis mine), but these polemics emerge from the development of his system.[14] Lockhart, in pursuing a counter-Enlightenment programme for a British audience, reorganised Schlegel's argument for his own ends by broadening his critique:

> Mankind are now every where ashamed of being, what the *philosophers* of the last age were pleased to call *unphilosophical*. Even the common people begin to take more pride in having some general ideas, than in retaining that warmth of attachment to one set of objects, which entirely depends, as they have [been] told, upon ignorance of that which is beyond their circle. The travelling regiments of books which pour in their heterogeneous impressions from the four quarters of the heavens, level all peculiarities before them, and turn the private enclosures of attachment and opinion into a thorough-fare.[15]

Kant's cautions, albeit paternalistic, become a pointed attack on the lower classes, one that reflects current concern about the diffusion of knowledge. While the passage is full of deeply coded phrases, the formulation 'general ideas' stands out. By framing the Enlightenment as an attack on empiricism, as well as on local and particular attachments, Lockhart draws together strains from Burke, Coleridge and Wordsworth. His use of metaphors of property in discussing the diffusion of ideas amplifies these claims. Lockhart is well aware that his readers would link the levelling work of books to the levelling principles of leftist or Jacobin politics, and the metaphor delivers subtle threats of instability, rootlessness and usurpation. Implicit in the formulation '*even* the common people' (emphasis mine) is the suggestion that such people should know their place and only so much as their betters see fit. Tellingly, Lockhart concludes this part of his analysis with a literary reference. He quotes Wordsworth's 'A Poet's Epitaph', which denigrates the moralist who overvalues reason as 'One to whose smooth-rubbed soul can cling / Nor form, nor feeling, great or small; / A reasoning, self-sufficing thing, / An intellectual All-in-all'.[16] In sum, then, Lockhart shows less interest in Schlegel's arguments than in the fitness of his conclusions for the current situation in Britain. Schlegel is valued less for being persuasive than for being resonant.

Other parts of Schlegel's analysis do not need such opportunistic reorientation. Lockhart's review simplifies and sharpens Schlegel's argument, as when he notes approvingly that the German philosopher has attempted 'to show how in every age, the action of literature upon nationality, and that of nationality upon literature, have been strictly reciprocal; and thus, by past examples, to warn the present generation of the dangers in which they have involved themselves'.[17] Literature, for Schlegel, should represent and promote religious faith, national history and national character by nurturing the feelings that are necessary to maintaining these central commitments.

> In doing so, literature gains, both by having a determinate purpose, and by being the conservator of associations, which grow more and more valuable as they grow older. As every nation has its own mental character and constitution propagated from generation to generation, no traditions or poetry can be so congenial to it, as those which originated with itself in early ages, constituting tests of its true bias and genius, and continuing, during the course of its history, to strengthen nature itself by reacting upon the same national temperament which at first produced them.[18]

Prominent here is the reflexive quality of the analysis: literature acts, but is then acted upon. Schlegel's analysis of Homer, from which Lockhart quotes extensively, bears this programme out. Homer's works became central only in the face of external threats, when they served as the means of making a nation: they 'nourish in the Greeks the pride of heroic feelings, and excite them to like deeds in the cause of their independence'.[19] In fact, the reflexive action of literature and culture is so entangled as to render cause and effect indistinguishable.

Significantly, and again in a calculated application and extension of Schlegel's points, Lockhart concludes his review with a consideration of the damage done to 'national sentiment and association' by abstract reasoners in England:

> nothing has contributed so much as the host of periodical publications to obliterate sentiment, and substitute metaphysical restlessness in its place. Our journals, with their eternal disquisitions, have been operating with slow but sure effect in mouldering down all large aggregates of association, which could form centres of gravity of sufficient power to control and regulate the orbits of our feelings. For a long while not many ideas have reached the people except through their medium. But these

journals are like sieves, that require every substance to be granulated before it can pass through them.[20]

Here, I think, we come to the centre of *Blackwood's* counter-Enlightenment project. Lockhart makes a sharp distinction between the detached, dissociated and desiccating cognition brought about by 'disquisitions' and the more homely, peculiar and, above all, connected habits of mind nurtured by a national literature. The production and maintenance of 'large aggregates of association' so crucial to feeling and national spirit become the ideological mission of *Blackwood's*.

In Maga, all the elements of a counter-Enlightenment come together. Hence its various attacks on Cockney or so-called Jacobin writers, its extremities of national sentiment and its heightened religious feeling are symptomatic. But in each case these features are not simply restatements of pre-Enlightenment positions but a complex response to them. For instance, nationalism in *Blackwood's* is hardly that of the 'John Bull' variety. It is a far more complicated formation, which includes its own articulated theory of national character as well as of the particular dangers of cosmopolitan tastes. The magazine's religious feeling is bolstered by a more historically informed perspective and an insistently pragmatic view of religious feeling as a means of pacifying and controlling the lower orders.

Most prominent is the dialectical quality of this particular strain of counter-Enlightenment thought. *Blackwood's* presents, at least on one level, a very knowing response; it seeks to clarify its difference from the reactionary and unimaginative monarchies recently restored on the Continent. On this level, Maga is unceasingly self-conscious and self-critical. It seeks something more than Burke's adherence to tradition and even simple prejudice, aspiring to Coleridge's goal of 'endeavor[ing] to walk in the Light of your own knowledge'.[21] Yet, on another level, it can never fully articulate its purposes, values and practices. This is evident in Lockhart's conclusion to the Schlegel essay quoted previously. He laments the pre-eminent role of 'periodical publications' in producing 'metaphysical restlessness' and breaking down old habits of feeling in a periodical essay. While he surely has newspapers in mind – 'our journals', as he calls them – the paradox, so obvious to modern readers, passes without remark. *Blackwood's*, despite its calls to an older tradition of conservative thought, cannot escape the disaggregation that the Enlightenment had unleashed.

Dialogism and Criticism: The October 1817 Number

These two strands, one formal and the other ideological, are evident in the October 1817 inauguration of the new *Blackwood's*.[22] The number formally opens and concludes with contributions that meld exuberance, intemperance, overstatement and a certain panache. Wilson's review of Coleridge's *Biographia Literaria* and the 'Chaldee Manuscript' comprise bold bids for notice, and Lockhart's 'On the Cockney School of Poetry. No. I' fits neatly between this booming hail and farewell.[23]

The extravagance of Wilson's attack on Coleridge is clear at once. Contributors to the magazine, Wilson prominent among them, praise Coleridge highly in later numbers. Here, however, Wilson dismisses the *Biographia* by likening it to work by Hume and Rousseau, whose sceptical and rational commitments ultimately engender a vicious egotism:

> His admiration of nature or of man, – we had almost said his religious feelings towards his God, – are all narrowed, weakened, and corrupted and poisoned by inveterate and diseased egotism; and instead of his mind reflecting the beauty and glory of nature, he seems to consider the mighty universe itself as nothing better than a mirror, in which, with a grinning and idiot self-complacency, he may contemplate the Physiognomy of Samuel Taylor Coleridge.[24]

The caricature here is harsh but is within what Bahktin termed the 'zone of crude contact' permitted by Menippean satire. It memorably marks the spot of the critical engagement that the genre allows. The charge of egotism is specific and, despite the exaggeration, coherent. Coleridge's poetry had charted the dark work of what in 'Frost at Midnight' he called 'abstruser musings', that is, the dangers of a solipsism in which the 'idling Spirit' becomes an 'echo or mirror seeking of itself' in nature.[25] Wilson's 'grinning idiot' reopens, forcefully, that meditation on the desiccating power of ratiocination.

The specificity of this critique of Coleridge is also evident in the contrast Wilson draws with Walter Scott's nationalism and seeming lack of self-consciousness:

> From the rude songs of our forefathers he has created a kind of Poetry, which at once brought over the dull scenes of this our unimaginative life all the pomp, and glory, and magnificence of a chivalrous age. . . . Since

he sung his bold, and wild, and romantic lays, a more religious solemnity breathes from our mouldering abbeys, and a sterner grandeur frowns over our time-shattered castles.[26]

For Wilson, Scott's genius lay in his reclamation and reshaping of the past, which turn upon reverence for the 'large aggregates of association' so dear to Schlegel. Coleridge's 'abstruser musings', conversely, run counter to the programme of cultural renewal and recreation. While cruel, the satire of this article is pointed and programmatic.

The last contribution in the October 1817 number, the 'Chaldee Manuscript', exceeded the *éclat* of Wilson's opening article. A faux-biblical parody of the Edinburgh literary scene and the particulars of the reorganisation of *Blackwood's Magazine*, the piece turns on rough humour, innuendo and riddling reference to well-known Edinburgh locals. Like Wilson's article, it emerges within the dialogic economy of Maga, echoing attacks on the *Edinburgh Review* launched earlier in the number. The biblical parody borders on blasphemy, and the personal insults – often aimed at physical defects and incapacity – are vicious. Yet here again the distortions and reductions of satire take on a critical aspect. While the 'Chaldee Manuscript' revels in partisan differences, it insists on the primacy of economic forces. Money, not party, motivates the combatants. Future contributors to *Blackwood's* will cite the magazine's profits and circulation and intimate that these trump almost all other concerns in the magazine; the freewheeling satire of the 'Chaldee Manuscript' not only anticipates this confession but asks readers to consider the operation of market forces that generate the partisan debates of magazines and reviews. Again, despite the flamboyance of the claim, the point here is essentially a critical one, and it merits careful consideration.[27]

The Cockney School Attacks *in Situ*

To read 'On the Cockney School of Poetry. No. I' in these terms is to put Hunt's work within the crosshairs of a very precise scope. The counter-Enlightenment imagined by Schlegel generates a series of programmatic responses to Hunt's cosmopolitan disposition and reform politics. The choice of Menippean satire provides a devastating comic approach to the task of opposition. And Lockhart inevitably subordinates his evisceration of Hunt to an attack on *Blackwood's* greatest commercial rival, the *Edinburgh Review*. The article opens with a transparent fiction:

> While the whole critical world is occupied with balancing the merits, whether in theory or in execution, of what is commonly called THE LAKE SCHOOL, it is strange that no one seems to think it at all necessary to say a single word about another new school of poetry which has of late sprung up among us.[28]

This is the sly overstatement of parody and satire, not a critical discourse that aspires to be judicious, reasonable or serious. The statement sets up the joke to follow, in which Lockhart begs 'the honour of christening' this new school.[29]

Hunt's 'Story of Rimini', the occasion for 'On the Cockney School of Poetry. No. I', could not have been better suited for Lockhart's purposes. The poem marks Hunt's first serious effort at poetry, and its light sentimentalism, precious colloquial turns and open couplets are poorly suited to its subject matter – the story of Paolo and Francesca so feelingly rendered by Dante. Lockhart's piece is justifiably reprehensible for its infamous use of personality, political rancour and exaggeration. Nevertheless, judged in terms of its contribution to a national literature, or, as Wilson puts it earlier, 'the pomp, and glory, and magnificence of a chivalrous age', the 'Story of Rimini' is a complete failure – even if one does not apply Schlegel's sharp criticisms of Enlightenment principles and his insistence upon a literature that speaks to deep religious faith. If, for Wilson and Lockhart, Scott's feudal narratives constituted the best of the national tradition, then the cosmopolitan, Italianate flippancy of 'Rimini' could only be anathema.

This ideological attack is bound up in a brilliant variant of Menippean satire. Lockhart builds a spectacular analogy to express the distaste readers might feel on reading 'Rimini':

> One feels the same disgust at the idea of opening Rimini, that impresses itself on the mind of a man of fashion, when he is invited to enter, for a second time, the gilded drawing-room of a little mincing boarding-school mistress, who would fain have an *At Home* in her house. Every thing is pretence, affectation, finery, and gaudiness. The beaux are attorneys'

apprentices, with chapeau bras and Limerick gloves – fiddlers, harp-teachers, and clerks of genius: the belles are faded fan-twinkling spinsters, prurient vulgar misses from school, and enormous citizens' wives. The company are entertained with lukewarm negus, and the sounds of a paltry piano-forte.[30]

Lockhart cleverly imagines spaces for 'Rimini' far different from the 'mouldering abbeys' and 'time-shattered castles' of Scott's 'bold, and wild, and romantic lays'. The terms here are powerful. Not only do they summon up class and sexual antagonisms but they present a pretentious, rival literary culture far from the traditions revived by Scott or championed by Schlegel. Manly feudalism is replaced by a cosy, feminised domestic scene. Lockhart targets the entire Huntian programme in this exaggeration – his poem's celebration of grace, surface, domesticity and charm. What is notable here is less the value Lockhart puts on these features than the clarity with which he identifies them. Different readers might handle these elements differently, but they must be accounted for in any critical treatment of 'Rimini'.

This combination of Menippean satire and counter-Enlightenment thought structures the memorable passages of 'On the Cockney School. No. I'. When read in terms of Lockhart's commitments, what seems an abusive flight of fancy becomes critical discourse. Here, Lockhart turns to Hunt's essayistic persona:

> As a vulgar man is perpetually labouring to be genteel – in like manner, the poetry of this man is always on the stretch to be grand. . . . He would fain be always tripping and waltzing, and is sorry that he cannot be allowed to walk about in the morning with yellow breeches and flesh-coloured silk stockings. He sticks an artificial rosebud into his button hole in the midst of winter. He wears no neckcloth, and cuts his hair in imitation of the Prints of Petrarch. In his verses he is always desirous of being airy, graceful, easy, courtly, and ITALIAN.[31]

The technique here is noteworthy. While Lockhart deforms and stretches Hunt's self-presentation to the point of grotesque, few would deny Hunt's deep affinity for the 'airy, graceful, easy, courtly, and ITALIAN' or the dash affected in his dress. It is Lockhart's nimble rhetoric that turns sympathies into pretensions, and preferences into shortcomings. In each case, Lockhart reliably locates essential elements of Hunt's work and artistic posture and then rereads them according to the counter-Enlightenment values he cherishes.

Among these satirical attacks on Hunt's vulgarity, Lockhart intersperses more straightforward critical comment which incorporates the Schlegelian programme in striking detail. Hunt's 'ignorance and vulgarity' are not his greatest transgressions:

> The two great elements of all dignified poetry, religious feeling, and patriotic feeling, have no place in his writings. His religion is a poor tame dilution of the blasphemies of the *Encyclopaedie* – his patriotism a crude, vague, ineffectual, and sour Jacobinism. His works exhibit no reverence either for God or man; neither altar nor throne have any dignity in his eyes.[32]

This effectively summarises the leading elements of Schlegel's *History of Literature* in the terms that Lockhart prefers to take it – with a calculated extension of Schlegel's anti-Jacobin rhetoric. This critique of Hunt, here presented with telegraphic brevity, will be developed more fully in the second instalment of the series.

After charting what 'Z.' styles Hunt's pretensions to admiration of or association with Wordsworth, Moore and Byron, the article returns to its financial and political competitor, the *Edinburgh*. That Lockhart concludes with this obsessive rivalry recalls the deeper commitments of Blackwood and *Blackwood's*. 'Z.', in the characteristically seesawing manner licensed by Menippean satire, cannot seem to decide whether Hunt's audience is alarmingly 'numerous' or comfortably 'paltry and pitiful'.[33] However impossible this seeming contradiction, there is no ambiguity about the role of the *Edinburgh* in the Hunt affair:

> The very culpable manner in which his chief poem was reviewed in the Edinburgh Review (we believe it is no secret, at his own impatient and feverish request, by his partner in the Round Table), was matter of concern to more readers than ourselves ... Mr Jeffrey does ill, when he delegates his important functions into such hands as those of Mr Hazlitt. It was chiefly in consequence of that gentleman's allowing Leigh Hunt to pass unpunished through a scene of slaughter, which his execution might so highly have graced, that we came to the resolution of laying before our readers a series of essays on the *Cockney School*.[34]

Recalling the *Edinburgh*'s reputation for savage reviews, such as those of Wordsworth, Byron and Moore, 'Z.' arrives at a more durable enmity, a rival periodical. 'The Cockney School. No. I' uses its criticisms of Hunt to sustain a commercial rivalry inflamed by politics and counter-Enlightenment ideology.[35]

My point here is not simply classificatory. We should – recalling the positive action of Menippean satire – be alert to the essentially critical gesture of Lockhart's opening move. The overriding metaphor for the Cockney School series, that these writers constitute a school, has ultimately shaped literary history. This basic figure not only generates the terms for brilliant satire but also sets out a specific field of critical enquiry. The topics of discussion that Lockhart makes visible through this figure – class, politics, pretension, stylistic traits – persist as facts and events that require interpretation. It is the value attached to each feature of the field that changes. If we reverse the polarities of Lockhart's sketch, we find the coalescence of a rich historical moment in a particular form – in fact, *through* this form. If Hunt heads a school, then we are prompted to investigate the interactions among the group and the conditions of the group's activity – as Jeffrey Cox has done in *Poetry and Politics in the Cockney School*. The 'school' figure implicates a politics as well, as Nicholas Roe has shown in *John Keats and the Culture of Dissent*. And 'school' as figure also suggests a style, as Marjorie Levinson has documented in *Keats's Life of Allegory*.[36] The figure becomes a heuristic that allows selection and exclusion of material. Instead of questioning the accuracy of the account or criticising Lockhart's exaggerations or tone, we are prompted to ask what Lockhart's way of handling the events of literary history allows us to see.

By comparison, the second instalment of 'On the Cockney School of Poetry', which appeared in the next number of *Blackwood's*, provides a more conventional response to Hunt's poem. It is as if, after the roistering opening instalment of the series, Lockhart felt compelled to make good on his assertions in familiar terms. Gone is the jest, and what remains is a remarkably controlled evisceration of 'Rimini'.[37] To demonstrate Hunt's shortcomings in handling his subject, Lockhart provides an impressive account of the incest theme in literature, including work by Sophocles, Euripides, Alfieri, Thomas Brown and Byron:

> In all these productions of immortal poets, we see the same desire to represent incest as a thing too awful to spring up of itself, without the interference of some revengeful power – the same careful avoidance of luxurious images – the same resolution to treat unhallowed love with the seriousness of a judge, who narrates only that he may condemn the guilty and warn the heedless.[38]

Hunt, by contrast, summons up neither a tragic atmosphere to suit the transgression nor extra-human intervention to explain it.[39] Lockhart's consideration of Hunt's source, the fifth canto of *Inferno*, is especially trenchant. Hunt departs from it in ways that downplay Dante's moral seriousness and soften his condemnation: 'The personages are all amiable, the sins all voluntary, and the sufferings sentimental.'[40] For Lockhart, the many attractive qualities of the 'Story of Rimini' – especially its characteristic lightness of tone – aggravate its moral shortcomings. Hunt's famous jauntiness, so charming in other moments, renders the poem 'a story not of incest, but of love'.[41]

These strictures are, in themselves, valid. Hunt himself later revised the poem for an 1832 volume accordingly, which suggests the force – if not the even-handed justice – of the review.[42] Hunt conceded the poem's faults in his *Autobiography*, while lamenting that 'nobody welcomed the pains I had taken to obviate those charges of too attractive a sympathy with error, which had surprised me when the poem first appeared'.[43] But Lockhart has more on his mind than simply correcting lapses of taste. He carefully frames his criticisms, like Schlegel, within a larger programme that considers the reciprocal effects of literature and national character. While 'noble' or 'lofty' spirits are proof against the pernicious morality of 'Rimini', others – specifically 'milliners and apprentice-boys'[44] – can be corrupted. As Schlegel argues, literature should properly offer readers 'recollections [that] have come down to them from a remote and a heroic ancestry', and these should shape behaviour. In his counterexamples, Lockhart lavishly praises feudal culture as an undervalued repository of national character, contrasting, for example, the 'austere and simple' account of Paulo and Francesca in Dante with the 'elegant rendering of the Cockney poet'.[45] The courtly elements of 'Rimini' have little to do with the flinty martial ethos of northern medieval literature or its contemporary refashioning in Walter Scott's poetry.

Subsequent attacks on the Cockneys build upon these two instalments. For the rest of the series, Z. seems content to draw Hunt into a series of vexing positions. Lockhart has done two very different things in the October and November articles: he has made a critical case, and he has shaped his antagonist to his liking. Hunt, like so many other figures in *Blackwood's*, has become less a human being than a brilliant caricature, a character formed of a few vivid elements, each of which can be reliably exploited. The 'Hunt' that emerges is a vehicle for further satire, a character that Lockhart, as well as other contributors to the magazine, can exploit as circumstance and occasion demand.

As we read the first 'Cockney School' essay – chuckling or clicking our tongues at Lockhart's excesses and distortions – we should give Lockhart a bit more credit as a critic. *Blackwood's* is made up of individual voices, but in their interaction – the dialogic play of contributors who can, by virtue of the magazine's particular formation, say and unsay what they might never really believe to be the case – a finer critical tool emerges. This is, after all, the ultimate work of Menippean satire: to put ideas and ideologues to the test. *Blackwood's* noisy dialogism – its welter of claim and counterclaim, solemnity and nonsense – performs the most basic of critical tasks: to define a field of enquiry. There is a critical edge to *Blackwood's Magazine*, but it is partly an institutional effect that emerges between and among individual contributions.

The elements of this textual dynamic are heterogeneous and ultimately unstable. What we might term the means – the genre of Menippean satire – is anti-authoritarian, restless and analytical, even in its comic exaggerations. The ideological commitment, to a variant of Schlegel's counter-Enlightenment programme, is essentially conservative. Menippean satire might, after the scathing dialectic of corrosive humour, reach a truth, but such truths show little respect for conservation of 'large aggregates of association' so dear to Schlegel. Finally, the material instantiation of this formation – the newly commercialised literary magazine – embodies a mode of production even more inimicable to Lockhart's ideological project. As the literary magazine sheds its genteel traditions – making essays, reviews and works of art into commodities; turning leisured contributors into workers paid by the sheet; seeking wider audiences by emphasising novelty, the scandal of pseudonyms and pleasures of dialogism; celebrating its sales and market penetration – Lockhart's 'aggregates of association' seem quaint and outmoded. A more reactionary form of conservatism emerges in *Blackwood's* after 1822, one content to forgo pleasures of Menippean satire and the comprehensive historical arguments of Schlegel's programme. What Lockhart might fondly wish to conserve cannot withstand the market forces to which *Blackwood's* is subject.

Notes

1. Hazlitt, 'The Periodical Press', p. 371.
2. Ibid. p. 371.
3. 'Noctes IV', p. 105. This is Maginn, writing in perhaps the finest of the *Noctes*.
4. Bakhtin, *The Dialogic Imagination*, p. 29.
5. See Macbeth, *John Gibson Lockhart*, pp. 64–83, esp. 73ff.
6. Schlegel, *Lectures on the History*, p. 2. This and subsequent references to Schlegel's *Lectures* are to Lockhart's 1818 two-volume translation.
7. Ibid. vol. 1, p. 6.
8. Ibid. p. 7.
9. Ibid.
10. Ibid. vol. 1, p. 11.
11. Ibid. p. 12.
12. Ibid. p. 15.
13. Ibid. p. 18.
14. Ibid. vol. 2, p. 310. Schlegel praises Kant's 'chief merit ... that he demonstrated the incapacity of pure reason to decide any thing at all respecting such subjects – that she can acquire some knowledge of God and divine things only by her power of gathering facts out of the experience of human life' but laments that he forgot his own lesson so quickly in 'erroneously assign[ing] her [reason in] the first [place]' (p. 297).
15. Lockhart, 'Remarks on Schlegel's History', p. 499.
16. Wordsworth, *Lyrical Ballads*, p. 236.
17. Lockhart, 'Remarks on Schlegel's History', p. 499.
18. Ibid. p. 500.
19. Ibid, p. 500.
20. Ibid. p. 511.
21. Coleridge, *Lay Sermons*, p. 121.
22. This number has a complex textual history. The 'Chaldee Manuscript' was suppressed in later printings of the number, and Lockwood's 'On

the Cockney School. No. 1' was revised. My chapter addresses the original version.
23. Lockwood wrote this essay under a pseudonym, 'Z.', which he slipped in and out of in later articles in the series.
24. Wilson, 'Observations', p. 5.
25. Coleridge, *Poetical Works*, pp. 453–6.
26. Wilson, 'Observations', p. 6.
27. This attention to market share and market segmentation pervades the October issue. While personality is prominent in the number, so too are gibes against competitors in the periodical market. In addition to edgy remarks *passim*, the number features an article that takes on the *Edinburgh* ('Strictures on an Article'), another critique of the *Quarterly Review* and a brisk assault on the *Edinburgh Monthly Magazine* for having slighted Wordsworth.
28. [Lockhart], 'On the Cockney School of Poetry. No. I', p. 38.
29. Ibid. p. 38
30. Ibid. p. 39.
31. Ibid. pp. 39–40.
32. Ibid. p. 39.
33. Ibid. p. 41.
34. Ibid.
35. Blackwood, in a September 1823 letter to Lord Dundas, makes much of his rivalry with the *Edinburgh Review* and desire to 'turn the laugh' on it. He exults in the transformation in opinion that he feels his magazine has achieved. See the Blackwood Papers, Ms. 30969, National Library of Scotland.
36. See Cox, *Poetry and Politics* (esp. chapter 1); Roe, *John Keats*; and Levinson, *Keats's Life*.
37. This shift in tone is echoed by other editorial decisions by Blackwood. Subsequent printings of the number did not contain the 'Chaldee Manuscript', and many expressions in Lockhart's article were softened. See Tom Mole's exhaustive account of these changes in *Selective Criticism*, pp. 53–61, 369–74. Mole demonstrates that the changes include shifts in agency: references to Hunt himself, his 'thought' or his 'mind' take the presumably less actionable form of his 'works', his 'writings' or his 'muse'.
38. [Lockhart], 'On the Cockney School of Poetry, No. II', p. 197.
39. Although to modern readers the term 'incest' applies somewhat awkwardly to an adulterous relation between a woman and her brother-in-law, the charge follows the list of prohibited marriages in the version of the *Book of Common Prayer*'s 'Table of Kinship and Affinity' applicable in Lockhart's time.

40. [Lockhart], 'On the Cockney School of Poetry, No. II', p. 201.
41. Ibid.
42. In his *Autobiography*, Hunt laments that his 'recasting of the poem was not a wise thing'. He sought to meet Lockhart's strictures by adhering more closely to historical fact, but his changes altered the character of Francesca and made weaker lines in the poem prominent. See Hunt, *Autobiography*, vol. 2, pp. 16–17.
43. In his *Autobiography*, Hunt combines docility and defensiveness in his discussion of 'Rimini', conceding: 'I had yet to learn in what the subtler spirit of poetry consisted. . . . I unfortunately chose the subject of Dante's famous episode. I did not consider, indeed at that time was not critically aware, that to enlarge upon a subject which had been treated with exquisite sufficiency, and to immortal renown, by a great master, was not likely, by any merit of detail, to save a tyro in the art from the charge of presumption, especially one who had not yet even studied mastery itself, except in a subordinate shape' (vol. 2, p. 15). Hunt's admission of 'presumption', given Lockhart's emphasis on it throughout the Cockney School series, would be surprising were it not for the famously amiable character of this poet.
44. [Lockhart], 'On the Cockney School of Poetry, No. II', p. 201.
45. Ibid. p. 199.

Chapter 6

'Some Grand Secreter': Secrecy and Exposure in *Blackwood's*

Mark Schoenfield

> The Secret, like a night-hag, rid his sleeps,
> And took the youthful pleasures from his days,
> And chased the youthful smoothness from his brow,
> That from a rose-cheek'd boy he waned and waned
> To a pale skeleton of what he was . . .
> Charles Lamb, 'The Wife's Trial', *BEM* (December 1828)

The wink of confidentiality, that blend of the secretive and the confident, was a characteristic gesture in Romantic-era *Blackwood's*: not unique to its rhetoric but suited to its understanding of the social world and the periodical world refracting it. The *Edinburgh Monthly Magazine*, *Blackwood's* initial incarnation prior to the firing of Thomas Pringle and James Cleghorn as editors, explained that the 'memoirs of princes' are

> always read with avidity, even though there be nothing very extraordinary in their details. We contemplate with interest any portrait, which exhibits the minds of such exalted personages without the disguise of court costume: we have a secret pride in comparing them with ourselves.[1]

Blackwood's deployed a double strategy of secrecy and exposure to secure its popularity, recognising that the construction of a secret world – whether of monarchic or editorial royalty – could produce readerly curiosity and identification, here named 'secret pride'. Whether claiming inside knowledge of William Hazlitt's journey to the Lake District, declaring to have read Lord Byron's memoir before it was burnt or exposing their own (admittedly fictionalised) inner dynamics at Ambrose's Tavern, the coterie of *Blackwood's* recognised that revelation – self-confession or exposure of others – would not exhaust their supply of secrets.[2] Rather, Maga's mixture of fiction and fact would prepare for more disclosures. This case study examines three distinct but resonant deployments of secrecy in Maga: first, the shift in editorial control in October 1817, which reconceptualised the genre of secret history; second, the notion of confidential and intimate communication between Christopher North and his multitude of readers evident in 'An Hour's Tete-a-Tete'; and, third, the confessional mode that aided *Blackwood's* in producing its own historiographic approach to the present.

These three examples, like early *Blackwood's* itself, are embedded in the development of the periodical industry from the era dominated by the polite essays crafted by Joseph Addison and Richard Steele. Throughout the eighteenth century, periodicals worked to establish, or ventriloquise, an intimacy between reader and writer. This intimacy, which implied shared or promised disclosures, was ensured by the exchanges, often of confidences, in letters to editors, chance essays whimsically submitted and recorded anecdotes or public queries offered in expectation of replies. The *Spectator*, as well as the *London Spy*, *Tatler*, *Adventurer* and *Rambler*, all declare their presence, at various degrees of mysteriousness, among their readers in spaces of public encounter. For Addison's silent, protean Mr Spectator, these included the coffee houses, theatres and the financial 'Exchange' where he has 'been [mis]taken for a merchant'.[3] He declares in the first number, 'Sometimes I smoke a pipe at Child's, and whilst I seem attentive to nothing but the Postman, overhear the conversation of every table.' Invisible in plain sight, Mr Spectator has gained hidden knowledge 'as standers-by discover blots, which are apt to escape those who are in the game'.[4] This idealised figure of an all-seeing individual was a guise for a developing corporate enterprise that traded on secrets and secrecy, circulation and currency. This 'symbolic reciprocity' offered a rich legacy to the romantic periodical.[5]

From the 1790s to the 1820s, as Jon Klancher has observed, the British periodical industry saw a 'productive disarray of early-nineteenth-century relations among writers, ideologies, discourses, and social audiences'.[6] This disarray propelled experiments in periodical productions, some grounding themselves in magisterial distinction, others depending on the simulacrum of intimacy, and many moving strategically between these rhetorics. The most successful reviews, the *Edinburgh* and the *Quarterly*, tended towards a distanced, impersonal stance, achieved by deploying procedures of reviewer anonymity combined with both professional levels of payment and policies directed towards securing greater circulation and cultural clout. By contrast, James Hogg's short-lived *The Spy* (1810–11) developed multiple strategies of intimacy, such as publishing a letter proffering marriage to 'the Spy' himself and his answer declining it, or printing a fictional character's confession, on the eve of battle, of his own secret marriage.[7] Each of these periodicals, in modes suitable to its goals and publishing moments, played with the potentials of secrecy and disclosure in order to construct its relation to its audience. *Blackwood's* shifts along the conceptual spectrum between the impersonality of the quarterlies and the confidentiality of *The Spy*, borrowing, mixing and transforming techniques from earlier periodicals. *Blackwood's*, thus, is at once typical in deploying strategies of secrecy and distinct in its particular formulations.

Secret History

Secret history, as a literary genre, emerges with uncertain origins and porous boundaries. Aimed at exposing the hidden or the personal, it is supplemental to the official, heroic or otherwise authorised histories, but that supplementary position allows it to reveal underpinnings or motives, to undercut or deauthorise public narrative. As Rebecca Bullard notes, popular secret histories have a tinge of scandal; they 'peer into secret spaces' and show the empowered 'in a metaphorical and literal state of undress'.[8] *Blackwood's*, for instance, presents the carvings of Sterling Castle, a series of heads that observed the passing of history, as a remarkable variant of secret history; in the book of prints restoring these representations to public awareness, 'we can distinguish nearly the whole paraphernalia of female beauty', while 'head No 3' represents (presumably) James I 'in a kind of undress. It is plain and simple, but very graceful'.[9] The article invites a familiarity that supplements the official record, just as the visual supplements the written; the carvings 'embody, corroborate, and elucidate' the available 'contemporary, historical, or poetical descriptions'.[10] In a comic faux-historical salaciousness, the 'Old Fellow' remarks in the January 1818 'Hint to the Ladies' that 'although nudity might have been a very appropriate *costume* . . . in the *very dawn* of society', he finds it 'doubtful whether the state of innocence of our modern beaux and belles admits of such an undress at an Edinburgh Assembly'.[11] A mostly favourable 1823 *Blackwood's* notice of Isaac D'Israeli's *Second Series of Curiosities in Literature* offers one recipe for secret histories in D'Israeli's own technique of 'bringing together' two elements, 'a good story and a good *hint*'; the review concludes by focusing on D'Israeli's final chapter, 'True Sources of Secret History', a theorisation of the relationship between hidden histories and their necessarily miscellaneous and accidental sources.[12]

The deployment of secret histories is part of the generic tactics by which periodicals relied on, exposed and breeched literary boundaries between news and fiction, satire and earnestness, and the social boundaries of public and private, city and country, high and low culture. Nicola Parsons has identified the 'affiliation to the double discourse of concealment and disclosure that characterises the secret history' as a prominent feature of the early eighteenth-century periodical, one bound to the implied intimate connections of readers and writers.[13] The secret history depends on the claim of its being produced, wholly or in substantial part, prior to an intent to publish. Consequently, for the Romantic era, secret history was a strategy for evading the commodification implicit in producing for publication and for sale. It maintained the veneer and values of amateur and gentlemanly social interest. In *Blackwood's*, the careless conversations and interrupted sentences of the *Noctes Ambrosianae* pretend to the authenticity of such secret histories, with characters seeming to expose in exclamation what they might prefer kept secret.

For Maga's precursor, the *Edinburgh Monthly Magazine*, secret histories took shape, in part, from Walter Scott's co-authored contributions on 'Scottish Gypsies'. Miranda Burgess argues that Scott's novels invoke an antiquarian perspective that seems to take 'flight from the political present, associating itself with the minor, the past, and the foreign' but reveals a persistent but oblique concern with central political questions of nation-based modernity.[14] The concluding and longest of the 'Original Communications' in the first issue, 'Notices Concerning the Scottish Gypsies', written by Scott and Pringle, adheres to this formulation. It is prefaced by an extract of a poem by Hogg that addresses the reader, 'Hast thou not noted on the bye-way side, / . . . a vagrant crew' and offers descriptions that 'Bespeak the remnant of a race of old'; the trace of ancientness leads to the couplet that is positioned to introduce the article: 'Strange are their annals! – list, and mark them well– / For thou hast much to hear and I to tell'.[15] The poem directs readers to their own observations to highlight their historical ignorance: from 'not[ing]' actual gypsies, the reader moves to 'mark[ing]' their 'annals' from the speaker's tale, a characteristic structure of secret history that renders the habitual strange and seeks its solution in history. The article's first paragraph repeats this structure at the level of 'men of letters' who, despite their 'endless disputes about Gothic and Celtic antiquities', have overlooked an ancient people that has 'retained almost unaltered their distinct oriental character, customs, and language' in 'the heart of Europe'.[16] Noticed but overlooked 'by philosophers and literati', the history of 'gypsies' has been told by 'poets and novelists' and needs only 'the historian' to 'affix the stamp of authenticity'. Both poem and opening paragraph move from a striking sight – gypsies 'far straggled through the glade' or 'pitched, perhaps, amidst the mouldering entrenchments of their [men-of-letters'] favourite Picts and Romans' – to the need for a literary supplement to explain what ought to strike the curious reader as strange.[17] The article, then, constructs itself within the genre of secret history, pausing to announce its structure:

> Having in the preceding pages endeavoured to give our readers a general outline of what may be termed the *public annals* of our Scottish Gypsies, we now proceed to detail some of those more *private and personal anecdotes* concerning them, with which we have been furnished chiefly from local traditions, or the observation of intelligent individuals.[18]

The first several of the anecdotes are attributed to Hogg; each is the story of a witnessed murder in which the witnessing does not result in prosecution but rather travels into the oral lore of Ettrick, preserved in retellings until published in this article.

The lead article of this first issue of the *Edinburgh Monthly* appears initially as a contemporary public secret history. The 'Memoir of the Late Francis Horner' begins by noting his 'splendid talents in the public councils', the 'inflexible integrity' of his 'private life' and the 'universal regret' caused by his death for 'the nation at large' and for those 'attached to him by the dearer ties of consanguinity and friendship'.[19]

This opening intimates knowledge of Horner's private life, but not to expose or to describe it, only to assert a formal consistency of character between the hidden private life and the known public one. This claim of consistency justifies resorting to strictly public information for the remainder of the article: the 'exalted estimation' of Horner's character is exemplified by 'the tone of deep and feeling regret with which his death was announced in all the public prints; and the strain of unexampled eulogy which was poured forth . . . in the House of Commons'.[20] The next six pages are almost entirely extracts from these parliamentary eulogies. Samuel Romilly, a legal reformer in Parliament, offers a tribute typical in alluding to private life only abstractly – no details – in order to bolster Horner's public consistency: 'Though no person better knew . . . the private virtues of Mr Horner than himself, yet, as he [Romilly] was not sure that he should be able to utter what he felt on that subject, he would speak of him only as a public man'.[21] The private life, unknown but hardly secret, persists in the emotional intensification of public grief. The 'Memoir' concludes with a résumé of accomplishments that runs from place and date of birth to those of death, the paradigm of official history. The secret history of the outcast gypsies can be exposed and expanded across four of the six issues of the *Edinburgh Monthly*. By contrast, Francis Horner's can only be gestured towards, his life told by official records.

Eschewing an exploration of the hidden while emphasising its availability, the 'Memoir' of Horner declines the play of personalities that, as Kim Wheatley has demonstrated, would come to characterise *Blackwood's* engagement with other periodicals and authors. For example, the opening article of the retooled magazine for October 1817, its attack on Coleridge's *Biographia Literaria*, is, as Wheatley says, an 'excellent example of the blurred line between personal attack and literary biography'.[22] As Tom Mole has shown, 'Maga seemed intent on distinguishing itself through both the personalities its reviewers constructed' for themselves and 'the personalities they perpetrated' on others.[23] This tactic extended beyond reviewers to the range of their writers and editorial apparatus, thus developing an extensive network of private connections, real and fictional, that they could insinuate, reveal or revise.

The 'Translation of an Ancient Chaldee Manuscript', also appearing in October 1817, further announced a break with, yet supplement to, the earlier approach of the 'Gypsies' articles by making the secrets of the present – cloaked in antiquarian guise – the subject of spectacle. It coalesced a series of secrets within its analogical narrative of the battle of Ebony and Crafty – William Blackwood and Archibald Constable – and their minions and in its falsified textual history as a translation of a manuscript 'preserved in the great Library of Paris' and part of a larger project in which the 'original' will be published, 'prefaced by an Inquiry into the Age when it was written, and the name of the writer'.[24] The 'translation', of course, had no original, and the authorship was not merely secret but unnameable because collective and corporate. Offered as a fragment of a non-existent whole, the 'Manuscript' ends on a moment of double secrecy. Confronted by the imminent battle between the arrayed forces of Ebony and Crafty, the narrator loses his nerve: 'And I fled into an inner chamber to hide myself, and I heard a great tumult, but I wist not what it was.'[25] Both authorial position and the cacophony of popular discourse are unintelligible, and the unravelling of these mysteries is projected not onto the completed translation of the manuscript but onto the continuous publication of *Blackwood's* itself.[26]

The 'Chaldee Manuscript' had another secretive aspect: it was quickly retracted and replaced in a new version of the October 1817 number by 'A Curious Old Song', a poetic attack on the Whigs, and the second part of 'Strictures on . . . the *Edinburgh Review*', which ended with sufficient blank space to mark an absence. According to R. Shelton Mackenzie, Blackwood had 'issued only two hundred' copies before making the substitution.[27] As R. P. Gillies recalls, 'Every purchaser expected to have his copy of the far-famed satire, and every one growled at its absence.'[28] In the midst of this affair, the magazine became, in Philip Flynn's words, 'momentarily noticed and notorious', a notoriety it exploited regularly thereafter by referencing 'The Chaldee Manuscript' and reviving the nicknames it had coined.[29] Although a wide audience knew about the text, in trying to find a copy, readers would instead uncover, in both poetry and prose, the wickedness of the Whigs. The strategy of replacement made the absent text an open secret, one that authorised a certain performance of Tory antiquarianism in resistance to Whig expansionism and the legend by which *Blackwood's* – measuring itself – could measure others. Over six years later, in the December 1823 number, a commentary on 'The Diary of Joseph Burridge' cycles through a series of hoaxes before concluding that none can match 'that state of ecstasy and excitement which some of our juvenile indiscretions produced, such as the Chaldee'.[30] This nostalgia invites readers' participation in the secret by insinuating that they were among those early readers.

Coining Confidence

While the secret history insinuated hidden knowledge, the pose of confidentiality was part of a strategy to bond the reader to the periodical, deploying signs of intimacy for projects of publicity. For example, the October 1820 number offers the peculiarly confidential 'An Hour's Tete-a-Tete with the Public', a title that echoes *Town and Country Magazine*'s series 'Tete-a-Tete', which ran from 1769 through 1793.[31] This earlier series publicly paired such celebrities as 'the Artful Lover and Miss C.lm.n' and 'the Reclaimed Rover and the amiable Miss D – rs – t', an accretive technique that balanced political and voyeuristic urges.[32] Similarly, North's tête-à-tête with his readers continues the earlier tradition of secret histories identified by Nicola Parsons:

> The temporality of serial publication combines with the tropes of the secret history to produce new reading possibilities. In particular, it demonstrates the ways in which the periodical contributes to the materialization of the secret, reifying a connection between secrecy and sexuality.[33]

Although North's sexuality is largely sublimated by appetites for eating, drinking and male camaraderie with its attendant shared reading, his periodical voice in 'An Hour's Tete-a-Tete' links such secrecy to the autobiographical character of recurrent scandal. Written, according to Alan Strout's *Bibliography*, by John Wilson, the 'Tete-a-Tete' opens by noting that, as the 'Chaldee Manuscript' was published in an October number, 'we cannot better conclude' this one than 'by communicating . . . a little private information concerning ourselves and our affairs' and distinguishing *Blackwood's* subscribers – 'those millions of souls who feel their temporal happiness' depends 'on our Miscellany' – from the world at large that 'is apt to be curious overmuch'.[34] In a collision of the text and the font in which it appears, *Blackwood's* asks 'just to whisper a few confidential words into the ear of the public' and presents those few words in a cacophonous couplet of loud capital letters:

'OUR SALE IS PRODIGIOUS – AND WE / ARE ABSOLUTELY COINING MONEY'.[35] In this presentation, as David Stewart suggests, 'the sale and spread of the magazine's fame themselves become the material of a playful fiction'.[36] Further, the secret of prodigious sales is only verifiable and publicly reinforced when announced: it becomes self-fulfilling by becoming a public secret.

Wilson animates Maga's contentious early history as a series of fights, a 'spirited sketch' of 'the difficulties we had to encounter' that leads North to allude to another tête-à-tête: 'We are Othello, and the public is Desdemona. She loves us for the dangers we have passed, and we love her that she did pity them.'[37] The analogy underscores the seductiveness of self-disclosure and locates the post-Chaldean *Blackwood's* as an autobiographical endeavour, aligned with Mr Spectator's declaration 'to Print my self out, if possible, before I die'.[38] But the analogy to Othello is truncated, disguising the homicidal jealousy of the publisher for a public that is indicated by Othello's fate within a web of secrets both malignant and benign. *Blackwood's* forestalls such a fate by committing itself to continual narrative seduction, repeating 'the same strenuous exertions, that first won her [the Public's] virgin heart'.[39]

Re-emphasising the lopsided intimacy of the corporate Christopher North and his multitudinous readers, the 'Tete-a-Tete' offers various assessments of circulation as proof of these recurring 'exertions'. North asserts, for example, Maga's presence in France and Italy, London and Glasgow, even aboard 'British packets' and other ships. The delineation of the geographic distribution shifts when North declares Maga one of the 'first periodical works that ever went up in a balloon' and perhaps the only one that 'ever went down in a diving-bell'.[40] He confuses circulation as a financial imperative and as an autobiographical, even scientific, excursion. Converting circulation into an adventure narrative uses the demonstration of *Blackwood's* as a financial endeavour, a commodity produced for sale, to conceal that very status.

Wilson performs a similar obfuscation when announcing Maga's profits. Proclaiming at first that 'any person can calculate the profits on 17,000 copies',[41] the next passages demonstrate the uncertainty of such a calculation (to say nothing of the hyperbolic number used as a starting point). After assigning one value for his income, North revises, 'We have, we perceive, made a very foolish and important error in this statement' and offers another estimate of profits. The next paragraph abruptly announces, 'Gracious Heavens! Another most egregious omission is just staring us in the face.' After another correction, he summarises, 'Add a few hundreds, for errors excepted, and you will have the amount of our income (from this one work at least).'[42] This vague, exasperated solution to a calculation initially declared straightforward conceals the very concealment of William Blackwood's financial model. In part, this revisionary presentation – moving from a simple calculation to errors, omissions, additions and subtractions – impersonates the immediacy of speech consonant with a tête-à-tête. But it is also a calculated presentation that discloses a key mechanism of finance, a balance between – and elision of – revelation and concealment. North concludes this analysis by abandoning monetary calculation for narrative declamation: 'We are inclined to suspect, that, with the exception of the author of the [Waverley] novels, whoever he may be, literature has been fully more lucrative to Christopher North than to any of his great contemporaries.'[43] Invoking desire ('inclined'), suspicion ('suspect') and feigned doubt ('whoever he may be'), this summation conceals its figures.

This economic braggadocio declared and obscured Maga's financial condition in a way that encouraged emotional investment in being identified as part of its readership. Tracing the emergence of financial journalism in the early Victorian period, Mary Poovey outlines its work in 'making the allure of investment vivid for Britons'.[44] Poovey demonstrates the supplementary aspect of financial writing: it reports on an industry dependent on, and altered by, its reporting; the dynamic corresponds to Derrida's formulation of value in autobiographical writing: 'The operation that substitutes writing for speech also replaces presence by value: to the *I am*, ... a *what I am worth* is preferred.'[45] In the performance of the 'Tete-a-tete', its writerliness appears in its exaggerated refusal of revision, highlighted by self-revelatory and speech-impersonating exclamations such as 'Gracious heavens!' North treats reading *Blackwood's* as a form of investment by the collective reader, and such an investment depends upon a 'tension' Poovey identifies 'between the imperative to disclose facts about finance and the need to keep aspects of business secret'.[46] Secrecy is maintained by excessive disclosure and elided by its relation to the open secret of Walter Scott's authorship. Just as, in Poovey's formulation, the 'distinction between rumor and information' caught financial journalism in the self-fulfilling web of a 'cleverly planted tip intended to incite speculation'[47] – and thus rendered the 'tip' true – *Blackwood's* speculations about itself became a literary-financial operation that fuelled readership, if not in terms of dramatic increases of print runs (which, though hard to reconstruct, David Finkelstein estimates as a fairly steady rise from around 3,000 to 6,000 in its first decade), then in terms of self-identification.[48] To coin money in secret was to forge readership in public.

Confession and Exposure

For *Blackwood's*, as well as the *London Magazine*, where De Quincey's *Confessions of an English Opium-Eater* was first serialised in 1821, confession was a blend of secret history and confidentiality, a mode of boasting and of exposing anxieties, of balancing pleasure and pain. The confessional article crystallised *Blackwood's* hyperbolic method of skewing the rhetorical strategies of competitors. Comparing *Blackwood's* Glutton with the *London's* Hypochondriac, David Higgins argues that both are haunted by 'a spectre of the *London's* former editor' as a figure of periodical excess; he suggests that the Glutton and Hypochondriac reflect 'the unpalatable possibility' that both magazines were 'as driven by market forces as their competitors'.[49] 'The Confessions of a Cantab', written by Francis Bacon and published across *Blackwood's* October and November 1824 numbers, offers a different and mediating approach to the genre, perhaps because Bacon was not a regular either at *Blackwood's* or within the periodical industry.[50]

Observing that 'everybody, from the "*Justified Sinner*," down to the "*Opium-Eater*" and the "*Footman*" have thought [it] proper to confess',[51] the narrator of 'The Confessions of a Cantab' announces his determination to enter this peculiar genre, which posits a balance between discretion and publicity, the reformulation of the private as publicly consumable, a simultaneity of the secret and its exposure. He compares confession – 'to pour forth one's follies and one's sins into [an] attentive ear' – to the medicinal 'tincture of rhubarb' for 'disordered bowels'.[52] Declaring that the 'selection of a confessor' must be 'extremely judicious', the Cantab reasons that, 'as secrecy' is a confessor's 'primary and indispensable qualification', he chooses for his 'the public . . . because I have a well-grounded conviction that *it will go no farther*'. His confessing exposes the hidden rituals that determine the collegiate experience and organises them to typify the modern character (which he presumes will shock the 'ancient pedagogues' attempting to shape it). In particular, the contemporary student is typified by misreading (of, for example, Greek history, modern manners and slang) amid chaotic textual circulations, culminating in an episode of stealing signs and relocating them to transform their meaning: 'another committed a depredation upon a board, with "men traps set here" upon it, and fastened the same to the dwelling of two maiden ladies'.[53]

Amid such interpretive chaos, the Cantab pivots to phrenology. When he is unpacking his books, the first are 'abridgments of the works of Lavater, and of Doctors Gall and Spurzheim', as 'I confess that I was then a very great Bumpiologist'. Although offered as a naive understanding of the secrets of personality, the narrator still believes 'Nature does sometimes write a very legible hand upon the *phizmahogony* of some people'; he 'would stake [his] existence' on being able to 'pick out Hazlitt's and Leigh Hunt's skull from those of the whole universe'.[54] The reference locates the Cantab within the orbit of the 'Cockney School' articles (a series that attacked Hazlitt and Hunt, in addition to Keats). In those articles, the dynamic of secrecy and disclosure was a weapon in a contest of periodical authority, with magazines exposing, threatening to expose or inventing the secrets of the other before accusing the others of those crimes. Hazlitt's and Hunt's secrets are presented as impossible to keep, already exposed by the shapes of their heads.[55]

For *Blackwood's*, phrenology represented a fantastical promise of science to disclose interiority – motive, disposition, intention – through a technology that would render human assessment redundant. Pretending to quote from the 'Judiciary Records for the year 1996', the epitaphs of the parodically pseudonymous Sir Tickletoby's 'Essays on Cranioscopy, Craniology, Phrenology, &c' (August 1821) portend that 'the truth of witnesses' will be obsolete for futuristic criminal trials, replaced by the evidence of the skull. The prosecutor points to the 'bumps', which 'all agree denote a thief', while 'Counsel for the Prisoner' notes the cranial symmetry that indicates 'such striking marks of rigid virtue' and challenges jurors to test the prisoner's bumps against the 'knob[s] upon your [own] skulls'.[56] Consistently satirised in *Blackwood's*, phrenology served as a hyperbolic version of confession that exposed its limits. The secret exposed by the Cantab to the public is the same secret the public experiences reading *Blackwood's* rejection of 'craniology': any amount of confession will leave a residue of the secret; full disclosure is a phantasm of the limits of logic and language.

The doubling implied by the single secret in its dual states of disclosed and hidden becomes, for *Blackwood's*, a shattering array of multiplicity; secrecy becomes a strategy for regulating information, transforming it into history, confession and accusation. Scott Mackenzie has demonstrated that secrets, for Walter Scott and James Hogg, are an intensification of the (unstable) distinction between interiority and exteriority. *Confessions of a Justified Sinner* offers a schematic doubling of Robert and Gil-Martin, in which the latter's omniscience constitutes the former's ignorance of interiorised self. In Scott's case, the doubling resides in the open secret by which Walter Scott and the Author of Waverley claim and reject identical literary space. Mackenzie argues that 'the secret of Scott's secrecy' is discovered by 'sketch[ing] relationships between authorship, authority, and ... nationality'.[57] While Scott Mackenzie primarily discusses Scott as novelist, Scott's tendency of secret literary engagement also concerns periodicals – his early machinations with the founding of the *Quarterly Review*, which he concealed from his friend, Francis Jeffrey;[58] his financial backing of *The Beacon*, exposed when the newspaper folded in scandalous circumstances;[59] and anonymous and pseudonymous publication are all part of his complex web. And such secrecy extended to his connections with the Maga coterie, partly through his son-in-law, John Gibson Lockhart.[60]

For *Blackwood's*, secrecy is epitomised by the concealment of William Blackwood's editorship by both the displacement onto Wilson and then the disguise into Wilson's unstable avatar Christopher North. More complex than the individualised doppelgänger confrontation as the uncanny, Christopher North and William Blackwood nonetheless encounter each other in 'The Tent' issue of September 1819. As North steps off the coach, he comes 'bob against Mr Blackwood', who exclaims, 'The cry for copy is most terrible ... come away up to Ambrose's'.[61] In the following scene, an undisclosed 'we' (perhaps the editorial 'we' or an unnamed coterie signified by it, or perhaps the self-plural North) devours food and drink and produces text, both at great rate and quantity, with a resulting productivity and 'versatility' the 'astonished'

Blackwood describes as 'most fearsome'.⁶² Seeming to disclose the mechanism of production, this scene is an allegory of its encryption: as Mackenzie contends for Scott's work, 'a secret is encrypted, which is to say both that it is sealed within a kind of psychic crypt and that it is rendered into language that misleads'.⁶³

Blackwood's presents a 'Singular Anecdote' (December 1818), which could as equally either parody or analogise Scott's own parables of historical encounter and secrecy – 'The crypt is sealed *within* the home at the same moment that home itself is founded', as Mackenzie puts it.⁶⁴ The anecdote is singular because of its compression of historical secrets, emblems and laws. Its prefatory note to 'Mr Editor' avers the 'authenticity' of the 'narrative', except that 'the family name has been altered', confirming secrecy within the exposure.⁶⁵ The story begins by noting the 'Maleverers' had both an 'ancient and extensive mansion' and an 'ancient descent', terms that spatialise history, creating spaces for concealment.⁶⁶ The family becomes increasingly insular following the Jacobite collapse, until the 'early part of the 19th century' when, by the action of an 'old entail', the estate is 'to go to a distant and protestant successor' unknown and despised by the current owner, the last of his branch. On his decease, the 'tarnished household furniture' is sold, alienating as many historical artefacts as possible from the 'respectable country gentleman' who arrives to take possession. He spends his first night reviewing 'musty deeds and age-stained parchments' that 'secure[d] and chronicle[d]' (to borrow Mackenzie's term, 'encrypted') 'the house of Maleverer'.⁶⁷ On the verge of sleep, he discovers first a keyhole and then a key, and opening a once-hidden cabinet, discerns a figure dressed in outdated 'English fashion' apparently 'deeply engaged in reading, but without any light' except 'the sickly beams of the moon'.⁶⁸ The modern Maleverer flees the perceived apparition, only to learn in the morning that it is a 'waxen image' of 'Charles Edward Stuart', revealed because the 'mirror' that had hidden both key and keyhole was sold off.⁶⁹ The encrypted wax figure replaces the mirror as the simulacrum of the historical, its pose of reading and its encryption in hidden chambers gesturing towards the unrecoverable, its waxen material towards the doublings of history.

As a furnisher of anecdotes and oddities to *Blackwood's* (such as those he provides for Scott and Pringle's article on 'Scottish Gypsies'), James Hogg exploited his role as a correspondent; his letter 'A Scots Mummy' (August 1823) serves as an early notice of *Confessions of a*

Justified Sinner. In another case, he provided 'A Strange Secret' (June 1828) as '*Related in a Letter from the Ettrick Shepherd*'.[70] The first page of this story epitomises how the construction of secrecy serves as a method for the dissemination of multiple perspectives, identities and information. When a poor man, Thomas Henderson, 'came to our door and presented me with a letter', Hogg's persona 'was kind to the man'; in response, the man 'gave me his history in that plain, simple, and drawling style, which removed all doubts of its authenticity'.[71]

This exchange of recognition, in the form of kindness, for narrative, constructs (hi)story as a type of currency, one Hogg signals is not counterfeit, based on style. The commodification of disclosure is thematically repeated in Thomas's speech, the bulk of which is worthless, except for 'one little story' that strikes Hogg as one of the 'fundamental documents of any sort relating to Scotland', namely, 'the secrets of a noble family'. What follows is a set of embedded secrets. When summoned by his new master, Thomas worries that he will become an unwilling confidante: 'Am I gaun to be made some grand secreter?' Instead, he is set upon a quest – spying on the Lady Julia, the master's sister. But the outcome is that he does become a grand secreter. He overhears Julia's secrets, which concern mysteries he cannot discern, including intimations of a murdered child. A child's 'coffin' contains not a body but the child's clothes, chronologically arranged to materialise his history and glossed, though mostly inaudibly to Thomas, by the presumed witch Eppie Cowan.[72] As with *Justified Sinner*, a cryptological imaginary, the simultaneous locus of death and inscription becomes the site of an obfuscating disclosure. On reporting back to the Earl, Thomas is dismissed with 'a very handsome present' on the condition he never return 'within a hundred miles of the house'.[73] Hogg presses Thomas for explanations, and he responds that 'the Bishop' is 'the only person who could explain the mysterious circumstances'.[74] Announcing he has 'written the Bishop', Hogg closes the letter, 'I am almost certain he will not withhold it; and if it be of such a nature as to suit publicity, I shall send it you as soon as it arrives.'[75]

Neither prediction – the bishop's response nor Hogg's despatch to *Blackwood's* – comes to pass. Instead, this letter becomes an advertisement for, and edited fragment within, a longer version published the following February in *The Shepherd's Calendar*.[76] There, it becomes a gothic tale that peels away the layers of the magical to disclose the commonplace fanaticism of religious prejudice, and the Bishop's non-response becomes entwined with the narrative, at the end disclosed as a secret history, the supplement to 'the evidence adduced before the courts of law for the rights of heritage, and before the Peers for the titles'.[77] The deployment of *Blackwood's* as a site for Hogg to create a mystery that his subsequent publishing does not solve, but rather defers to official sites of judgement, both suits and exploits *Blackwood's* own compulsions towards secrecy and display.

Conclusion

Blackwood's treatment of secrets answers to a number of theoretical imperatives. It becomes a public text by following the Derridean understanding that a text 'hides from the first comer, from the first glance, the law of its composition and the rules of its game'.[78] It exploits what Jesse Rosenthal notes as the 'modern flow of information, dating back to the nineteenth century', that 'requires that our most closely guarded secrets – amorous, financial, political – pass through unknown hands'[79] while also partaking in the formulation of the restoration of secret histories, which, as Melinda Rabb demonstrates, 'suffuse the print marketplace with an atmosphere of suspicion'.[80] These tendencies are visible in individual articles – the 'Chaldee Manuscript', 'An Hour's Tete-a-Tete', 'A Strange Secret' – and in the mystified operations of the journal and its patterns of obfuscations and information performed by various pseudonyms and recurrent series, metaphors, self-allusions and gags. Maga was at once an imitator and innovator in the management of secrets, and other journals – Leigh Hunt's *Examiner*, James Silk Buckingham's *Calcutta*, the *London Magazine*, later *Fraser's* – deployed and engaged secrets for purposes that overlapped or contested the goals of Maga, and in doing so, reshaped it, themselves and the media of print as the holders and hiders of cultural secrets.

Notes

1. The article, reviewing the *Private Memoirs* of the Duchess d'Angouleme, paraphrases the preface's claim that its secret production indicates its authenticity: 'It is composed from notes, either made by stealth at the

moment, with pencils [she concealed from her persecutors], or added immediately after her release.... It was written without any view to publication' ('Review of Duchess', p. 172; D'Angouleme, *Private Memoirs*, p. vi).

2. The interrogatories that comprise 'Hazlitt Cross-Questioned' claim to demonstrate Hazlitt's secret propensities: 'Did you, or did you not ... infamously vituperate and sneer at the character of Mr Wordsworth?' Having accused Hazlitt of plying secrecies, *Blackwood's* deems that method opened to exploitation and asks, 'Is it, or is it not, true ... that you once owed your personal safety, perhaps existence, to the humane and firm interference of that virtuous man, who rescued you from the hands of an indignant peasantry?' ([Wilson], 'Hazlitt', p. 550). Odoherty declares in 'Noctes XV', 'But, as for Byron's Memoirs, why, I can tell you, I have read the book myself, twice over; and, what is more, you will read it yourself within a month or six weeks' time'; he adds that Byron 'puffs' the 'Chaldee most stentoriously' ([Lockhart], 'Noctes XV', p. 709). In September 1819, Christopher North is named as always-already editor (emerging from the shadowy man 'clothed in dark garments, having a veil upon his head' assigned editorial control in the 'Chaldee Manuscript' [p. 92]) with the announcement of his three-volume autobiography in the fictional 'Works Preparing for Publication' (Lendrum, '"Periodical Performance"', p. 67; also discussed by R. S. Mackenzie, 'History', p. xiii).
3. Addison, '*Spectator*, No. 1', p. 6.
4. Ibid. p. 6. Although 'blots' references exposed single pieces in backgammon, its figurative sense of flaws or weaknesses is invoked by Mr Spectator declaring his neutrality between parties unless he is provoked by 'the hostilities of either side'.
5. Klancher, *The Making*, p. 20.
6. Ibid. p. 172.
7. Hogg, *The Spy*, pp. 433–4, 269.
8. Bullard, 'Introduction', p. 1.
9. Fraser-Taylor, 'Remarks', p. 209.
10. Ibid. p. 206.
11. 'Hint to the Ladies', p. 377.
12. [Lockhart], 'New Series', pp. 166, 174–5. Lockhart's discussion of D'Israeli's uncertain native language and religious practice emulates the combination of 'story' and '*hint*'. Miranda Burgess contends that for 'the antiquarian Isaac D'Israeli', the 'relationship of secret history to the moral significance of literature and private character is explicit' (Burgess, 'Secret History', p. 194).
13. Parsons, 'Secret History', p. 147. In addition to reviews and notices of books declaring themselves secret histories, the phrase 'secret history' was

familiarised in the periodical context by series that deployed it; the 'Secret History of the Court' ran in nineteen issues, 1761–63, of *Court Magazine* and characterised the magazine's approach; the *Lady's Monthly Museum* ran 'A Mystery Developed, or, the Secret History of the Countess of Cambria' in nine issues from January to September 1818.

14. Burgess, 'Secret History', p. 189. Burgess shows that Romantic-era secret history was available to a variety of genres that managed 'public chatter about secrecy in which government and its agents engaged', and she highlights Walter Scott's antiquarianism as one mode of such management (pp. 188, 193–7).
15. [Scott and Pringle], 'Notices', p 43; the poem appeared in considerably different form as 'The Gypsies' in Hogg, *Poetical Works*, vol. 4, pp. 281–3.
16. [Scott and Pringle], 'Notices', p. 43.
17. Ibid.
18. Ibid. p. 49.
19. 'Memoir', p. 3. Horner was a close friend of Francis Jeffrey, editor of the *Edinburgh Review*, and had written several articles on economics during the journal's early years.
20. Ibid. p. 3.
21. Ibid. p. 7.
22. Wheatley, *Romantic Feuds*, p. 84.
23. Mole, '*Blackwood's* "Personalities"', p. 90.
24. [Hogg et al.], 'Chaldee Manuscript', p. 89.
25. Ibid. p. 96.
26. Other secrets constructed in 'Chaldee' include the shrouded 'seven young men' who reappear in, for example, [Wilson], 'Pilgrimage to the Kirk of Shotts', pp. 674–79); [Wilson], 'Old North and Young North' (p. 810), and multiple 'Noctes', including [Maginn?], 'Noctes VI', p. 374 and [Lockhart], 'Noctes LI', pp. 419–21. R. S. Mackenzie describes them as 'contributors to Constable's Scots' Magazine ... ridiculed by Maga, for years, on all occasions' (in Wilson, *Noctes Ambrosianae*, vol. 4, p. 138).
27. Mackenzie, 'History', p. ix. Thomas Constable, in *Harper's* (1874), repeats that figure (p. 510). 'An Hour's Tete-a-Tete', discussed below, offers a different, somewhat self-contradictory assessment: 'Nothing else was talked of for a long while; and after 10,000 copies had been sold, it became a very great rarity' ([Wilson], 'An Hour's', p. 80).
28. Gillies, *Memoirs*, vol. 2, p. 235; quoted in Oliphant's *Annals* vol. 1, p. 130, and by Philip Flynn, 'Beginning', p. 27.
29. Flynn, 'Beginning', pp. 28–9.
30. [Lockhart], Review of *The Diary*, pp. 702–4.

31. Mitchell, 'The Tête-À-Têtes', p. 14.
32. Bleackley, 'Tete-a Tete Portraits', pp. 344, 463. The series was kept current by various literary allusions (Mitchell, 'The Tête-À-Têtes', p. 13). Cindy McCreery points out that its readers were both social critics and celebrity watchers ('Keeping Up', p. 211).
33. Parsons, 'Secret History', p. 148.
34. [Wilson], 'An Hour's', p. 80.
35. Ibid.
36. Stewart, 'WE ARE ABSOLUTELY COINING MONEY', p. 32.
37. [Wilson], 'An Hour's', p. 81.
38. Addison, 'The *Spectator*, No. 1', p. 6. The passage concludes with Mr Spectator declaring that should he succeed, he will die 'with the secret satisfaction of thinking that I have not lived in vain'. Writing himself out at 'a sheet full of thoughts' daily, a final comforting and justifying secret remains, a consequence of the exposure of all others.
39. [Wilson], 'An Hour's', p. 81. Variations of overheard tête-à-têtes arise early in the article, including Milton's Adam and Gabriel, boxers toe to toe, and undergraduates 'devour[ing]' Maga in chapel as 'bread eaten in secret' (pp. 80–1, 84).
40. Ibid. p. 88.
41. Ibid.
42. Ibid.
43. Ibid. p. 89.
44. Poovey, 'Writing about Finance', p. 18.
45. Ibid. p. 32; Derrida, *Grammatology*, p. 155.
46. Poovey, 'Writing about Finance', pp. 29–30.
47. Ibid. p. 31.
48. Finkelstein, 'Selling *Blackwood's*', pp. 80–1. During this same period, as Finkelstein calculates from compiled sources, print runs of the *Edinburgh Review* and *Quarterly* dropped about 50 per cent and 25 per cent respectively ('Periodicals', p. 191).
49. Higgins, 'From Gluttony', pp. 53, 51.
50. Strout identifies Francis Bacon as from Trinity College, Cambridge (*Bibliography*, p. 124). According to Venn's *Alumni Cantabrigienses*, Bacon attended Cambridge from 1822 to 1826 and later became a lawyer and both theatre critic and assistant editor at the *London Times* (II, i, p. 109); he died in 1840, according to the 'Obituary', *Gentleman's Magazine* (July 1840), p. 107.
51. [Bacon], 'The Confessions', p. 459.
52. Ibid. p. 459.
53. Ibid. p. 467.
54. Ibid. p. 463.

55. The first 'Cockney School' article declared the 'culpable manner' in which Hunt was reviewed by the *Edinburgh*: 'We believe it is no secret, at his own [Hunt's] impatient and feverish request, by his partner in the Round Table [Hazlitt]' ([Lockhart], 'On the Cockney School, No. I', p. 41). From the perspective of Jeffrey's editorial policy, review authorship was definitely a secret, here disclosed as if already evident and impugning that policy. For a reading of the Cockney School attacks as they extended into the fabric of *Blackwood's*, see Mark Parker's 'Maga as Medium: Cockneys in Context' in this volume. Speaking equally as metaphor for the *London* and commentary on London, in 'An Hour's Tete-a-Tete' North laments, 'Hardly a vehicle . . . is to be seen without a Cockney taking the reins' ([Wilson], p. 105).
56. Vary, 'Essays', p. 73.
57. Mackenzie, 'Confessions', p. 9.
58. Lockhart, *Memoirs*, vol. 2 (Boston), pp. 102–5.
59. Walter Scott, a 'silent, non-circulating sponsor' of *The Beacon*, became 'implicated in the utterances of others' when 'fiscal responsibility' was traced to him (Caroline McCracken-Flesher, *Possible Scotlands*, p. 63).
60. Leonidas Jones outlines Scott's concealed connections with the fatal duel between Jonathan Christie, Lockhart's 'former college classmate', and John Scott, editor of the *London* ('The Scott–Christie Duel', p. 608). As Strout relays, Lockhart was terrified that Walter Scott would discover his secret authorship of *Letter to Lord Byron*, which was consequently reviewed in *Blackwood's* with '[Jeremy Bentham, Esq.]' as supposed author ([Wilson], Review of *Letter*, p. 421).
61. [Lockhart and Wilson], 'The Tent', p. 627.
62. Ibid.
63. Mackenzie, 'Confessions', p. 8.
64. Ibid. p. 20.
65. [Utterson?], 'Singular', p. 330.
66. Ibid.
67. Ibid.
68. Ibid. p. 331.
69. Ibid. p. 332.
70. Hogg, 'A Strange Secret', p. 822.
71. Ibid.
72. Ibid. pp. 824–5.
73. Ibid. p. 822.
74. Ibid. p. 826.
75. Ibid.
76. The textual history for the *Shepherd's Calendar* is detailed in Douglas Mack's 'Introduction'. Noting that 'the revisions to the *BEM* part of

the story were almost certainly made by Hogg's nephew, Robert Hogg', Thomas Richardson offers several possibilities for why the rest of the story never appeared in *Blackwood's* (*Contributions*, p. 549).
77. Hogg, 'Chapter II. A Strange Secret', *Shepherd's Calendar*, p. 107.
78. Derrida, *Dissemination*, p. 69.
79. Rosenthal, 'The Untrusted Medium', p. 289.
80. Rabb, *Satire and Secrecy*, p. 18.

Chapter 7

Blackwood's Pastoralism and the Highland Clearances

Alexander Dick

Published in September 1829, 'Noctes Ambrosianae XLVI' is one of several *Blackwood's* articles to mention the evictions of Gaelic-speaking communities to make way for massive sheep farms, known today as the Highland Clearances.[1] Midway through this instalment of Maga's series of tavern dialogues, the discussion turns to debating whether Scotland has become a 'province' of the Empire and, if so, if Maga might found its own colony, governed by its imaginary editor, Christopher North.[2] The fictitious *Blackwood's* contributor Timothy Tickler then laments that Highland gentry have abandoned their feudal obligations by evicting their subsistence-farming tenants and leasing the land to Lowland sheep-breeders. Concurring, the Ettrick Shepherd (James Hogg's alter ego in the *Noctes*) remarks, 'If the gentry lose the land, the Highland anes at ony rate, it will only be the Lord's righteous judgment on them for having dispossessed the people before them.'[3] The Shepherd then recollects sailing around the Scottish isle of Arran and admiring the peat fires rising above the inhabitants' dwellings. This prompts North to report:

> I have a letter this morning from a friend of mine now in Upper Canada. He was rowed down the St Lawrence lately, for several days on end, by a set of strapping fellows, all born in that country, and yet hardly one of whom could speak a word of any tongue but the Gaelic. They sung heaps of our old Highland oar-songs, he says, and capitally well, in the true Hebridean fashion; and they had others of their own, Gaelic too.

His friend having translated one of these songs, North proceeds to 'croon' it.[4]

In just three short pages, 'Noctes XLVI' brilliantly takes up a range of subjects that remain troublesome to this day: the divide between Highland culture and Lowland improvement; the rights and responsibilities of landowners; the displacement, migration and mobilisation of Scotland's Gaelic population. The song North sings encapsulates these issues. Titled 'Canadian Boat-Song – (*from the Gaelic*)', it begins with a call for Highland emigrants to 'sing long ago the song of other shores' (l. 2). The second stanza recalls how

> From the lone shieling of the misty island
>   Mountains divide us, and the waste of seas –
> Yet still the blood is strong, the heart is Highland,
>   And we in dreams behold the Hebrides[.] (ll. 7–10)

Lamenting that they 'ne'er shall tread the fancy-haunted valley' of their youths, the song nevertheless recalls fondly the Highlanders wrapping their 'arms around the patriarch banner' and taking 'the soil' and 'the keep' before they 'would be banish'd' so a 'degenerate Lord might boast his sheep' (ll. 13, 15, 20–2). But it ends with a call to

> Come foreign rage – let Discord burst in slaughter!
>   O then for clansman true, and stern claymore -
> The hearts that would have given their blood like water,
>   Beat heavily beyond the Atlantic roar[.] (ll. 25–8)

In typical *Noctes* fashion, though, this violent call to arms is countered by sentimentality, misdirection and aloofness. 'Hech me', the Shepherd remarks, 'That's a very affectin' thing . . . what say you? Another bowl?'[5]

'Canadian Boat-Song' has gone on to become a classic of Scots-Canadian emigrant lyric.[6] Both the poem and the episode of the *Noctes* where it appeared are prime examples of what this essay will call *Blackwood's* pastoralism. This term conjoins two discourses not usually discussed together, animal husbandry and literary genre, to explain how the ideologies, affects and media surrounding the Highland Clearances constellate and clash in Romantic periodicals. On one hand, *Blackwood's* never opposed the conversion of Highland agriculture to animal pasture, a process called pastoralisation, or the resettlement of Highlanders; on the other, it used pastoral conventions to depict Highlanders as living monuments of a proud, but tragically lost culture. *Blackwood's* pastoralism is thus neither the same as literary pastoral nor did it prompt pastoralisation, which was well under way by the time *Blackwood's* appeared. Rather, it is an aesthetic supplement that attempts to comprehend – and to some extent ameliorate – an ecological transformation that has already happened. As 'Canadian Boat-Song' intimates, *Blackwood's* was also attuned to the connections between Highland pastoralisation and colonial issues such as emigration and military recruitment. As a result, *Blackwood's* pastoralism provides an important point of departure for understanding the vexed relations between periodicals and colonialism.[7]

Georgic and Pastoral

It is well known that *Blackwood's* opposed the Whig mandate of the *Edinburgh Review*. It is less well known that the *Edinburgh*'s support for progressive social change and distrust of enthusiasm and sentimentality was built on an established eighteenth-century genre that has come to be called 'prose georgics'.[8] The *Edinburgh* emerged out of the Scottish Enlightenment milieu of Lord Kames's *Gentleman Farmer* (1771), Adam Smith's *Wealth of Nations* (1776), Alexander Hunter's *Georgical Essays* (1777) and John Sinclair's twenty-one-volume *Statistical Account of Scotland* (1791–6). Influenced by both classical georgic and the mode's mid-eighteenth-century revival, these landmark Scottish books emphasised the importance of labour, industry and commercial exchange; attended to the minutiae of agricultural processes and scientific experiment; and encouraged the circulation of local knowledge through the nation, supervised by a professional, managerial elite. Arriving on the scene a generation later, the *Edinburgh*'s varied interests, critical perspicacity and nationalist orientation extended this georgic paradigm. Eventually, as Clifford Siskin notes, the *Edinburgh* helped convert prose georgic into the formal platform for the disciplines of the social sciences.[9] Eschewing the outmoded fashion for the 'dull and prosaic' precepts of 'Didactic poetry', the *Edinburgh* downplayed its georgic roots.[10] But the *Farmer's Magazine* – another periodical published by its proprietor, Archibald Constable, launched the year before the *Edinburgh* in 1801 to circulate news of local agricultural experiments – was more sanguine about classical georgic's continuing relevance: 'Considering the period at which Virgil penned his Georgics,' his magazine's introductory essay explained, 'the similarity between the system he lays down and our modern husbandry is astonishing.'[11]

The Highlands were ground zero for the experimentalism encouraged by georgic. Highland lairds were already enclosing lands and embracing market exchange by the 1740s, but defeating the Jacobites presented an opportunity to British authorities to modernise the region more systematically. Constituted in 1755, based in Edinburgh and including many of the aforementioned figures who popularised prose georgic, the Board of Annexed and Forfeited Estates built roads, canals and forts; established fishing villages and manufacturing towns; and standardised education and religious practice in English. Through the auspices of Highland Societies, many of these same men encouraged the preservation of Gaelic language and customs. All of this was mediated by reports, treatises and reviews which assessed the successes and, often, failures of new farming and management techniques. By the 1780s, the Highlands were a 'laboratory' of improvement with a panoply of publications and journals covering and debating its progress (or lack thereof).[12] Among the experimentalists were enterprising sheep-breeders who replaced local species with hardier Cheviot and Black-face in hopes of making the Highlands a base for the wool industry. As other agricultures foundered, with some commentators declaring the Highlands a 'stationary state' and its people incapable of economic development,[13] the sheep industry grew, albeit at further cost to local communities forced to migrate in increasing numbers to the coasts and colonies. By the 1820s, the Highlands were thoroughly *pastoralised*.

Highland pastoralisation exposed rifts in the georgic media. Several contributors to the *Farmer's Magazine* and Constable's other journal, the *Scots Magazine,* claimed the Clearances were a humanitarian tragedy that could only be ameliorated by more agricultural improvement. These were answered by those who insisted sheep were the only resource on which Highland landlords could profit. Meanwhile, the *Edinburgh Review* used the Clearances to double down on its reduction of the georgic improvement mandate to commercial principles, insisting that the sheep economy signalled the success of the global market economy. Already in 1803, it favourably reviewed the Earl of Selkirk's plan to emigrate whole communities to Canada, arguing that the migration of people to the colonies was a natural outgrowth of the spread of free markets to the Highlands.[14] Reviewing the Highland Society of Edinburgh's *Transactions* the following year, the *Edinburgh* complains that the Society, in preferring agricultural experimentation over sheep-farming, ignored the global demand for wool.[15] In a sense, the *Edinburgh*'s determination to narrow the georgic mandate to these principles reflects Britain's increased reliance on wool production. Sheep became a node around which the edifice of colonial trade, commerce and migration turned. In its commitment to principle, the *Edinburgh* takes responsibility for defending that system.

Given this context, the *Blackwood's* set's use of pastoral motifs is especially canny. Pastoral appeals to the Blackwoodian mindset precisely because, in contrast with georgic, its various conventions produce intersecting, even clashing effects rather than a unified mandate. Hence, Maga's conservative view that 'inequality of power' between landlords and tenants is 'the most natural, the surest, and safest *basis* of Government' recalls pastoral's 'hearty relation', as William Empson calls it, 'between rich and poor'.[16] Yet, as historians of pastoral affirm, that 'beautiful relation' is a view of rural life from without; as Frank Kermode famously remarks, 'The first condition of Pastoral is that it is an urban product.'[17] Blackwood's 'sense of place', as Joanne Shattock describes it, is a homosocial fiction of urbane, convivial masculinity built around *Blackwood's* offices and, of course, Ambrose's Tavern.[18] Conviviality too is a generic protocol that originated in the light-hearted debates and contests of Virgil's *Eclogues* and that, revived by Romantic poetry (Wordsworth's especially), spotlights the negative effects of improvement and mobilisation of the rural poor during the 1790s without offering any economic alternative. This is, of course, exactly the criticism levied at Wordsworth by Francis Jeffrey in the *Edinburgh*. In contrast, *Blackwood's* sees Wordsworth's poems as touchstones for its own aesthetic complexity. As Ian Duncan argues, *Blackwood's* partisan attacks on the *Edinburgh Review* focus on its 'immersion' in commerce and offered 'national culture' as an alternative basis for social stability.[19] By conjoining this cultural nationalism to Highland pastoralisation through the medium of literary pastoral, a more varied and self-reflexive genre that conveniently also happens to be concerned with sheep, the Blackwoodians confound the *Edinburgh*'s georgic mandate without jeopardising aesthetic integrity.[20]

The result is a new genre: 'prose pastoral'. As Paul Westover has shown, Victorian critics saw prose pastoral as memorialising the virtues of local communities even as it acknowledges the inevitability of their passing through economic change.[21] John Wilson had already elaborated the terms of this genre against the georgic mandate in one of *Blackwood's* defining essays, 'Burns and the Ettrick Shepherd'. Agriculture, Wilson contends, 'is a life of severe and incessant labour' which leaves the farmer 'few opportunities for the cultivation and enjoyment either of his moral or intellectual nature'. Its 'knowledge' is 'narrow and worldly' and thus 'not linked with objects fitted to awaken much enthusiastic or imaginative feelings', while a 'density of population' in agricultural districts has alienated the people from their natural 'superstition'.[22] Although Burns was certainly gifted, he was also, in Wilson's view, preoccupied with 'the men who walk around him in this our every-day world', and this concern with present circumstances renders his poetry fragmented and pedestrian.[23] While there are glimmers of 'bliss' and 'joy' in Burns's poems, these are overshadowed by a 'melancholy air' that stems from an inability to rise above the 'hard and oppressive fate' of the farming life. Burns's attachment to worldly affairs entails that, even in his religious poems, his voice seldom 'elevated' above ridiculing the clergy.[24]

By contrast, Wilson argues, the Ettrick Shepherd, who is 'connected with a pastoral life', is unconcerned with the banalities of secular modernity. He shows little 'knowledge of human nature' or 'profound insight into its passions'; instead, he 'deals with imaginary beings' who embody Scotland's 'mild and gentle superstitions' as well as 'the historical traditions that people them with the "living dead"'.[25] Whereas Burns barely registers the 'images of external nature' that the poetry of landscape is meant to convey, Hogg 'loves to bring before him, as a shepherd still in his solitude, the far-off images of human life, dim and shadowy as dreams'.[26] Wilson cultivated this alter ego for Hogg to delineate a more suitable poetic identity than Burns's struggling farmer to speak for an era in which sheep had already become a crucial economic resource, but which could also convey the desultory effects of that transformation. This historical connection renders Wilson's essay not simply an early example of prose pastoral but also an example of the way *Blackwood's* supplemented current events. Put another way, for Wilson, Hogg's imaginative landscape is a cleared landscape: it both invokes sublime vistas created by animal husbandry and registers the economic challenges wrought by its intensification.

To be sure, Hogg chafed under the mantle of the Ettrick Shepherd. His career as a shepherd and his use of pastoral modes were more varied than Wilson's characterisation implies. Before moving to Edinburgh in 1810 to pursue his literary career, he was one of many experts who travelled north to encourage animal husbandry. In a series of letters to Walter Scott recounting his journeys to the Highlands and Western Islands in the summers of 1802, 1803 and 1804 (excerpts of which appeared in Constable's *Scots Magazine*), Hogg recorded, as Alex Deans notes, 'the underdevelopment of sheep farming in the Highlands', and 'propose[d] its systematic expansion as a solution to the region's apparently "stationary state" of unproductivity'.[27] Yet, Deans shows, Hogg also empathises with evicted Gaelic tenants and describes the sublimity of harsh mountain landscapes confounding agricultural improvement.[28] From his early poetry collections, *Scottish Pastorals* (1802) and *The Mountain Bard* (1807), to the 'Tales of Pastoral Life' that appeared in Maga's predecessor, the fledgling *Edinburgh Monthly Magazine*, and extending through the *Shepherd's Calendar* (1829) and *Tales and Sketches* (1837), Hogg developed an 'unimproved' style that, as Antony Hasler argues, reflected his sense that rural land, animals and people were connected in ways that commercial principles could never adequately encompass.[29] In 'Sheep', Hogg remarks that ovine creatures are all pliable and stupid, but also have a 'strong attachment to the place of their nativity' and can find their way home even in harsh weather.[30] In the late essay 'Emigration', published originally in *Chambers's Edinburgh Journal* in 1832, Hogg expressed the view that anyone 'obliged to emigrate', be it from the Highlands or the Borders, is in a condition 'most deplorable'.[31]

Wilson's later views of the Highland Clearances similarly demonstrate how combining pastoral elements with references to pastoralisation creates ambiguous aesthetic effects. In 'Remarks on the Scenery of the Highlands', which originally appeared in 1836 as the preface to the second edition of *Swan's Views of the Lakes of Scotland*, Wilson again invoked the principles of prose pastoral to read the Highland landscape as a memorial of its own transformation and abandoned shielings as silent epitaphs. 'We think,' he writes, 'that we almost remember the time when those glens were in many places sprinkled with huts, and all animated with human life. Now they are solitary; and you may walk from sunrise till sunset without seeing a single soul.'³² Yet 'those sweet pastoral seclusions,' he muses, 'lie, sometimes, embosomed in their own green hills, among the most rugged mountains, and even among the wildest moors. They have no features by which you can describe them; it is their serenity that charms you, and their cheerful peace.'³³ In a passage that warrants quoting in full, Wilson posits:

> For while the rocks continue to frown aloft for ever, and the cliffs to range along the corries, unbroken by trees, which there the tempests will not suffer to rise, the woods and groves below, preserved from the axe, for sake of their needful shelter, shall become statelier, till the birch equal the pine; reclaimed from the waste, shall many a fresh field recline among the heather, tempering the gloom; and houses arise where now there are but huts, and every house have its garden: – such changes are now going on, and we have been glad to observe their progress, even though sometimes they had removed, or were removing, objects dear from old associations, and which, had it been possible, but it was not, we should have loved to see preserved.³⁴

Wilson dignifies clearance aesthetically, even as he notes its trauma. As in his earlier essay on Burns and Hogg, Wilson's pastoralised Highland landscape, though not explicitly identified here with sheep farming, is not a bucolic alternative to georgic improvement because the pastoral landscape is already improved. Pastoralism thus signals a shift in periodical writing from improvement to reflexivity, providing a framework through which to both express misgivings about economic progress and indulge in the aesthetic pleasure that the sheep industry's apparent economic security allowed.

Pastoralism and Primitivism

Pastoral, I am arguing, gave the Blackwoodians a generic platform on which they could develop a more nuanced and complex understanding of the effects, both aesthetic and economic, of the Clearances than that offered by prose georgic and the *Edinburgh Review*. Pastoral characters, its rustic swains and benevolent landlords, also provided archetypes for *Blackwood's* to explain how dispossession was affecting the rural population. Like the 'shadowy beings' who, in Wilson's account, populate the Ettrick Shepherd's 'pastoral vallies', Highlanders appear in many *Blackwood's* articles as living relics of Scotland's ancient traditions.[35] But in their new roles as labourers, migrants and soldiers from a global commercial superpower, Highlanders exhibited enthusiastic loyalty, physical resilience and brute strength, qualities that could threaten imperial security as well as support it. To an extent, this ambivalence confirms *Blackwood's* colonialist sympathies. As Peter Womack and Murray Pittock explain, popular depictions of Highlanders caricature them as part ferocious barbarians and part mischievous clowns, desperately hungry and contentedly ignorant, an 'elastic' monster to be both ridiculed and feared.[36] This stereotype is also apparent in Scottish Romanticism's trademark 'savages', including Macpherson's Fingalian heroes; Scott's Fergus MacIvor and Rob Roy; and the 'Romantic Indians' who thrilled British audiences.[37] *Blackwood's* indulged in many of these primitivist stereotypes even when it was defending Highlanders' 'virtues'. A May 1819 article, 'On the State of Religion in the Highlands', for instance, described Highlanders as 'half-clothed, shrivelled, poor, speechless, and a-gaze' in 'miserable huts' and compared them to the 'ignorant savages' of America and the Pacific, while also arguing that Highland people were endowed with a 'love' for 'their native soil' that is equalled only by their religious enthusiasm.[38]

The origin of this stereotype is the 'pastoral state' delineated by Scottish Enlightenment stadial historians. Pastoral conventions had already been used in early ethnographic accounts of 'noble savages' encountered throughout the European colonies in Africa, Asia and America.[39] Gradually, this conventionalism was reversed by the idea that pastoral poetry originated in a pre-historical era. Adam Smith in his *Lectures on Jurisprudence* (1763) notes that in the 'Age of Shepherds' people retained the independent but authoritarian temper of their 'savage' forbears even as they were organising themselves into societies or clans through husbandry and, eventually, agriculture.[40] Adam Ferguson in *An Essay on the History of Civil Society* (1767) further claims that those owning the most cattle became 'chieftain[s]' who, in Ferguson's words, were 'distinguished from [their] tribe' but were also 'considered as the common bond of connexion, not as their common master'.[41] From this pastoral state, government developed 'the ground of a permanent and palpable subordination' necessary to the proper organisation of society. Yet pastoral cannot be called civilised because its social organisation is grounded in loyalty rather than law. It thus marks a transition from primitivism to civilisation – Ferguson calls it 'barbarism' – in which there is a potential for improvement, but only with the abandonment of primitivism, including nobler qualities like loyalty and enthusiasm, represented especially in its art. In *Origin of the Distinction of Ranks* (1770), John Millar finds in 'pastoral' passages from Homer and *Ossian* evidence of a settled but not yet fully organised social life. 'There is good reason to believe', he reflects, 'that these representations of the pastoral life were not inconsistent with the real condition of shepherds, and that the poets, who were the first historians, have only embellished the traditions of early times.'[42]

Several writers associated with *Blackwood's* used these aesthetic conventions and ethnographic stereotypes in their descriptions of the 'Highland character'. In 1815 while 'tramping' in the 'deepest glens' around Loch Lomond, Lockhart wrote to a friend: 'There is something abundantly delightful in the naked-heartedness of the Highland people. Bating the article of inquisitiveness, they are as polite as courtiers.'[43] That sense of simple nobility, for Lockhart, marks an appealing compliance towards social hierarchy that he would encode into his depictions of pastoral Scottish borderers in *Peters Letters to his Kinsfolk* (1819). Hogg, though he sympathised with the plight of evicted Highlanders, had little faith in their economic capacity. In his 'Essay on the Utility of Encouraging the System of Sheep Farming in some districts of the Highlands', included in his 1807 *Shepherd's Guide* and excerpted in the *Scots Magazine*, Hogg explains that the Highland economy was best served by experienced Lowland shepherds like himself rather than native farmers. 'How easy and agreeable is it', Hogg writes,

> to give orders to two or three shepherds, perhaps once or twice in a month, compared with raging and swearing in Gaelic, among a great retinue of ragged, emaciated wretches, whose natures did commence with sufferance, and times hath made hard in it.[44]

A particularly derogatory example of this characterisation in *Blackwood's* is 'The True and Authentic Account of the Twelfth of August' from August 1819. Along with 'The Tent' in the following issue, this prelude to the *Noctes* sees a band of *Blackwood's* regulars (Tickler, Odoherty, The Shepherd, The Editor, Buller of Brazennose) venturing on a shooting party to the Highlands replete with tent, food, booze and a full arsenal of guns and sporting equipment. At one point, a party of Highlanders appears, complaining that a dog belonging to two English tourists has killed their sheep, and demanding £20 in recompense. After Tickler intercedes and they make a 'treaty of peace', the rest of the company

> could not help having our suspicions, that the whole story of the worried sheep was got up for the occasion, and that these bashful Celts preferred, as it were, storming our intrenchments to get at the grouse and whisky, to that more pacific and more regular approach which they were prevented from adopting by their well-known national modesty.[45]

References to treaties, shyness and a fondness for liquor appropriate widely circulating stereotypes of Indigenous peoples. Later the Highlanders return with 'wild cries' that 'echoed far and wide, from rock to rock over that sublime solitude, as every glen sent pouring down its torrents of shouting hunters' to celebrate the arrival of the Belgian Prince Leopold, who had married the Prince of Wales's daughter Charlotte in 1817 and retained close ties to the British monarchy after her death. His chieftainship thus becomes something of an ironic joke, especially as it conjures up such violent emotions: 'The primitive loyalty of the Scottish mountaineer', North quips, 'is still as pure as the air which he inhales.'[46] In 'Noctes XXII', North and Tickler agree that English tourists wandering the Highlands should always be prepared to pay their Celtic guides:

> Recollect, old or young hunks, that you are on a tour of pleasure – that you are as fat as a barn-door fowl; and these two boatmen – there they are grinding Gaelic – as lean as laths; – what the worse will you be of being cheated a little? – but if you grudge a guinea, why, go round by the head of the loch, and twenty to one you are never seen again in this world.[47]

Comic foils to louche Lowland tourists, the Highlanders also embody scarcity and murder often associated with indigeneity in the period.

Three years earlier, in September 1822, 'Noctes VI' introduced a Highland Chieftain who came to Edinburgh for 'the King's Jaunt'. The issue in which 'Noctes VI' appeared was devoted entirely to George IV's visit and featured day-by-day accounts of the king's arrival at

Leith and his stay in Edinburgh, as well as processions of 'chieftains and clans' paying homage, less than a century after Culloden, to the Hanoverian monarch. When, in 'Noctes VI', Morgan Odoherty, the fictional Irish Ambrosian (later linked to William Maginn), reminds the Chieftain that it is easier to hunt eagles after they have eaten sheep, the Chieftain agrees. The mighty bird, he mysteriously asserts, 'sits as heavy as a Dutchman – cannot take wing – and you may bag him alive if you chuse . . . but let him take wing, and he darkens the sun-disk like an eclipse'. Highland life, he suggests, is not so easy to contain by the introduction of sheep. Ebony then asks the Chieftain for an 'Article on the State of the Highlands' consisting of 'sound, sensible, statistical articles, full of useful information . . . with less fun and more facts' because 'there is much misrepresentation as to the alleged cruelty and impolicy of large farms'. The Chieftain, clearly a supporter of the Clearances, wishes he 'could write an article of the kind you mention . . . In twenty years the Highlands will be happier than they ever have been since the days of Ossian. Lowland Lairds have no right to abuse us for departing from the savage state'. He then adds that Ossian was as 'authentic as the heather and the hail on our misty mountains'.[48] From here, the company discusses the geographic accuracy of Macpherson's poem to counter Wordsworth's complaint that it is bad poetry. 'Our conversation', North quips, 'is degenerating into literature'.[49] The Highland Chieftain, a 'primitive' figure, embodies *Blackwood's* pastoralism, the 'degeneration' of periodical conversation to its roots in improvement and the Ossian controversy. But as an advocate for clearance, the Chieftain also speaks for a landlord class who cultivates this primitivism to screen the effects of improvement through clan loyalty. In drawing comic attention to this conundrum, the encounter with the Chieftain crystallises the ambiguous combination of colonial modernity and cultural nostalgia that defines pastoralism.

Wilson, Hogg and other writers of *Blackwood's* tales employ pastoral tropes to depict those stuck in an unimprovable 'stationary state' or, as in the case of the Chieftain, use those tropes to project a fashionable image of that state as a corollary to its improvement. But peasant Scots also appear in *Blackwood's* as hardy, resilient and environmentally sensitive. William Laidlaw's 'Narrative Illustrating the Pastoral Life' (1819), Wilson's 'The Snowstorm' (1820) and Hogg's 'Snowstorms' (1819) all feature isolated families struggling against terrible winter conditions. In the last of these, Hogg's narrator's effort to walk to a book-club meeting is blocked first by terrible snow and then by the loss of sheep, suggesting affinities not only between the repetitive tasks associated with reading and shepherding but also between the challenges of the Scottish landscape and the convivial pleasures of aesthetic experience. A similar pattern occurs in Hogg's 'Rob Dodds' (1823), which, like most of Hogg's stories, is set in the Borders: a father is inspired to locate the body of his supposedly murdered son in a snow storm by watching a 'momentary glimmer o' light'. He discovers discolourations at the bottom of a creek and, from there, hunts with his dog among the peat-stacks where his son's body lies, even though it had been examined 'again and again, so minutely, that a dead bird could not have been there without their having seen it'.[50] Dead bodies appear in these stormy landscapes as reminders of a primitivism that cannot be absorbed completely into an improvement mandate, its threat or support to the imperial zeitgeist being an open question. Though harsh weather is a feature of the Scottish countryside, it is hard not to see these pastorals as parables for the Clearances, long accomplished in the Borders and well under way in the Highlands. As Anthony Jarrells and Ron Broglio have argued, *Blackwood's* tales often symbolically convey senses of 'opposition' and 'resistance' to forces of economic change through the stubborn instincts of 'primitive' people.[51] Published at the same time as the high point of Highland eviction, and among *Blackwood's* defences of it, pastoral tales overdetermine the Clearances as the locus of possible critique.

Shepherds and Soldiers

While supplanting the prose georgic mandate of Constable's journals with a prose pastoral platform, *Blackwood's* also embraces colonial primitivism to legitimate the ongoing pastoralisation of the Highlands, promulgating borderline racist stereotypes of Highland people. But, I have been arguing, *Blackwood's* aesthetic reflexivity also opens the magazine's readers to the ways that such colonial impulses could be exposed and even resisted. This ambiguity is especially apparent in *Blackwood's* treatment of a particular subclass of Highlanders: soldiers. Highland men made up a sizeable proportion of the British military during the eighteenth and nineteenth centuries. In this capacity they were praised, albeit with a good dose of stereotyping, for their 'war-like' spirit and tenacious loyalty, qualities also associated with the very peoples – in America and then in India – that the Highland regiments were fighting.[52] By and large, these traits were not what inspired so many Highlanders to enlist. The leading historian of Highland soldiering, Andrew Mackillop, shows that youth from the region primarily entered military service to gain employment, avoid famine, retain land at home or start a new life abroad.[53] Military recruitment also played a role in accommodating Highland men and their families to the Clearances, providing them with a new and sometimes lucrative identity to replace the community that was lost. The violence that Highland soldiers faced on the battlefield, not to mention the cruel injustices they encountered coming home, forms an important part of the historical record of the Clearances.

A key instance of *Blackwood's* engagement with Highland militarism is its April 1822 review of Major General David Stewart's hugely popular *Sketches of the Character, Manners, and Present State of the Highlanders of Scotland*. Born in 1772 at Garth Castle in Perthshire, Stewart retired from the Black Watch in 1815 and devoted the rest of his life to promoting Gaelic language (which he spoke fluently), culture and military history, primarily through the Celtic Society of Edinburgh, which he co-founded with Walter Scott in 1820. Stewart also teamed with Scott to organise George IV's royal visit to Edinburgh in August 1822. Honoured with the task of dressing the king in Highland garb, Stewart pronounced His Majesty to be 'a verra *pretty* man'.[54] Unlike Scott's writings on the subject, as Kenneth McNeil explains, Stewart's *Sketches* do not call for the wholesale 'immersion' of the Highland identity into British national culture. Rather, it insists that Highlanders should retain as much of their 'native' character as possible.[55] *Sketches* is thus an 'autoethnography' wherein the colonised writer comes to see himself dialectically through the eyes of the coloniser as both same and different.[56] Such feelings of affinity for Highland culture did not stop Stewart from leading the Black Watch regiment in putting down an anti-clearance protest in Ross-shire in 1792 or from evicting most of the Gaelic tenants from his Perthshire property.[57]

The argument of his *Sketches* is as contradictory as Stewart himself. Throughout, he emphasises the Highlanders' physical agility, military prowess and fierce loyalty to clan and country. He asserts that Highlanders descended from 'pure stock' and lived in an 'insulated community' that needed at all costs to be defended from the incursions of improvement.[58] Yet he also states that their heritage and loyalty made them perfect soldiers who would defend the Empire at all costs. Stewart also insists that the current generation of Highland landlords have made their tenants weak and disconsolate, transforming 'the abode of a brave, vigorous and independent race of men, into scenes of desolation' and forcing them 'pennyless and unskilful, to seek a refuge in manufacturing towns, or, in a state of helpless despair, to betake themselves to the wilds of a far distant land'.[59] *Sketches* is especially harsh on the Marquis and Marquise of Sutherland and their factor Peter Sellar, who, in allowing the most violent removals, had betrayed the clan. Recalling that Sellar was acquitted of murder following the particularly harsh evictions of 1814, Stewart argues that it by no means would 'diminish the general feeling of culpability' that his trial had shown the public.[60] Landlords can restore their tenants' loyalty, Stewart urges, if they protect their culture (through Highland societies), regulate emigration, encourage labour and, above all, establish new regiments that will exercise the Highlanders' native 'military character' and fierce devotion.[61]

Stewart's description of Highland soldiers was not uncontroversial. Recognising the debt Stewart owed to Scott's *Waverley* and other 'fashionable' fiction, the *New Monthly Magazine* argues that he 'overrated' Highland 'Jacobitism', noting instead that most Highlanders had benefited from their relocations to the coasts and cities; in popularising a fantastic Highland character based on 'prejudices and misrepresentations', Stewart had 'done no great service either to the truth or credit of Highland character'.[62] In contrast, *Blackwood's* unknown reviewer of the *Sketches* praises Stewart's effort to identify the Highland regiments with the region's cultural traditions, though it does so with an eye to literary effect rather than historical accuracy. 'Altogether', Maga's reviewer opines,

> this book is one of the few we see coming out now-a-days that is sure to last. It must form a part of every library: the future historian must resort to it for materials: the heroes of a future age will look to it for bright examples.[63]

Blackwood's represents Stewart's book as a literary repository for pastoralism's martial heritage. Even before this review, however, *Blackwood's* had praised the *Sketches*' literariness in the previous month's inaugural instalment of the *Noctes*. In this dialogue, Odoherty asks the magazine's editor if there is 'any thing new in the literary world'. North proceeds to single out 'Colonel Stewart's History of the Highland Regiments', calling the *Sketches* 'one of the most entertaining books that have been published this long time'. It has, the editor remarks, 'not much of the flash that's in vogue, but a great deal of feeling and truth'.[64] A month later, 'Noctes II' returned to the *Sketches*, with North remarking that 'Stewart tells a fine story of his heroism at the battle of Fontenoy', to which Buller of Brazenose adds 'like somebody in Homer'.[65]

In reading *Sketches* as epic romance, *Blackwood's* exposes the aesthetic imprint of the Highland Clearances that Stewart himself embodies. Indeed, *Blackwood's* excessive praise of Stewart may well be sardonic, especially given that *Sketches* was published by *Blackwood's* nemesis, Archibald Constable. What Stewart lacks, *Blackwood's* review suggests, is a sufficient understanding of the relation between aesthetic codes and political effects. If Stewart's goal is to convert his readers – including, preferably, Highland landlords – into regimental officers and clan chiefs, then, *Blackwood's* assumes, he needs to create that fantasy for them rather than berate them into acknowledging their failures. Landlords must understand that the showy trappings of war are not an alternative to imperial policy, but their aesthetic supplement. Yet what becomes apparent in *Blackwood's* review is just how difficult it is for even this aestheticised militarism to completely accommodate the effects of the new commercial economy, especially the Clearances. The magazine's anonymous reviewer agrees with Stewart that 'the instrument of lowering to a prodigious extent the population of these regions . . . must ere long . . . destroy altogether . . . an invaluable nursery of British soldiers'. He concedes that the Sutherlands and other Highland landlords will likely regret this depopulation:

> acquitting the Marquis and Marchioness of Stafford, as we most sincerely do, of any evil intention, we can have no hesitation in expressing our doubts whether the reduction . . . in the population of these vast estates may not hereafter be repented very bitterly by those at the head of them.[66]

Yet, the reviewer also admits, the administration of land operates by way of self-interest like every other aspect of a market economy. It is thus not surprising that Highland landlords pursue the most lucrative options available rather than adhere to military custom:

> nobody can expect that a great landholder is to sacrifice so much of his own income for the good, not of himself, but of the state. A few very liberal minded and reflective landholders in the Highlands may indeed be wise enough to prefer other things to the mere calculations of pounds, shillings, and pence: but it is not perhaps fair to blame those who conduct themselves on the more common-place and prosaic principle quite so severely as Colonel Stewart has done . . . *Make the Celtic lord or laird understand, that whenever he raises a regiment, or a company, he shall receive such and such substantial advantages, and then perhaps there will be less difficulty about persuading him* that the race of men is a better thing than the race of sheep.[67] (emphasis added)

Highland policy, *Blackwood's* suggests, has to balance interests and loyalties. Only a system in which the state reimburses landlords for raising regiments will compensate for their trouble. But since the state cannot do this without contravening landlord rights, landlords must be persuaded that finding alternative employment for their tenants – such as in the army – will provide at least some compensation for the moral risk attending the removals. Stewart's mistake is believing that strength and allegiance, while necessary to soldiering, are sufficient to overcome landlords' economic interests. What is needed instead, Maga suggests, is an aesthetic that elucidates the hardships of clearance and militarisation and the benefits of progress and tradition. What is needed, in short, is not epic, but pastoralism.

To suggest what this aesthetic looks like, I conclude with a story from Wilson's *Lights and Shadows of Scottish Life* (also published by Blackwood in 1822) that illustrates how Blackwoodian pastoralism endorses the imperialist agenda (as Stewart did), but also clarifies the difficulties that attend it (which Stewart misses). In 'The Shealing', Wilson brings together prose-pastoral conventions – death, religion, nostalgia – to represent the 'character' of a Highland solider. Auld Lewis Cameron, a shepherd himself and a veteran of both Jacobite rebellions and the British victory at Quebec in 1759, lies on his deathbed watched over by his granddaughter Flora; Hamish Fraser, a piper; and Catholic, Episcopalian and Presbyterian ministers. For

Katie Trumpener, this gathering of Britain's three religions signifies national unification, further embodied in Cameron's transformation from rebel to imperialist.[68] But Cameron's name, alluding both to seventeenth-century radical Covenanters and to the Cameronians, the infantry regiment that defeated a Jacobite insurgency at Dunkeld in 1689, also hints at the uneasiness of these alliances. This mixture of historical contexts suggests that Scottish military identity is much more varied and conflicted than Stewart's racially simplistic military epic will allow: it is both loyal and resistant, in the same way that religion in Scotland can be both quiescent and obstreperous. Such ambiguity is further apparent in Cameron's lament that the 'Glens that could once have sent out a hundred bayonets, belong entirely now to some fat Lowland grazier. Confound such policy'.[69] Echoing Stewart's criticism of the Sutherlands, and also the latent complaint against the sheep industry in 'Canadian Boat-Song', Cameron comes to speak for a resentment against the Clearances that also dies with him. As the three ministers depart, though, Cameron's granddaughter, Flora, and friend, the piper Hamish Fraser, are left to watch over the body. Fraser plays a final 'Lament' on the pipe,

> a mournful but martial tune which the old Soldier had loved and, in which if there were any superstitious thoughts in the soul of him who was playing, might be supposed to soothe the spirit yet lingering the dark hollow of his native Mountains.[70]

The story ends, then, with a lingering sense of lamentation and dispossession.

Sentimental though it may be, Wilson's story shows how the pastoralism he and other contributors cultivated in *Blackwood's* elucidates moral and political contradictions that attend the Highlands even as they demonstrate the aesthetic means by which clearance can be justified. To the Highland landlords and factors who might read *Blackwood's*, appreciating these tensions is one way to understand how and why clearance might elicit resistance. To a great extent, the Highland Clearances were too problematic an issue to be reducible to simple generalisations, which is why *Blackwood's* required a different generic platform from the economically focused georgic perspectives encouraged by the *Edinburgh Review*. Yet, as I have shown, it is important that we do not thus regard Maga's intervention in discussions of the Clearances as simply a by-product of their

Toryism. *Blackwood's* was by no means an 'improving' magazine, but neither was it devoted exclusively to a sentimentalised cultural nationalism, nor can it be classed entirely as a conventionally Tory or brazenly colonialist publication. Rather, the ambivalence of *Blackwood's* pastoralism and the aesthetic critique that it opened is a result of an uncanny conjunction of literary genre – pastoral – with historical events – pastoralisation – that required a new form of journalistic enquiry. Pastoralism thus not only played a significant role in cultivating the *Blackwood's* ethos, but also helped articulate the mixture of currency and nostalgia that in many respects defines the temperament of modern media.

Notes

1. As Eric Richards explains in *The Highland Clearances* (pp. 6–7), until the late nineteenth century, only the terms 'eviction' and 'removal' were used to describe the practice of dispossessing farmers, whereas 'clearance' referred to the conversion of agricultural land into pasturage. The term 'Clearances' (usually capitalised) generally encompasses both the conversion of land and the policies and practices of mobilising and migrating communities off it. However, the historical events covered by the term 'Clearances', extending from the late seventeenth to the early twentieth centuries, involved a huge range of agricultural practices and economic policies with an even wider array of social effects. See Devine, *The Scottish Clearances*.
2. [Lockhart], 'Noctes XLVI', p. 399.
3. Ibid.
4. Ibid. p. 400.
5. Ibid.
6. The authorship of 'Canadian Boat-Song' remains a mystery.
7. See Jarrells, 'Tales of the Colonies', and Roberts, 'Mediating Indian Literature'.
8. The term comes from Leask, *Robert Burns*, p. 31; for the imprint of georgic on the eighteenth century generally, see Goodman, *Georgic Modernity*, and Crawford, *Poetry*.
9. Siskin, *Work of Writing*, p. 224.
10. [Jeffrey], 'Grahame's *British Georgics*', p. 213.
11. Anon., 'Introduction', p. 9.
12. Jonsson, *Enlightenment's Frontier*, p. 249.
13. Ibid. pp. 255–6.

14. Douglas, *Observations*, pp. 185–202.
15. 'Transactions of the Highland', pp. 63–75.
16. Anon., 'Ricardo and the *Edinburgh Review*', p. 60; Empson, *Some Versions of Pastoral*, p. 198.
17. Kermode, *English Pastoral*, p. 14.
18. Ibid.
19. Duncan, '*Blackwood's* and Romantic Nationalism', pp. 74, 71.
20. On *Blackwood's* playful 'conversational' style, see Stewart, *Romantic Magazines*, pp. 133–50.
21. Westover, 'At Home', p. 78.
22. [Wilson], 'Burns and the Ettrick Shepherd', pp. 523.
23. Ibid. p. 527.
24. Ibid. p. 524.
25. Ibid. p. 529.
26. Ibid. p. 527.
27. Deans, 'Pastoral Optimism', p. 136.
28. Ibid. 147–8.
29. Hasler, 'Reading the Land', p. 62.
30. Hogg, *Tales and Sketches*, vol. 4, p. 197.
31. Ibid. p. 266. I do not have space here to elaborate further on Hogg's many 'pastoral' poems, tales and essays. Hogg's views on the Clearances and its effects are discussed in De Groot, 'Hogg and the Highlands'; Deans, 'Pastoral Optimism'; Hasler, 'Reading the Land'; and Mackenzie, 'Pastoral Against Pastoral Modernity'.
32. Wilson, 'Remarks on the Scenery', p. xix.
33. Ibid. pp. xxi-xxii.
34. Ibid. p. xxi.
35. [Wilson], 'Burns and the Ettrick Shepherd', p. 529.
36. Womack, *Improvement and Romance*, p. 41; Pittock, *Celtic Identity*, p. 56–61.
37. See Fulford, *Romantic Indians*; Makdisi, *Romantic Imperialism*; McNeil, *Scotland, Britain, Empire*.
38. [Wilson?], 'On the State of Religion', p. 138.
39. See Crandall, '"The Great measur'd by the Less"'.
40. Smith, *Lectures on Jurisprudence*, p. 15.
41. Ferguson, *Essay on the History*, p. 168.
42. Millar, *The Origin*, p. 79.
43. Lang, *The Life and Letters*, p. 85.
44. Hogg, *Shepherd's Guide*, pp. 271–2.
45. [Lockhart and Wilson], 'The True and Authentic Account', p. 609.
46. [Lockhart and Wilson], 'The Last Day of the Tent', p. 727.
47. [Wilson], 'Noctes XXII', p. 502.

48. [Maginn?], 'Noctes VI', p. 372.
49. Ibid. p. 373.
50. Hogg, *Shepherd's Calendar*, p. 34.
51. See Broglio, *Beasts of Burden*, p. 62; Jarrells, 'Provincializing Enlightenment'.
52. On the contradictions attending Highland soldiers' encounters with and comparisons to Indigenous people in America, see Calloway, *White People*, and Trumpener, *Bardic Nationalism*, pp. 267–70.
53. Mackillop, 'More Fruitful than the Soil', pp. 172–5; see also Dziennik, 'Through an Imperial Prism' and *The Fatal Land*.
54. McNeil, *Scotland, Britain, Empire*, p. 84.
55. Ibid. pp. 103, 108.
56. Ibid. p. 88.
57. McNeil, *Scotland, Britain, Empire*, p. 115; Calloway, *White People*, p. 243.
58. Richards, *Patrick Sellar*, p. 260.
59. Stewart, *Sketches*, p. 123.
60. Ibid. p. 164.
61. Ibid. p. 234.
62. Anon., 'Remarks on Col. Stewart's Sketches', pp. 169, 171.
63. Anon., 'Colonel David Stewart's Sketches', pp. 394–5.
64. [Lockhart], 'Noctes I', p. 359.
65. [Wilson], 'Noctes II', p. 475.
66. Anon., 'Colonel David Stewart's Sketches', p. 390.
67. Ibid. p. 391.
68. Trumpener, *Bardic Nationalism*, p. 266.
69. Wilson, *Lights and Shadows*, p. 383.
70. Ibid. pp. 389–90.

Part IV

Gender, Race and Romantic Periodicals

Chapter 8

Crashing the *Blackwood's* Boys' Club: Caroline Bowles and Women's Place in Romantic-era Periodicals

Nicholas Mason

Conventional accounts of how, from October 1817 onward, the upstart *Blackwood's Edinburgh Magazine* muscled its way into national and international debates on literature, politics and culture have emphasised the exploits of an all-male cast of characters. In the vanguard were the magazine's founder and namesake, William Blackwood, and his spirited lieutenants John Wilson, John Gibson Lockhart, James Hogg and William Maginn. At their sides were trusty, battle-hardened veterans like David Macbeth Moir, Thomas Hamilton, George Croly, Thomas Doubleday, William Howison, John Galt and Thomas De Quincey. While some among their ranks, notably Wilson and Moir, displayed an occasional weakness for sentimental lyrics on rural sunsets or dying maidens, such tender-hearted fare generally provided but a brief interlude between bare-knuckled takedowns of Edinburgh's Whig establishment, merciless cudgellings of dandified Cockneys and spirited defences of such 'manly' recreations as boxing, cock-fighting and fox-hunting.[1]

Soon after its founding, *Blackwood's* became renowned across much of the anglophone world as a Tory gentlemen's club that was as off-limits to women as to Whigs. This androcentric image would survive largely intact through to the 1890s, when it was rekindled by Margaret Oliphant's *Annals of a Publishing House: William Blackwood and His Sons* (1897), the authorised house history that remains the most detailed account of the firm's and magazine's inaugural decades. Oliphant focuses her first volume on the presiding spirits of Romantic-era *Blackwood's*, devoting full chapters to Blackwood, Lockhart, Wilson, Hogg and Maginn and half-chapters to Galt, De Quincey, Samuel Taylor Coleridge and John Wilson Croker. She then affords a mere two paragraphs, in contrast, to Maga's earliest women contributors, justifying this imbalance by explaining how, in perusing *Blackwood's* contributors book, 'I find few women's names'. 'Mrs Hemans and Miss Bowles', she continues, 'are the only lasting representatives of the half of the world, up to that time chiefly silent.'[2]

Fortunately, in the case of Felicia Hemans, scholars have recently filled many of the sizeable gaps left by Oliphant's narrative, offering valuable analyses of the poet's relationship with William Blackwood and how publishing poems in his magazine helped her build a loyal readership and stay financially afloat during the late 1820s and early 1830s.[3] The contributions to *Blackwood's* by the other woman Oliphant mentions, however, remain largely overlooked, despite Caroline Bowles having preceded Hemans by several years as the magazine's first regular female contributor. This, alas, is consistent with a broader pattern of scholarly neglect of Bowles's life and work. While important research has appeared of late on her 'Chapters on Churchyards' series and her complex relationship with long-time mentor and eventual husband, Robert Southey, Virginia Blain's *Caroline Bowles Southey, 1786–1854: The Making of a Woman Writer* (1998) remains the only detailed study of large stretches of her career.[4]

Tasked with reintroducing Bowles to a new generation of readers and scholars, Blain structures her book as a hybrid between an anthology and critical biography. Although this approach precludes exhaustive coverage of any one phase of Bowles's career, she nevertheless provides a detailed and insightful overview of the writer's decades-long relationship with the house of Blackwood. Building therefore upon Blain's pioneering research, this chapter delves more deeply into Bowles's often witty and unusually candid correspondence with William Blackwood and the resulting string of submissions, especially in prose, that saw her enthusiastically participating in his magazine's long-term effort to create and sustain a distinctive ethos. By chronicling how this rural 'poetess' broke into one of the era's premier boys' clubs, I aim to challenge enduring notions of the single-mindedly masculinist, even misogynist, agendas of Maga's early years and highlight the surprising influence women writers were coming to have in even the most staunchly conservative corners of the literary world.

Constructing a Blackwoodian Masculinity

Insofar as *Blackwood's* privileged male voices and perspectives, it was hardly alone. Early nineteenth-century periodicals as varied as the *Edinburgh Review* and *The Examiner* on the left and the *Quarterly Review* and *The British Critic* on the right proceeded, like Wordsworth's poetry, under the rhetorical premise of 'a man speaking to men'.[5] Except for instances when either a specific periodical (e.g., *The Lady's Magazine*) or submission ('To Our Fairest Readers') directly engaged women, readers were led to imagine the writer as a learned gentleman and his primary audience as men of comparable background and beliefs. While seasoned editors and writers undoubtedly understood that much of their audience consisted of women of all ages, the female reader was envisioned, if at all, as a silent eavesdropper learning what she might from the discourse of formally educated men. And, on the rare occasions when Romantic-era periodicals foregrounded women's interests and writing, they were no less prone than their forebears to indulge in what Jonathan Swift dubbed the 'fair-sexing' of women.[6]

Even within a periodical culture characterised by de facto masculinity, however, *Blackwood's* quickly became notorious for taking laddishness to new extremes. This is perhaps nowhere more evident than in *Hypocrisy Unveiled, and Calumny Detected: in a Review of* Blackwood's Magazine, an anonymous exposé that, after being widely advertised and discussed in newspapers from London to Inverness, went into four editions within three weeks of its 20 October 1818 release and occasioned one of the year's leading literary feuds. Today attributed to Macvey Napier – a long-time ally of William Blackwood's cross-town nemesis Archibald Constable – this pamphlet castigates Maga as a purveyor of a puerile masculinity that bastardises the gentlemanly ethos cultivated in Britain's landmark periodicals from *The Spectator* to the *Edinburgh Review*. In an opening simile that spans two pages, Napier equates *Blackwood's* 'Veiled Editor' and 'his associates' with 'a set of mischievous boys, who station themselves in a gutter for the purpose of throwing dirt on all who pass them'. While these imps had initially been left unimpeded out of fear that 'no one can approach without being bespattered', it was high time for 'thrusting the nose of the urchins into the filth which they had been so liberal in distributing to others'.[7]

True to form, upon this pamphlet's release, *Blackwood's* principals chose to counter-punch rather than retreat. In a move the powerhouse publisher John Murray called a 'palpable absurdity', Wilson and Lockhart took Napier's bait and published signed rebuttals implicitly outing themselves as Maga's fearsome 'Leopard' and 'Scorpion'.[8] Then, rather than repenting of its ways, the magazine increased its displays of manly bluster and schoolboy tomfoolery. In its first issue after *Hypocrisy Unveiled*, *Blackwood's* denounced the *Edinburgh Review* insiders responsible for the offending pamphlet as 'antichristian' and 'fatuous menials' who, having long since 'dismissed ordinary decorum from their own attacks', now hypocritically demanded 'a tame and feeble courtesy' from others.[9] A month later, Lockhart, Wilson and J. H. Merivale penned a new instalment of 'The Life and Writings of Ensign and Adjutant Odoherty' in which this fictionalised embodiment of Blackwoodian bluster regales readers with such bellicose boasts as:

> I'm a swapper [thumper], as every one knows,
>   In my pumps six feet three inches high
> 'Tis no wonder your minikin [puny] beaux
>   Have a fancy to fight rather shy
> Of a Gulliver chap such as I[.][10]

While partially self-satirising, the machismo of this and countless other *jeux d'esprit* in its line set the tone for the full-issue celebration of homosociality of 'The Tent' (September 1819) and the boozy *Noctes Ambrosianae* dialogues that became the epicentre of Blackwoodian masculinity between 1822 and 1835.

Given the central place these pieces still occupy in the *Blackwood's* canon, it is little surprise that the magazine remains widely known, in Lisa Niles's words, as the Romantic age's 'ultimate bachelor party'.[11] In recent studies, Maga has matter-of-factly been referred to as 'masculinist turf', a 'masculine stronghold' and a bastion of 'Regency hegemonic masculinity'.[12] Lucasta Miller has gone so far as to argue that the *Noctes* promulgated a 'hyper-sexualized' view of women that led Emily and Anne Brontë to write novels 'responding at a distance to a sadomasochistic model of sexual relations which they had imbibed as child readers of *Blackwood's*'.[13] More compellingly, if less provocatively, Niles has revisited the same contributors books that informed Oliphant's study and found that, between 1817 and 1825, 'fewer than five percent of *Blackwood's* contributors were women'. This abysmal statistic understandably leads her to conclude that early *Blackwood's* functioned as 'a space of male homosociality' that was purposely 'free from intellectually-minded women'.[14]

Some scholars, however, have hesitated to treat such tallies as the final word on the subject, suggesting that the magazine was not nearly as chauvinist as the raw numbers would suggest. David Stewart, for instance, has asserted that 'Blackwoodian masculinity is often tempered by a sense of a correspondent femininity', and Pam Perkins has contrasted the enthusiasm *Blackwood's* demonstrated from its founding for the likes of Hemans and Anne Grant with the coverage the putatively progressive *Edinburgh Review* only began begrudgingly affording women writers 15 years into its run.[15] Most recently, Lindsy Lawrence has supplemented Niles's data with her own counts showing women poets' growing presence in *Blackwood's* between 1827 and 1835. Over this nine-year period, 25 per cent (139 out of 547) of the magazine's poems 'were by women poets, with 102 explicitly signed under their own names'.[16]

Bowles's Two Mentors

Somewhat surprisingly, none of these revisionist accounts makes more than passing reference to Bowles, who should serve as Exhibit A in the case for reconsidering the gender politics of *Blackwood's* first decade. The unpublished correspondence between Bowles and Blackwood now at the National Library of Scotland is especially compelling in this regard, as it shows her rapid metamorphosis from a self-doubting novice into a respected professional who was granted wide leeway within the magazine. Perhaps even more extraordinary is the portrait that emerges of William Blackwood. Far from an unreconstructed chauvinist and fierce protector of male privilege, he consistently figures as a champion of women's writing intent on bringing significant more female voices to his magazine.

In recruiting Bowles to be his first regular female contributor, Blackwood quickly discovered her habitual disinclination to shatter glass ceilings. Born in 1786 as the only child of a retired East India Company captain and the daughter of a powerful local family, Bowles spent her entire life, save her four years as Southey's wife (1839–43), in the village of Lymington on the Hampshire coast.[17] After her father's death in 1801, she became her mother's closest companion. Between this duty and her own chronic ailments, Bowles apparently made few efforts towards matrimony, planning to live out her days in quiet, rural gentility. In 1817, however, her mother suddenly passed away and a financial agent's mismanagement put her inheritance in jeopardy. Until her father's adopted son offered her a £150 annuity two years later, Bowles faced the prospect of sudden eviction and lifelong dependence. Desperation to forestall this fate therefore led her to a common expedient of genteel women facing imminent poverty, trying to monetise the poems and tales she had previously written entirely for her and her parents' entertainment.[18]

Instead of immediately approaching publishers, Bowles rather boldly chose to cold-call Britain's poet laureate, Robert Southey. She was drawn to Southey, of all poets, not only by their shared conservatism and her long-time admiration for his work, but also, as Blain points out, by his reputed 'catholic taste' and 'readiness to help both women and working-class poets to find their way into print'.[19] Accordingly, in a query dated 25 April 1818, Bowles timorously introduced herself and asked Southey to offer a candid assessment of her verse tale *Ellen Fitzarthur*.[20] Five anxiety-filled weeks later, she received his lengthy reply. After warning that 'not one in twenty, – perhaps I might say in fifty' verse collections recovered its costs, Southey offered a more encouraging, if decidedly gendered, assessment of Bowles's poem:

> There is a great deal of beauty in it, – a female fluency, a womanly fluency, a womanly sweetness, a womanly truth & tenderness of feeling, which I have enough of my mother in me perfectly to understand. It is provoking to think that if the same powers had been displayed in prose instead of verse, in a novel instead of a poem, there would have been little or no doubt of finding a publisher[.]

From here, Southey magnanimously offered to show her work to Murray, who, he suggests, might potentially 'take the risque upon himself, & give you half the eventual profits'.[21] In reply, the euphoric Bowles gratefully accepted the proffered assistance. Flashing the self-deprecating wit that would become a hallmark of her later correspondence, she responded to Southey's hint that she might earn more by writing novels by quipping, 'I could as easily compose a treatise on chemistry'.[22] Southey soon assumed the role of Bowles's mentor, providing copious feedback on her drafts, repeatedly coaxing Murray to take her on, and, when that effort came to naught, introducing her to his own publisher, Longman, who eventually published *Ellen Fitzarthur* in June 1820.[23]

Up to this point, Bowles's budding career had been entirely independent of both William Blackwood and his magazine. A month after the publication of *Ellen Fitzarthur*, however, and likely without her knowledge, Southey wrote to John Wilson, saying, 'If you could recommend a little poem called Ellen Fitz-Arthur to a kind notice in the Magazine, I should feel myself greatly obliged.'[24] This was presumably intended in a spirit of quid pro quo, as three months earlier the laureate had acceded to Wilson's request to support his controversial bid for the Chair of Moral Philosophy at the University of Edinburgh.[25] Wilson, though, apparently felt under no such obligation, providing neither the desired puff nor even a passing mention of *Ellen Fitzarthur* in Maga. Quite possibly, Wilson considered this payback for Southey's refusal in 1812 to write a review, favourable or otherwise, of his own *Isle of Palms* for the *Quarterly*, the taste-shaping journal where he enjoyed insider privileges. Despite their shared conservative values and supposed membership in the 'Lake School of Poetry', the two had long clashed. Southey made little effort to hide his contempt for the younger poet, explaining in 1815 that he refused to puff the *Isle of Palms* because it was 'made up of the grossest imitations of Wordsworth, with not a few from myself'. He went on to assert that only Wilson's friendship with Wordsworth and reputation as a berserker 'prevent me from giving him the very hard knock which would otherwise fall to his share'.[26]

Upon *Blackwood's* launch two years later, not even Southey's strong affection for Hogg and desire to please Murray – who had a minor stake in the magazine – could outweigh his disdain for anything associated with Wilson. Recognising that including even a few lines by the current laureate would lend the fledgling monthly a certain respectability, Murray repeatedly requested Southey's assistance. The poet responded in January 1818 with a scrap from his commonplace book that was apparently so unremarkable that Maga's editors decided against publication.[27] Renewing his efforts in September, 'Maximus Murray', as Southey privately dubbed him, stopped in Keswick while journeying northward with Blackwood to introduce the writer to his 'brother Bibliopole'. 'They were full of his [Blackwood's] Magazine', Southey sneered to a friend. 'I let them talk & throw out their hooks . . . & set them off well pleased', as 'nothing had been said to put them out of humour with themselves & their own projects'.[28] But when Murray again requested a submission a month after their visit, Southey came clean:

> You ask why I will not assist you in Blackwoods Magazine? It would be a sufficient answer that it stands in no need of any new assistance, – & that I have no time. But the truth is that . . . I have a mortal dislike to that sort of personal warfare: & tho I heartily approve of the political principles of the Magazine, I disapprove as heartily the principle of personality upon which it is conducted.[29]

So sour was Southey on the new magazine that a few months thereafter he would even gripe about a fictitious travelogue in Maga by 'Philip Kempferhausen', who rhapsodises over Southey's timeless genius, enviable library and idyllic Lakeland home.[30] Upon learning that 'Kempferhausen' was in fact Wilson, Southey carped, 'Much personal opportunity of knowing me [Wilson] has not had, – for I could not tolerate his manner of life enough to accept the advances which he made towards an intimacy.'[31]

Considering this long history of antipathy towards Wilson and *Blackwood's*, it is all the more remarkable that Southey's protégée and future wife not only found a home in the magazine but participated actively in its satirical and sentimental agendas for over two decades. While Bowles's initial letter to Maga's publisher and his reply have been lost, later correspondence suggests that sometime in June or early July 1821, and likely without Southey's blessing, she once again summoned the courage to cold-call a conservative literary icon, penning an introductory letter to Blackwood that included samples of her verse and an offer to become a semi-regular contributor. Judging from the incoming correspondence the publisher left behind, Bowles was apparently the first woman to make such an offer.[32]

In her initial letter to Blackwood, Bowles had concealed her name and authorship of the well-received *Ellen Fitzarthur*. Even lacking this information, though, the publisher thrilled at the prospect of adding a gifted woman to his ranks. In fact, his exuberant response – manifest most conspicuously in his featuring two Bowles lyrics, 'Autumn Flowers' and 'To a Dying Infant', at the head of his magazine's July 1821 issue – impelled Bowles to temper his expectations. Her 30 August letter expresses gratitude for Blackwood's 'liberal proposals' and 'the favourable opinion entertained of my partial attempts' but warns that chronic ailments taught her to be 'scrupulous in making promises which it may not be in my power to fulfill'. Less sombrely, she adds,

> My Pegasus is a very wayward palfrey, and will by no means go thro' his paces at my will and pleasure; I can only say that when I find him a tractable mood, he shall do his best for Mr. B's service.[33]

Further demonstrating her versatility with both 'the *dulce*' and 'the *utile*' desired of *Blackwood's* 'correspondents',[34] Bowles closes by affirming her ability to keep confidences, noting, 'I have nothing to talk to but birds & flowers, an old Nurse, and a deaf spaniel'.[35] With this, the poet clearly passed her audition. Before the close of 1821, Maga would publish her devotional poem 'Gracious Rain', her Wordsworthian lyric 'The Primrose' and her debut effort in prose, the 11-page adventure tale 'The Smuggler'.

Nanora Sweet, one of the few scholars to mention Bowles's early contributions to Maga, has argued that 'during the journal's early misogyny', its editors systematically obscured women's contributions and even set about 'tracking and monitoring' Hemans's 'progress onto its conservative and masculinist turf'. She goes on to suggest that, upon enlisting as a regular contributor in 1827, Hemans 'would join only one other woman poet at Maga, Caroline Bowles, whose verse of sensibility appeared in a demure near-anonymity'.[36] While, as detailed above, there is ample room for criticising the gender dynamics of early *Blackwood's*, this account of the environment in which Bowles in particular toiled is largely refuted by the documentary record. Bowles's name being excluded from her early Maga publications had nothing to do with an exclusionary agenda, as anonymity for all but the most famous contributors, male or female, was the norm in Romantic-era periodicals.[37] Moreover, rather than completely bowing to this convention and relegating Bowles to 'demure near-anonymity', Blackwood published fourteen of her first sixteen Maga publications under her first initial, 'C.', and for years to come reserved this mark exclusively for her work.[38] Indeed, *Blackwood's* largely overlooked effort to highlight its first regular female contributor resembled and coincided with the *Literary Gazette*'s significantly more celebrated late-1821 campaign to hype its own house poetess, Letitia Elizabeth Landon, by printing her verses under what Edward Bulwer-Lytton dubbed 'the three magical letters of L. E. L.'.[39] As I have argued elsewhere, literary historians have tended to be far too credulous of tales about the entrancing effect of Landon's initials. Besides the fact that most such accounts appeared with the *Literary Gazette* itself, readers had become fully accustomed to magazine verse appearing under real or pseudonymous initials.[40] That said, even if this form of quasi-anonymity was far from revolutionary, *Blackwood's* and the *Literary Gazette*'s consistent deployment of the initials 'C.' and 'L. E. L.' was genuinely noteworthy insofar as both heralded the integration of their pages by a woman who would become one of their leading voices in the years ahead.

Perhaps what was most remarkable, however, about the welcome Bowles received at Maga was the creative liberty she was almost immediately afforded. Blackwood granted her the same freedom as Lockhart, Wilson and Maginn to follow the muses wherever they led, whether that be towards prose or verse, the sublime or the sardonic. Above all, he was intent on preventing her from being pigeon-holed as the magazine's sentimental poetess, telling her on 22 December 1821:

> I hope you will favor me with some more of your prose. Besides articles such as the smuggler, [I] feel confident you could send us capital articles of a gayer cast. The Magazine would be greatly enriched from a Lady's pen on life, manners, literature or in short any subject. [Ladies] view many things so differently from Gentlemen that it would be quite a new feature in Maga.[41]

To boost her confidence, he routinely forwarded praise for her publications. On 2 November 1821, he reported, 'I have heard Ellen Fitzarthur very favorably spoken of'.[42] The next month, as 'The Smuggler' went to press, he assured her that 'a few friends have seen the nos. and admire very much your Tale'.[43] Soon thereafter, he informed her 'your tale has been almost universally admired' and 'people here think it from the pen of my friend Prof. Wilson'. He went on to urge her to 'give us some other tales illustrative of ordinary English life & manners'.[44]

Meanwhile, in direct contrast to two years earlier, when, despite Southey's solicitations, Maga failed to notice *Ellen Fitzarthur*, Blackwood ensured it immediately and warmly reviewed Bowles's follow-up, *The Widow's Tale*, after its February 1822 release. He found an ideal candidate for the task in R. F. St Barbe, an occasional contributor who had mentioned to Blackwood that he was Bowles's neighbour and considered her 'by far the cleverest young woman I am acquainted with'.[45] Unsurprisingly, St Barbe's review, which appeared in March 1822, effusively praised the poet's powers of observation and pronounced her 'fully participant in what Southey calls the great *revival* of our days'.[46] Blackwood promptly thanked St Barbe for an 'excellent article' that did 'full justice' to Bowles's volume, noting, 'I have not told her who is the author of it'.[47] The reviewer himself, however, felt no scruples over the matter, apparently confessing his authorship to Bowles. For on 9 March, she wrote to Blackwood, 'Your forthcoming critique of my little book is from the pen of a friend, so you cannot expect me to be <u>flattered</u> by it—grateful I will be tho' – a better feeling.'[48]

Entering the Fray

Any reinforcement Blackwood offered Bowles on the one flank was consistently matched by Southey on the other. A day after receiving *The Widow's Tale*, Southey shared the elation he felt in seeing her 'become such a poetess as I believed and hoped from the first'.[49] Notably, however, neither this nor other congratulatory letters he sent her during this period so much as hint at her simultaneous successes in *Blackwood's*. In late 1824, as Bowles prepared to replace Longman with Blackwood as her book publisher, she and Southey playfully began calling the Edinburgh bookman her 'Monster'.[50] Even then, though, they steered the discussion away from the 'Monster's' magazine. Only one surviving letter from Bowles to Southey from the early 1820s mentions her work for Maga, a 17 July 1822 note that minimises her commitment to the magazine in remarking, 'Now and then, during a sunny interval . . . I compose a few scraps of verse or prose, most of which remain incomplete, and a few find their way to Blackwood – all idle nothings.'[51]

Clearly, Bowles's 'idle nothings' were a sensitive topic in their relationship. That her insider status at Maga did little to soften Southey's views is suggested by his remarking in February 1825 that the magazine's habitual 'blackguardism' led it and its imitators to 'degrade what ought be good, & render imperious what would otherwise be useful'.[52] Overall, then, the two appear to have adopted a 'don't ask, don't tell' policy regarding *Blackwood's*, an approach made all the more expedient by the conflicting professional advice Bowles received from Blackwood and Southey. Since 1818, Southey's career vision for Bowles had kept her squarely within the sentimental 'poetess' tradition, and his praise had typically been steeped in diminutives and familiar notions of womanhood. Whether speaking to his protégée or a third party, he habitually returned to the 'great sweetness' and 'real feeling' of her 'little volumes', reserving special praise for poems displaying 'a womanly fluency, a womanly sweetness, a womanly truth and tenderness of feeling'.[53] Meanwhile, Blackwood, as we have seen, initially advocated a more expansive and experimental path, prodding her to move beyond melancholic and devotional modes and to take up genres and themes of 'a gayer cast'.

Perhaps wisely, then, Bowles began compartmentalising the two halves of her literary career, counselling with Southey on her book collections and with Blackwood primarily on her magazine work. While chronic health problems and the distance between Hampshire and Edinburgh prevented her from joining the Maga gang *in situ*, she would prove an even more reliable contributor over stretches of the 1820s than Lockhart, Wilson or Maginn. Between her July 1821 debut and the end of 1825, Bowles published thirty-one identified works (seventeen in verse and fourteen in prose) in *Blackwood's*; over the ensuing 12 years (1826–37), she contributed at least fifty more (thirty in verse and twenty in prose).[54] All told, over a 16-year period, her work appeared in nearly every other issue of the magazine, a fact that should definitively quash notions of early *Blackwood's* categorically excluding women writers.

Bowles's verse contributions to Maga remained largely unchanged over the years, as, like many poets, she regularly returned to her favourite themes (nature's bounty, mortality's trials and God's mercy) and modes (Wordsworthian effusions, sentimental lyrics and medieval ballads). She took considerably more risks with her prose, especially early on. In 'The Smuggler' she experimented with short fiction, narrating how a respectable Isle of Wight family is reduced to trading in contraband in the voice of an 'eccentric old bachelor' who feels 'indulgently tender' to women's 'little whims and foibles'.[55] Bowles's general preference, though, was for non-fiction, and her successful forays into the personal essay mode popularised by Lamb, Hazlitt and De Quincey include 'Childhood' (August 1822), 'Beauty' (December 1823) and her 'Chapters on Churchyards' series (started April 1824).[56]

It was in prose satire, however, that she most fully abandoned any lingering inhibitions and threw herself into the Blackwoodian revels. Four remarkable pieces from 1822 to 1825, in particular, mark the apogee of Bowles's participation in the magazine's collective project. Tellingly, only the last of these appeared under her trademark 'C.'[57] Otherwise, the strategy seems to have called for keeping her sentimental and satirical personae separate. Bowles's first publication in this new mode was 'Thoughts on Letter-Writing', a meandering, witty rumination on the hollowness of modern correspondence that *Blackwood's* published in March 1822 under the initials 'M. G.' After musing over such angles as whether manufacturers might invent 'an epistolary steam-engine', the essay closes by annotating a typically banal letter with the arch thoughts actually flowing through the writer's mind. Hence, when the letter innocuously enquires, 'Where are your two lovely boys? Dear fellows!', Bowles suggests its author may well be thinking, 'I'd as lieve have a couple of wild cats turned loose into the drawing room, as let in those two riotous cubs.'[58]

Two years later, Bowles brought this relatively gentle satirical style more squarely into the Maga universe in 'To the Author of "The Shepherd's Calendar"'. Writing as the pet-lover 'E.', she opens by praising Hogg's Scottish tales before haranguing him at length for heartlessly parting with his loyal dog, Sirrah.[59] Far and away, though, Bowles's most audacious experiment in the Blackwoodian style was the 'Letter from a Washerwoman' published in the February 1823 issue, a bruising send-up of the 'Greekish' airs of Cockney School poseurs. In the spirit of famously elaborate *Blackwood's* satires like 'The "Luctus"' (May 1820) and the *Noctes*, Bowles's 'Letter' is an amalgam of prose and verse, supplementing the titular bill of complaint with pitch-perfect parodies of Hunt's and Shelley's poetry. Most strikingly, she exchanges the light-hearted, Horatian mode of her earlier satires for the cutting, Juvenalian wit generally deemed the exclusive province of men. So far does the 'Letter' venture beyond the conventional bounds of female literary propriety that it would prove her only major prose contribution to *Blackwood's* never republished under her name.[60] Prior to 1959, when Alan Lang Strout attributed the 'Letter' to Bowles on the basis of Blackwood's contributors book, it was widely believed to be by Maginn and even anthologised in a posthumous collection of his works.[61]

Without countervailing evidence, Maginn was a reasonable guess, as after his arrival at *Blackwood's* in late 1819, the pugnacious Irishman had re-energised the anti-Cockney crusade. As a dedicated reader of the magazine, Bowles was well versed in its long-running offensive against Hunt's metropolitan band of progressive poets. She also was privy to Southey's similar disdain for the Cockneys. Bowles's mentor considered Hunt 'a conceited writer, & a man of the most villainous principles' and was even more scornful of Shelley, his one-time Keswick neighbour. In 1820, Southey ended a long-running epistolary feud with Shelley by flatly charging the younger poet with driving his first wife to suicide:[62] 'You corrupted her opinions, you robbed her of her moral & religious principles, you debauched her mind'.[63] Animosity between the laureate and the Cockneys further escalated while Bowles was writing the 'Letter from a Washerwoman' in late 1822. In early October, Hunt and Byron launched *The Liberal*, the radical journal they had dreamed up with Shelley prior to his drowning that July. Their periodical's long-delayed inaugural issue savaged Southey both in Byron's *The Vision of Judgment* and its preface, which advised prospective contributors: 'Cut up SOUTHEY as much as you please. We all think him as great a coxcomb as you do, and he bores us to death'.[64]

However unlikely it might initially seem for a writer later known for her 'pathetic novelettes' to have enlisted in this battle, Bowles undoubtedly saw in the anti-Cockney crusade the rare cause that allied both Southey and Blackwood.[65] The first hint of her training her sights on the Cockneys comes in the partially torn postscript to her 4 June 1822 letter to Blackwood, which reads, 'I suppose news from Cockaigne would be out of date now'.[66] Supportive as usual, he replied, 'News from Cockaigne or any thing of yours would never be out of date or stale to us'.[67] From here, Bowles seems to have plied Southey for information on Hunt and Shelley in a now-lost letter. For, on 7 July 1822, he wrote, 'You mention Shelley: I should like to show you some letters which passed between that wretched man and me about two years ago'. He goes on to lament that, since leaving Keswick at the age of nineteen, Shelley had failed to 'outgrow the insane opinions which had their root, as I then thought, in mere ignorance, not in a corrupted heart and will'. Elsewhere in this letter, Southey forwards the regards of the popular poet William Lisle Bowles, who, while no relation, was pleased to claim her as 'my namesake' and called her 'deeply affecting' verse the antithesis of 'the golden-silvery-diamond-alabaster-Pontypool-style of the present Cockney race of dandy poetasters'.[68]

After being slowed by 'general debility' for much of 1822, Bowles finally sent Blackwood her contribution to the anti-Cockney offensive on 1 February 1823, characterising it as 'a scrap to be dealt with at your pleasure'.[69] Three weeks later, this 'scrap' appeared in Maga under the signature of 'Patience Lilywhite' of 'Puddleditch-Corner, Islington', an orthographically challenged 'lone widder woman, left with five fatherless children to purvide for in a wicked world'. Mrs Lilywhite opens her 'Letter' by explaining that, having received no assistance from the authorities over the 'oudacious treetment' meted out by the lodger who 'hockipied my apartments last', she had been encouraged by a new lodger to 'tell your story to the larned Kristophur North', whom he considered 'a sort of Scotch gustice'. The case, as she proceeds to detail, is that in July 1821 a 'thin spindle shanked gentleman' named Mr Pennyfeather had enquired about her empty rooms, saying he wanted 'a little country hair and quiet, after the noise an' smoke of Lunnon'. Apparently inexperienced with the genuinely picturesque, he was delighted by her 'private an' rural' retreat, which was 'parted off by a ditch an' an elder hedge from the backs of the sope manifacktory, an' Mr Bullock's slawtur-house'. What sealed the deal, however, was Pennyfeather's discovery that her 'urn' could hold two full gallons of tea.[70]

For *Blackwood's* regular readers, this was the first signal that an article that never directly names Shelley, Hunt or the Cockney School marked the latest effort to discredit their rivals' literary and political agendas by lampooning them as half-educated, effete suburbanites with a fondness for dressing up as poets. From its earliest issues, Maga had rendered tea the ultimate symbol of Cockney effeminacy and pretentiousness, gleefully invoking an 1817 *Round Table* essay in which Hunt muses upon the 'clear and gentle powers of inspiration' associated with sipping tea.[71] Over five years later, Bowles slyly alludes both to this and an earlier *Round Table* essay where Hunt concedes, 'my tea-kettle, – I frankly confess, – has long been displaced, or rather dismissed, by a bronze-coloured and graceful urn; though, between ourselves, I am not sure that I have gained any thing by the exchange'.[72]

She also, as Gregory Dart has suggested, grounds her anti-Cockney satire in an emergent trend among conservatives to eye lodging-houses with suspicion, casting them as 'an ambiguous, aspirational realm somewhere between the polite and the plebeian'.[73]

The rich intertextuality of Bowles's 'Letter' does not stop, however, with her invocation of tea and lodging-houses, as she turns to yet another of Hunt's works from 1817, his disquisition 'On Washerwomen', to flesh out her title character. In this essay, Hunt aims to show how even 'that laborious and inelegant class of the community, – *Washerwomen*', with 'their brawny arms and brawling voices', might be depicted so as to evoke empathy and moral insight.[74] To this end, he transports us to an average morning in a washerwoman's life, interlacing descriptions of her labour with snippets of her earthy, solecistic diction and glimpses of the pleasure she takes in 'a dish of good christian souchong'. 'A washerwoman's cup of tea', Hunt informs us, 'may vie with the first drawn cork at a bon-vivant's table'.[75]

Although several of the most humorous passages in Bowles's 'Letter' require no special knowledge of her targets, she clearly envisions an ideal reader who recognises allusions to such sources as this and will thereby appreciate her turning of Hunt's rhetoric upon himself. In effect, she treats Hunt as he does his washerwoman, snickering at delusional 'refinement' of the less educated and using rites of tea-drinking to burlesque their self-importance. Hunt is hardly her only mark, however, as Shelley comes in for equal ridicule with the appearance of a 'shamblin', 'unholesum lookin' acquaintance of Pennyfeather who goes by his first and middle names and has an eye for under-aged girls.[76] In keeping with *Blackwood's* credo of 'abus[ing] Wickedness, but acknowledge[ing] Wit', Bowles displays no qualms over maligning Shelley less than eight months after his drowning, taking pains, in fact, to set her plot in 1821, when Shelley was still alive.[77] In an unmistakable dig at the poet's having twice stolen off with 16-year-old girls, Mrs Lilywhite recounts how, upon first visiting Pennyfeather in Islington, Shelley's unnamed proxy 'took peticklar notice of Nance, as was mi eldest, an' just turned fifteen'.[78]

From here, Bowles turns to more obscure rumours, possibly conveyed by Southey, about Shelley's having erected altars to pagan deities for the re-enacting of Hellenic ceremonies.[79] After surveying

Mrs Lilywhite's premises, Bowles's Shelley puts 'wild vagarys' into Pennyfeather's head. Soon, without the landlady's permission, the two begin refashioning her garden into Mount Helicon and her pigsty into the Temple of Apollo.[80] After 'two or three more chapps of there one sort comd in', the would-be classicists coax Nance and eight other local girls to adorn themselves as the muses and partake of 'Nektur an' Hambrowsy', which Mrs Lilywhite explains is simply 'oshuns an' oshuns of tea'.[81] Midway through their rites, however, a ceremonial torch sets fire to the repurposed pigsty. In the ensuing commotion, the 'cowwardly currs' slip away, taking Nance as their new plaything and leaving behind a ruined garden, unpaid bills and half-drafted poems.[82] We soon learn that Christopher North has generously purchased these poetic scraps from Mrs Lilywhite, as he appends to her letter fragments that unmistakably parody Hunt's overcharged diction ('Spangling about the jaunty greenery') and jarring eroticism ('Come, ye little cunning jade ye, / Come and see what I've got here, / In my pocket, pretty dear!') and Shelley's notorious impiety ('They were not married by a mutt'ring priest, / With superstitious rites, and senseless words' in an 'old house, that fools do call *a Church*!').[83]

While neither Hunt nor the surviving members of his circle directly responded to the 'Letter from a Washerwoman', Bowles's satire did not go unnoticed. In early March, the poet and journalist Alaric Watts opined to Blackwood: 'The letter from a Washerwoman and extracts bearing on Hunt & Shelley, were exquisite. Smollett himself could not have done the thing better'.[84] Eight months after Bowles's 'Letter', Maga published a 'Letter from a Contributor in Love' that tells of 'King Leigh's' return from Italy. Only after reporting Hunt's residence in 'the White Conduit House Tea Gardens' does it occur to the 'Contributor' that 'White Conduit-House is so near Islington; and that affair of the washerwoman; it can hardly be!'[85] That Patience Lilywhite's tale resonated beyond *Blackwood's* is evidenced, as Sara Lodge suggests, throughout 'An Address to the Steam Washing Company', one of the showpiece poems in Thomas Hood's 1825 satirical collection, *Odes and Addresses to Great People*.[86]

Having delivered one of the magazine's most incisive send-ups of the Cockneys and proven herself as adept with Juvenalian as Horatian modes, Bowles largely retired from the fray. That, at least in private, she indulged her satirical sensibilities is suggested by a

Cornhill Magazine retrospective published 20 years after Bowles's 1854 death, which reports that her 'strong sense of the ridiculous, and her utter absence of sentimentality, disappointed comparative strangers, who expected something pathetic from the writer of so many touching poems'.[87] Her later publications, however, generally shied away from controversy, never again displaying the parodic genius of the 'Letter from a Washerwoman'.

Ironically, Bowles's general turn from satire in the late 1820s partly stemmed from the counsel of the magazine publisher who had originally promoted venturing beyond conventional sensibility. In a 22 December 1828 letter to Southey, she includes Blackwood among 'the worthies' who 'discourage my comic vein', complaining, 'Whenever I treat the Monster in that [comic] way he thanks me for "the admirable production", but hints that "in the pathetic I am super-admirable"'.[88] The date here is important, as Blackwood's apparent reversal on the desirability of 'the pathetic' coincided with the keepsakes and annuals boom that suddenly created a rush on sentimental 'poetesses'. A generous reading would suggest that, as before, he was directing Bowles towards genres he thought would sell. To the writer, however, his volte-face seems to have signalled that any artistic freedom Blackwood had offered had always been contingent on market demand.

If, however, it would be a stretch to label the publisher or his magazine proto-feminist, both were considerably more forward-thinking on women's literature than most scholarly accounts would have it. In the decade before his 1834 death, Blackwood only redoubled his efforts to narrow the gender gap at Maga. According to Lawrence's counts, between 1827 and 1835, women accounted for 11 per cent of Maga's content, roughly twice as much as before.[89] Obviously, 11 per cent seems, at best, a Pyrrhic victory. But, in both tone and content, *Blackwood's* had largely outgrown its frat-house roots and become considerably more gender-inclusive than most of its rivals. Fittingly, the strongest testament to these gains comes in a letter Maga's original female regular sent one of its staunchest detractors on the eve of its founder's death. Disconsolate over the news, Bowles writes to Southey: 'My poor Monster! Always a kind Monster to me he has been'. Then, in a final display of pluck, professional confidence and self-satisfaction for not succumbing to her original mentor's anti-*Blackwood's* bias, she gibes, 'My Monster was worth ten of yours, autocrat of fashion as he has been in his line'.[90]

Notes

1. On *BEM*'s celebrations of 'manly' sports, see Strachan's 'Fighting Sports' and 'John Wilson'.
2. Oliphant, *Annals*, vol. 1, pp. 493–4. A decade earlier, Oliphant had pointedly observed that, while Maga 'has her ladies', she 'perhaps loves them less' ('In Maga's Library', p. 127).
3. See Feldman, 'The Poet and the Profits'; Sweet, 'All Work and All Play'; Peterson, 'Nineteenth-Century Women Poets'; Perkins, '"She has her ladies too"'; and Lawrence, '"Afford[ing] me a Place"'.
4. See especially chapter 2 of Blain's *Caroline Bowles Southey* (pp. 74–88). For annotated versions of several Bowles contributions to *BEM*, see Mason (ed.), *Selected Verse*, pp. 237–41, 257–71 and Jarrells (ed.), *Selected Prose*, pp. 245–56, 265–74. On her relationship with Southey, see chapter 2 of Low, *The Literary Protégées*. On 'Chapters on Churchyards', see Westover, 'At Home in the Churchyard'.
5. Wordsworth, 'Preface', p. xxviii.
6. Swift, *Journal to Stella*, vol. 2, p. 482.
7. Napier, *Hypocrisy Unveiled*, pp. 2–3. This pamphlet was first advertised in the Edinburgh newspapers *The Scotsman* and the *Caledonian Mercury* on 17 October 1818. For examples of nationwide advertisements, see *Durham County Advertiser* (24 October), *Inverness Courier* (29 October) and *Morning Post* (10 November). For reports on the controversy, see *Morning Chronicle* (29 October), *Carlisle Patriot* (31 October) and *Military Register* (11 November).
8. Murray to Blackwood, 27 October 1818, in Smiles, *A Publisher*, vol. 1, pp. 487–8.
9. [Wilson], 'Is the Edinburgh Review', pp. 228–9.
10. [Lockhart et al.], 'Some Account', p. 321.
11. Niles, '"May the married be single"', p. 115.
12. Sweet, 'All Work and All Play', p. 240; Blain, *Caroline Bowles Southey*, p. 74; Newbon, *The Boy-Man*, p. 156.
13. Miller, 'The Brontës', pp. 290–1.
14. Niles, '"May the married be single"', pp. 102–3, 109.
15. Stewart, *Romantic Magazines*, p. 57; Perkins, '"She has her ladies too"', p. 253.
16. Lawrence, '"Afford[ing] me a Place"', p. 400.
17. Other valuable life sources beyond Blain's biography are Dowden's introduction to *Correspondence*; De La Vars's *DLB* entry; Blain's *Oxford DNB* entry; and chapter 2 of Low, *The Literary Protégées*.
18. Bowles to Southey, 21 September 1818, in Dowden, *Correspondence*, p. 12.

19. Blain, *Caroline Bowles Southey*, p. 21.
20. Dowden, *Correspondence*, pp. 1–4.
21. Letter 3140 (28 May 1818) in Southey, *Collected Letters*.
22. 3 June 1818, in Dowden, *Correspondence*, p. 8.
23. See Letters 3149, 3154, 3181, 3184, 3241 and 3268 in Southey, *Collected Letters*.
24. Letter 3515 (27 July 1820) in ibid.
25. Letter 3469 (21 April 1820) in ibid.
26. Letter 2550 (Southey to G. C. Bedford, 8 February 1815) in ibid.
27. Letter 3066 (Southey to Murray, 11 January 1818) in ibid.
28. Letter 3187 (Southey to Bedford, 6 September 1818) in ibid.
29. Letter 3201 (7 October 1818) in ibid.
30. [Wilson], 'Letters from the Lakes', pp. 401–4.
31. Letter 3255 (Southey to Bedford, 27 February 1819) in Southey, *Collected Letters*.
32. The three women's letters to Blackwood predating Bowles's earliest surviving letter are from Lady Mary Clerk (24 November 1817), Anne Grant (30 July 1820) and Jane Wilson (10 April 1821). None touch upon potential contributions to Maga.
33. Bowles, Letter to Blackwood, 30 August 1821.
34. [Lockhart], 'Notices'. See also Flynn, 'Beginning *Blackwood's*'.
35. Bowles, Letter to Blackwood, 30 August 1821. Another Bowles letter (NLS MS 4005.284) initially seems to precede this one, but internal details suggest it should be dated 22 June 1830, not 1820.
36. Sweet, 'All Work and All Play', pp. 239–40, 243.
37. Rare instances of signed poems in early *Blackwood's* are 'Three Original Sonnets by W. Wordsworth' (January 1819) and 'Fancy in Nubibus' by 'S.T. Coleridge' (November 1819).
38. Bowles's two early submissions not signed 'C.' were 'Thoughts on Letter-Writing' (by 'M. G.') and 'Letter from a Washerwoman' (by 'Patience Lilywhite'). So closely was Bowles associated with this initial that the 1855 index of *Blackwood's* first fifty volumes mistakenly credits her with two poems signed 'C.' before her earliest communication with Maga (*General Index*, p. 63).
39. Bulwer-Lytton, Review of *Romance and Reality*, p. 546.
40. Mason, *Literary Advertising*, pp. 89–92. Earlier *Blackwood's* poems published under initials include one by 'F. D. H.' (Felicia Dorothea Hemans), another by 'P. M. J.' (P. M. James) and several by 'Δ' (David Macbeth Moir, using the Greek equivalent of his first initial).
41. Blackwood, Letter to Bowles, 22 December 1821.
42. Blackwood, Letter to Bowles, 2 November 1821.
43. Blackwood, Letter to Bowles, 22 December 1821.

44. Blackwood, Letters to Bowles, 28 January and 22 February 1822.
45. St Barbe, Letter to Blackwood, 26 November 1821; Blackwood, Letter to St Barbe, 22 December 1821.
46. [St Barbe], Review of *A Widow's Tale*, p. 287. Emphasis in original.
47. Blackwood, Letter to St Barbe, 20 February 1822.
48. Bowles, Letter to Blackwood, 9 March 1822.
49. 9 February 1822, in Dowden, *Correspondence*, p. 24.
50. See Southey to Bowles, 17 November 1824, and Bowles to Southey, 8 January 1826, in ibid. pp. 74, 95.
51. Dowden, *Correspondence*, p. 30.
52. Unpublished letter from Southey to Mary Ann Watts Hughes (24 February 1825; courtesy of Lynda Pratt; original in the New York Public Library's Pforzheimer Collection).
53. Unpublished letter from Southey to Humphrey Senhouse (11 February 1822, courtesy of Lynda Pratt, original in University of Rochester's Southey Papers); Letter 3140 (28 May 1818) in Southey, *Collected Letters*.
54. These counts are derived from Strout's *Bibliography*, the *Wellesley Index* and the *Curran Index*.
55. [Bowles], 'The Smuggler', pp. 635–6.
56. Blain, *Caroline Bowles Southey*, p. 19.
57. [Bowles], 'Gentlemanly Expostulation', p. 352.
58. [Bowles], 'Thoughts on Letter-Writing', pp. 302, 304.
59. [Bowles], 'To the Author', pp. 655–6.
60. Bowles reprinted 'Childhood', 'Beauty', 'Thoughts on Letter-Writing' and 'The Smuggler' alongside various early Maga poems in *Solitary Hours* (1826), her first book published by Blackwood. Her churchyard essays were gathered in her second Blackwood volume, *Chapters on Churchyards* (1829).
61. Strout, *Bibliography*, p. 105. For the misattribution to Maginn, see *The Odoherty Papers*, vol. 2, p. 279.
62. Letter 3114 (Southey to Murray, 8 April 1818) in Southey, *Collected Letters*.
63. Letter 3538 (12 October 1820) in ibid.
64. [Hunt], 'Preface', p. ix.
65. 'Caroline Southey', p. 969.
66. Bowles, Letter to Blackwood, 4 June 1822.
67. Blackwood, Letter to Bowles, 25 June 1822.
68. Dowden, *Correspondence*, pp. 26–8.
69. Bowles to Southey, 17 July 1822, in ibid. p. 29; Bowles, Letter to Blackwood, 1 February 1823.
70. [Bowles], 'Letter from a Washerwoman', p. 232.

71. Hunt, 'No. XLI', p. 150.
72. Hunt, 'No. XXXIX', pp. 122–3.
73. Dart, *Metropolitan Art and Literature*, p. 93.
74. Hunt, 'No. XLIV', pp. 182–3.
75. Ibid. pp. 184–6.
76. [Bowles], 'Letter from a Washerwoman', p. 233.
77. [Lockhart], 'Odoherty on Don Juan', p. 282; see also Morrison, '"Abuse Wickedness"'.
78. [Bowles], 'Letter from a Washerwoman', p. 233.
79. Wallace, *Shelley and Greece*, p. 92.
80. [Bowles], 'Letter from a Washerwoman', p. 233.
81. Ibid. p. 234.
82. Ibid. pp. 235–6.
83. Ibid. pp. 236–8.
84. Watts, Letter to Blackwood, 8 March 1823.
85. [Thomson], 'Letter', p. 472.
86. Lodge, 'Sally Brown (1822)', pp. 107–8.
87. [Orlebar], 'Robert Southey's Second Wife', p. 222.
88. Dowden, *Correspondence*, p. 149.
89. Lawrence, '"Afford[ing] me a Place"', p. 403.
90. 16 September 1834, in Dowden, *Correspondence*, pp. 310–11.

Chapter 9

Mary Prince 'At Home' in *Blackwood's*: Maga's Origins and the End of Slavery

Caroline McCracken-Flesher

In 1828, Mary Prince, an enslaved woman who had been brought to London from Antigua, walked into the Anti-Slavery Society at 18 Addle Street, Aldermanbury. The claim she there initiated against her current masters, the Wood family, impacted the ongoing debate for abolition. Prince's appeal to be recognised in England as a person of freedom with the right to choose a home for herself echoed, less predictably, in Scotland. It evoked particular ire in James MacQueen, a *Blackwood's* contributor and West Indies proponent, who led a vituperative battle in the magazine over who could claim the discourse of homecoming. This chapter draws on MacQueen's published attacks and on correspondence in the National Library of Scotland's Blackwood archive to show how Prince's case reawakened long-ago grudges, exposing tensions between *Blackwood's* advertised values and its own history. *Blackwood's* had played a considerable role in popularising Scotland as a hub for ideas of home, and Prince's claims coincidentally echoed *Blackwood's* language. But given its early establishment as the *Edinburgh Monthly Magazine* and then its recreation as *Blackwood's*, the journal's own origin narrative was uncomfortably doubled, and its role in any discourse of homecoming consequently overdetermined. Thomas Pringle, a Scot who in 1828 was serving as secretary to the Anti-Slavery Society and who formulated Prince's case for the public, had been a partner in William Blackwood's first editorial team. His fellow Scot, MacQueen, had begun his association with Blackwood's new magazine on the heels of Pringle's ejection. Both men, the case of Mary Prince made clear, had been formed by their experience. Prince, appealing to Pringle, found her case entangled in the uncanniness of *Blackwood's* as contested literary home.

Mary Prince's life is the most important strand in this complex web. Although the traffic in slaves had become illegal across the empire in 1807, West Indian slave holding was permitted until 1833 and its coercive substitute, 'apprenticeship', was not overturned until 1838. Arriving in London, Prince stood between British law and Caribbean practice, on the cusp of change. *The History of Mary Prince, a West Indian Slave*, though a relatively late contribution to the West Indian slave narrative, also stood out for dwelling on a woman's experience.[1] Its challenge and uniqueness pushed it to three editions within a year of its February 1831 release.[2] Prince's voice resonates strong and unapologetic, despite being transcribed by Susanna Strickland, then edited and supplemented by Pringle. As Barbara Baumgartner shows, Prince's suffering body accomplishes a powerful 'rhetoric of complaint'.[3] Pringle's biographer, Randolph Vigne, asserts the book considerably increased the popular support that brought abolition to prominence in Parliament.[4] Assuredly, Prince's narrative foregrounded human be-ing in the Caribbean.

Tracking how Prince's narrative was co-opted and contested by *Blackwood's* personalities helps us understand more fully the difficulties Prince faced and the uncertain trajectory of abolition in period journals. *Blackwood's*, for instance, as a Tory journal, typically took the part of West Indian colonists.[5] Even when decrying slavery in the United States as late as 1854, it temporised in the direction of conservatism: 'we are not entitled to usurp the right, which every separate nation possesses, of regulating its own laws'.[6] Attention to the vagaries of Prince's case in *Blackwood's* pages also illuminates the weave of pasts and presents that made up the magazine as it stood in 1831. This chapter, therefore, triangulates discourses, cases and people; highlights their unexpected intersections; and recounts how *Blackwood's* past played a blocking role against Prince's plea to choose a home of her own. It speaks to the complexity, the interwoven causes, experiences and affects that lie behind any life – and behind the magazine named for one William Blackwood.

Blackwood's and the Scottish claim on 'Home'

Perversely, the simplest and most direct part of Mary Prince's appeal was what especially roiled *Blackwood's*. Throughout her *History*,

Prince asserted her right to determine her own home. To Kremena Todorova, the ramifications of Prince's book extended into period debate about 'what constituted "Englishness"'.[7] Yet Prince's insistently expressed desire aligned with a discourse of homecoming prevalent more among Scots than among the English, and dear to *Blackwood's*. It thus drew her into a loaded debate over terms, their meaning and their application.

The Scottish nineteenth century is bookended by ideas of home. From Robert Burns's poem 'The Cottar's Saturday Night' (1786) to the Kailyard authors' celebration of village life, Scottish culture resonated with home idealised, lost and sought. Why so? The decline of rural society throughout Britain was intensified in Scotland by the economic imperatives and opportunities that followed Union (1707), the exile that came after the rebellions of 1715 and 1745 and the clearances encouraged by agricultural improvement. During the early decades of the nineteenth century, Walter Scott's novels inscribed themes of exile and return as Jacobite (*Waverley*, 1814) and Covenanter (*Old Mortality*, 1816), and thus decidedly Scottish. Indeed, through the author's idealised housekeepers (Jeanie Deans in *The Heart of Midlothian*, 1818) and crazed keepers of family secrets (Meg Merrilies in *Guy Mannering*, 1815), Scots claimed the hearth. These works circulated beyond Scotland. 'The Cottar's Saturday Night' not only featured in the *Pennsylvania Packet* of 14 June 1788, it also, as Rhona Brown says, foreshadowed in America an 'appetite for the sentimental, pious Heaven-taught ploughman'[8] – both Burns and his cottage patriarch. Scott became the most commercial and international author of his day. Scotland, that is, in 1831 was already generating, and serving as a focus for, ideas of homecoming.

Contemporary Scottish journals, *Blackwood's* included, thus dwelt on exile and concerns about who could come home. In its first number (1802), the whiggish *Edinburgh Review* affirmed that the 'history of the Highland emigrations is intimately connected with that of the agricultural improvements of the island'.[9] In 1826, the Tory *Quarterly* (under the editorship of the Scot and former Maga insider John Gibson Lockhart) recounted that Scotsmen 'are very remarkable for attachment to home and kindred; but they are compelled to leave their native land'.[10] That same year, the Scottish Christian Isobel Johnstone (ultimately of *Tait's Magazine*) constructed an ideal space to which to return. Her *Cook and Housewife's Manual* assembled disparate characters from a range of fictions – most come home from empire, war or England. At Meg Dods's inn (reprised from Scott's *St. Ronan's Well*, 1823), these recreated the home comforts of cookery. For its part, *Blackwood's* discussed the evils of depopulation and the yearning for home in 'Noctes XLVI' of September 1829, where the Ettrick Shepherd imagines a punishment on the gentry for 'having dispossessed the people': the Duke of Hamilton's cottars, the Shepherd maintains, 'are a' gaun away, man and mither's son, frae the Isle o' Arran'.[11] This leads Christopher North to recite a lament received, supposedly, from a reader in Canada: 'From the lone shieling of the misty island / Mountains divide us, and the waste of seas – / Yet still the blood is strong, the heart is Highland, / And we in dreams behold the Hebrides'.[12] Here, as in much of Scottish writing from this period, home is made of loss and, especially for *Blackwood's*, desire.

Blackwood's, moreover, appropriated home with a unique and political intensity. For George IV's 1822 visit to Edinburgh, Scott helped to orchestrate events by operationalising the idea of Scottish homecoming. Although the king's roots lay in Hanover, Scott, in his *Hints Addressed to the Inhabitants of Edinburgh, and others, in Prospect of His Majesty's Visit*, urged his countrymen to offer their visitor a homely welcome. The 'blood of the . . . Bruce' was come over the border; the king was 'our kinsman'; 'we are THE CLAN, and our King is THE CHIEF'; Scots and king together were 'ae man's bairns'.[13] Positioning itself in direct opposition to its Whig rivals, *Blackwood's* embraced the language and the cause. Whereas the *Scotsman* saw the king as the 'first Magistrate of a free state',[14] *Blackwood's* 'Royal Number' of September 1822 welcomed him as kin, sharing Scotland's blood. In Edinburgh, George IV would 'grace the Halls of his Ancestors', sit at the Scottish fireside and eat 'the bread and salt of Scotland'.[15] This was quite a welcome for an unpopular and outsider monarch.

In short, *Blackwood's* had seized homecoming for its Tory discourse. 'The homelier the symbol [of welcome], the holier is the oath', the magazine insisted, as it bound itself to monarchy and, it hoped, a future of recognition and importance through royal favour.[16] So far, so conservative, romantic and sentimental. But the king was not the only one arriving in Edinburgh. With him came a London retinue of courtiers and hangers-on; to see him, Glaswegians, Highlanders and hordes of non-Scots assembled. In the moment, *Blackwood's* went with the flow, gushing that '[f]riends from the most distant parts of the kingdom recognised each other'.[17] The traffic was only beginning, however, and would prove problematic. Already, J. G. Lockhart worried about Scott's 'Celtified pageantry'.[18] In the long term, the elaborate entertainments boosted Scotland towards a tartan tourism that would produce Queen Victoria resident at Balmoral and all the knick-knackery of today's Edinburgh Royal Mile. Not surprisingly, then, a few years later, *Blackwood's* registered in Mary Prince an unexpected challenge. Having cultivated a discourse of welcome, how should it engage the West Indian slave as she sought a home – even though the home she sought was a place of imagination? Through Prince, *Blackwood's* pages were usurped by a discussion that hit to the heart of the magazine's self-image. Who, exactly, could be 'at home' in Britain – at least from *Blackwood's* fraught, Edinburgh perspective?

Mary Prince, Thomas Pringle and the Language of 'Home'

The clash between Prince and *Blackwood's* may have been inevitable, then – just as a matter of terminology. If *Blackwood's* helped shape the discourse of home in late-Romantic Scotland, *The History of Mary Prince* makes 'home' one of its limit terms. For instance, for the narrative's slaveholders, 'home' is constructed through choice. Captain Williams, Prince's first master, is 'seldom at home long together', but his stays 'at home' bode ill for the slaves.[19] Having a right of property and presence in 'home', masters come and go at will. By contrast, for Prince and her fellow slaves, 'home' is the space that requires their attendance. Only once does Prince invoke this 'home' positively. When preparing to give up the relative safety of Mrs. Williams's care and thus to move away from her mother, the 12-year-old Prince is assured by 'good Mrs Williams' that she will 'still be near the home I was about to quit'.[20] Otherwise, 'home' is a site of orientation to which one trends perforce, but where one never truly lives.

Yet to Prince, 'home' is not solely a site of entrapment; it is also a locus of power. For most of her service, Prince was a 'house' slave. Her duties were domestic. Both her punishments and her attempts to resist pushed her into field service, as with her time in the horrendous salt pans. Prince's hope is to return free to Antigua, where she can be at home with her husband, a freeman. She fears that punishment in the form of field work will be the consequence of her desire to be both home and free. Thus, Prince appropriates and deploys domestic terms as part of her resistance narrative. Recalling the cruel words of potential buyers, she describes them as cayenne to her sorrows. As Barbara Baumgartner observes, this metaphor signals pain, yet it also 'underlines the centrality of domesticity to her emotional life'.[21] Prince, then, issues a claim on 'home'.

Going further, Prince plays off ideas of house and home, questioning their appropriation for particular communities in ways that would anger *Blackwood's*, which treated 'home' as its sentimentalised property. After her first master disrupts home with his brutality, Prince is hired out to a 'strange house . . . among strange people'; sold on, she reaches a 'new home', where it turns out that the 'stones and the timber . . . were not so hard as the hearts of the owners'; at odds with her masters in London, Prince makes the servants witnesses to her performative declaration that 'I am going out of this house . . . but I have done no wrong . . . my mistress . . . has ordered me out of doors . . . and now I am going out'.[22] Twice, too, she shows the colonial home as subject to retributive destruction. A flogging is followed by an earthquake; when the colonists tear down a prayer shelter, 'a flood came down . . . and washed away many houses . . . and I do think that this was for their wickedness'.[23] For Prince, home is not just a site of desire, but a locus for critique. It is a place, thereby, in which she has a peculiar right.

Notably, Prince's narrative is intensified through the efforts of her facilitator, Thomas Pringle. Pringle had spent his post-Blackwood career in South Africa, where he developed his abolitionist principles. Schooled in Scotland's discourse of home, as a poet he sympathetically represented the African stolen away from his family. 'The Bechuana Boy', seized from his hut, stands 'upon the stranger's ground', declaring that 'I have no home!'; 'The Captive of Camalú' carries a 'homeless heart'.[24] Evidently, for Pringle, too, 'home' served as a term of art. He thus begins his 'Supplement to the History of Mary Prince' by noting how she checked her desire to return home to Antigua over fear it would prove no home to her: 'Her words were, "I would rather go into my grave than go back a slave to Antigua, though I wish to go back to my husband very much!'"[25] Indicting the notion of a home within slavery, Prince, as quoted, 'would rather go into my grave!' She nonetheless is aligned with home insofar as it should be the site of intimacy and trust – home, Pringle reminds us, is where her husband is. Pringle takes pains, too, to show that Prince deserves confidence in domestic spaces. Statements he marshals in her support witness that although the Wood family, her current 'owners', defame her, in Antigua and London she had 'the charge of [their] house in their absence ... and was always considered by the neighbours and visitors as their confidential household servant'.[26] Having himself employed Prince after she left the Woods and sought help from the Anti-Slavery Society, Pringle stresses her work as 'a domestic servant in my own family'; he claims that 'we have no hesitation in leaving every thing in the house at her disposal'.[27] To Pringle, the discourse of home extends to Mary Prince.

From Pringle's perspective, the Woods abuse the idea of home and thus fall subject to its exclusions. Attempts to negotiate Prince's manumission before turning to print had proved fruitless, producing only exculpatory claims from Wood in a letter of 20 October 1830 to Sir Patrick Ross (another Scot, and the governor of Antigua).[28] Here, the Woods stand ostentatiously invested in 'home', yet they are prone to hoard it as place and in prose. They contend over whether Prince lived in an outhouse, as she claimed, or in a house they had gifted. The supposed gift of a house serves as a test of Prince's home qualities. Wood claims that he gave Prince and her husband a house because she was of a wandering disposition. Now, Wood says, Prince's husband has left her. A home is supposedly available to Prince, but she is unhomely and unhomed. Wood further insists, in terms designed to unhouse Prince from British and colonial sympathy – terms replete with irony when applied to an Afro-Caribbean slave in England – that she 'is not a native of this country'.[29] For the slave in the matrix of British capitalism, no house could be home. But Pringle promptly challenges Wood on his inconsistencies, focusing on his core term. Wood, he observes, 'prefers losing entirely the full price of the slave, for the mere satisfaction of preventing a poor black woman from returning home to her husband!'[30] Pringle well knows that home, as much as the slave's body, is the site of contention and the field on which battle is to be fought.

James MacQueen and the Problem of 'Home'

It was the claim on home, made not just by Prince but by Pringle – since 1817 divorced from Blackwood – that exercised James MacQueen. Pringle had left under a cloud for failing to produce the success Blackwood had hoped; MacQueen had been enlisted by Maga in the wake of his fraught departure. Moreover, if Pringle trended liberal, MacQueen brought a contesting politics and attitude. He had previously spent years in Grenada, serving as overseer on the Westerhall sugar plantation – itself named for an estate in Dumfries.[31] He arrived there in 1797, just after Fédon's rebellion, and as David Lambert points out, he likely was 'influenced by the paranoid, anti-French, negrophobic, white community that he joined'.[32] Returning to Glasgow in 1816, he became editor of the *Glasgow Courier* and a powerful voice in opposition to anti-slavery movements from what he claimed as his 'perfect knowledge' and 'perfect confidence' across the Atlantic.[33] That activity, and a convergence of interests, brought him to Blackwood's attention. On 20 November 1817, the Edinburgh publisher wrote to MacQueen, 'I am happy to learn . . . you are willing to give your assistance to my Magazine'.[34] Thus began MacQueen's ongoing contribution of West Indian commercial reports to the 'Monthly Register' that concluded each number. And Blackwood's letters show the publisher and the polemicist in close collaboration through succeeding years – with Blackwood congratulating MacQueen for 'the cutting you are cordially giving our pretended Liberals . . . in [the *Glasgow Courier*]', and even soliciting MacQueen's favourable notice in that paper for his own Maga.[35]

By 1831, then, Thomas Pringle might seem a dusty figure receding in Maga myth. James MacQueen, on the other hand, was ensconced as an ongoing contributor. Indeed, outside the commercial reports, he was a named contributor of feature articles. But old rivalries burgeoned to new politics. Prince's story appeared in February. MacQueen, that month, was already fulminating in *Blackwood's* against the 'gigantic fabric of falsehood' raised by the *Anti-Slavery Reporter* – which Pringle edited.[36] MacQueen took the next eight months to get thoroughly worked up about Prince as a representative evil in his campaign to preserve colonial rights.[37] Then, in a November letter in his series to government, this one originally intended to lay out 'the magnitude and importance of the trade, the commerce, the revenue, the industry, and the wealth of the whole Colonial Empire of Great Britain', he railed against the 'despicable tool' Prince. Less predictably, he also assailed '"*the well known*" Mr Pringle'.[38] From Prince and, I will suggest, especially from Pringle, he strove to seize back the discourse of home for *Blackwood's* and the colonial cause.

In MacQueen's screed, the term of art is that code substitution for home, 'family'. It appears nineteen times in the nine pages he devotes to Mary Prince. 'Family' privileges intimacy and relationship. These are attributes allowed to the Woods but denied to, and supposedly by, the ingrate Prince. MacQueen's Caribbean sources consider Mr Wood 'a respectable father of a family'.[39] 'The conduct of Mrs Wood to the slaves about her is . . . that of a parent'; her relations with Prince 'partook more of the familiarity and kindness of an alliance by blood than by bondage'.[40] MacQueen insists that Prince has been kept 'in [Wood's] family' and 'treated with superior kindness and confidence', but Prince has 'rendered the family of Mr Wood miserable'.[41] Wood deserves 'redress for the cruel injuries which himself and his family have sustained', particularly 'the wife of his bosom', for Prince, a onetime '*confidential and favourite servant*', is a viper in that bosom.[42] Prince has supposedly abandoned Wood's house 'without any communication with him or any of his family, and proceeded to fraternize with her new friends and advisers, till we find her planted in Pringle's family'.[43] According to MacQueen, she has betrayed the discourse of family – which of course, never included her. Thus, no family for her, in his terms, and no home.

In Mary Prince's person, indeed, MacQueen sees the idea of home – the home that appeared in *Blackwood's* pages – as subverted. Prince had a complicated sexual history. This came out in Wood's 1833 libel case against Pringle, which Pringle lost.[44] Here, Prince had to testify to her forced and consensual relationships – associations not unusual for a woman in such exploitative circumstances (as Angela Davis made explicit in her impassioned 1971 attack on the scholarship of slavery and gender, and as Margo Madison-MacFadyen thoughtfully explains for Mary Prince).[45] But MacQueen's letter of 1831 already insinuates Prince's threat to the idealised home that *Blackwood's* readers had come to expect. Perversely, but perhaps predictably, that home had been elaborated in the sentimental stories of John Wilson – the Maga insider and problematic Professor of Moral Philosophy, who was son-in-law to a slave trader driven out of business by the 1807 Act.[46] Thus, MacQueen describes Prince not just as 'planted in Pringle's family, and at his washing-tub'.[47] From this post, he recounts, 'she was frequently called to [Pringle's] closet to give a narrative of the severities inflicted upon her'.[48] MacQueen imagines Pringle's 'secret closetings and labours with Mary', elaborating, should we miss the innuendo, that 'in London maidservants are not removed from the washing-tub to the parlour without an object'.[49] Moreover, Pringle's family – and particularly 'the females of his family', whom Pringle had invoked as witnesses to Prince's '*decency* and *propriety* of conduct' – stands impugned.[50] MacQueen sneers:

> Pringle's labours afford a criterion to determine that the delicacy and modesty 'of the females of his family' cannot be of the most exalted character. His continued labour by night and by day in the study, in the parlour, and in the drawing-room, is to call for and to nestle amidst all kinds of colonial immorality and uncleanness.[51]

'Home' is fenced about as British, in need of protection from Mary Prince's pollution. Worse, Prince's presence has the power to eject a family from this hoarded and protective cultural location. It is only justice that Pringle's is the family so ejected.

The Colonial Contest for Home

MacQueen surely could not have been surprised that an enslaved person might yearn for a 'home' and want their own family, or be grateful for such welcome as they could receive. Scots, indeed, were well poised to understand such circumstances, and not just by their recent history of exile and emigration. For Scotland, and also for Britain more widely, Scots claim credit for some of the major decisions towards emancipation. Lord Mansfield, who in 1772 made it impossible to assert slaveholder rights over someone in England, was born a Murray in Perthshire. Crucial cases, such as that of Joseph Knight, were argued in Scotland.[52] In 1778, an appellate panel of twelve law lords assembled for Knight, though only three were required. They concluded by a vote of eight to four that 'the defender had no right to the negro's service' – in practical terms, ending slavery in Scotland.[53] Lord Auchinleck emphasised the principles that directed their decision: 'I do not think [slavery] is agreeable to humanity, not to say to the Christian religion. Is a man a slave because he is black? No. He is our brother; and he is a man.'⁵⁴ Still, Auchinleck concluded in terms that prefigured the tussle for home for Mary Prince, arguing that the black man 'is in a land of liberty, with his wife and child: let him remain *there*'.⁵⁵

But if cases like that of Knight or invocations of Christian spirit like that from Auchinleck might suggest Scotland as a place of sympathy for enslaved people, in 1831 it was not a place that could be occupied unproblematically by Pringle or MacQueen themselves. Scots flung as far as South Africa and Grenada were the constituency directly appealed to by the discourse of homecoming. That discourse, though strong in principle, was proving weak in practice.

MacQueen, importantly, had actually come home from away. Iain Whyte points out that a 'large number of the colonists in the West Indies saw themselves as temporary sojourners who intended to return home when they had made their fortunes'.⁵⁶ MacQueen may have been one of these. Certainly, in Glasgow he found a home to which to go. He had been born in nearby Lanarkshire.⁵⁷ Moreover, his welcome was ratified through employment at the *Glasgow Courier* – which Lambert observes was established 'to profit from Glasgow's trans-Atlantic trade' – and his enlistment to Maga.⁵⁸ Yet Scotland was changing, and MacQueen soon found himself on the wrong side of history. The year 1826 saw a huge Edinburgh anti-slavery meeting, born of frustration that slavery had not dwindled under current pressures, and Glasgow joined in with a petition of 39,000 signatures; in 1830, an Edinburgh meeting 'as numerous . . . as could be' lobbied for abolition 'at the earliest possible opportunity'; before the meeting was over, a call came for immediate abolition.⁵⁹ That same year, MacQueen was succeeded as editor of the *Glasgow Courier*. Though he continued to write for the paper, he no longer controlled that platform.⁶⁰ *Blackwood's* itself, typically hospitable to MacQueen's ideas, had followed his July 1831 article on the course of the Niger with an implicit critique of his position on slavery.⁶¹

MacQueen's intensification of the language of home in his *Blackwood's* attack on Prince and Pringle, then, signalled anxiety. Britain, and perhaps even Scotland, had become unhomely for repatriated colonialists like him. In an early sign of this sensitivity, in 1825, MacQueen published *The West India Colonies*, with the subtitle *The Calumnies and Misrepresentations Circulated Against Them*. Returning to this theme, his 1831 attack on Mary's *History* foregrounded 'the hideous falsehoods . . . which are advanced against the colonists by their enemies in this country'.[62] Colonists, he declared, find themselves unparented: they 'must think that they are despised by the mother country'.[63] 'I am one of those', he claims, 'who, from experience, know how greatly . . . feelings of affection and respect for our native country are increased by being removed to the distance of many thousand miles'.[64] So much the more does he feel Britain's rejection of her children. Against the government's implication that 'it is impossible to be at the same time a colonist and a humane man', in outrage and outrageously MacQueen cries, 'It is impossible to conceive any state more degrading or debasing than this'.[65] Britain, he rails, 'has no right to call upon the colonists to become her slaves'.[66] It was this anxiety that stoked the attack against the presumptuous Mary Prince and that erstwhile Blackwoodian, Thomas Pringle.

Pringle, however, was no more at home in Scotland than was MacQueen. As recently as 1826, he had returned from South Africa, where he had emigrated with his extended family and the aim of settlement.[67] There, he had melded home and away, comparing himself to a 'petty "border" chief', and his biographer records that he rode out against marauding bushmen.[68] But if the epigraph to Pringle's *Narrative of a Residence in South Africa* invokes his father, 'Sprung from a stalwart line of Scottish sires, / [to] be thou the patriarch on Afric's strand / of a young race', Pringle was not the stereotypical colonist.[69] His neighbours relied on him to care for Africans made vulnerable by the death of better masters, thus he 'strengthened our own hands, while . . . protecting and benefiting those oppressed and despised people'.[70] Pringle was also a newspaperman of conscience. For these virtues, manifested in his 1826 'Letter from South Africa' to the *New Monthly Magazine*, for his history with *Blackwood's* known even on the Cape and earning him the (dis)respect of being 'an arrant dissenter', and for his co-editing of the deliberately assertive *South African Commercial Advertiser* – in which he 'attacked despotism and called for "open discussion of differences" which could be achieved "by means of a Free Press, its liberty (not licentiousness)" protected by law' – he found himself unwelcome in the colonies.[71] This made Pringle just the man to serve the Anti-Slavery Society. But unlike MacQueen, he did not feel he could live again in Scotland. And *Blackwood's* was to blame.

Blackwood's and the Uncanniness of 'Home'

From South Africa, Pringle had written to Scott asserting his desire not to figure in Scottish contexts any more, and certainly not amid the personal/political broils enacted in the pages of the Edinburgh journals:

> I . . . would wish my name . . . to have no connection with them. In leaving my native country (probably forever) I buried all my personal resentments . . . and having forgiven my foes (if I had any) I would willingly be permitted to forget and be forgotten by them.[72]

He took his cue from the inception of Blackwood's first journal, the *Edinburgh Monthly Magazine*. Thus, he suggests that the febrile response to Mary Prince, from foe and friend alike, lay only secondarily in *Blackwood's* appropriation of the discourse of home and in the failure of that discourse under the challenge of Pringle and MacQueen's experiences abroad. It lay, first and foremost, in *Blackwood's* as a contested literary home for both men.

Sigmund Freud explains and Tom Wolfe affirms that we can't go home again, for home is both the site of our origins and the origin of our (mis)recognition.[73] *Blackwood's*, with its complex origin and contesting editorial teams, for its early authors – whether exiled or simply anxious – constituted a site of intensified desire and impossible return. How so? We know well the tussle between Hogg, Lockhart and Wilson for the credit of priority with the reborn *Blackwood's*. But we could usefully remember, too, the story of the magazine's short-lived forerunner, the *Edinburgh Monthly Magazine*. Together, these constituted *Blackwood's* inception not just as a doubling but as a redoubling. For literary men, that made Maga, Edinburgh, even Scotland the uncanniest home of all.

Mary Prince, then, stumbled into a deeply dysfunctional Blackwoodian family. Some little-considered details make the case. In the mid-1810s, Gillian Hughes says, Hogg 'had been discussing the establishment of a new magazine with his friends', especially Thomas

Pringle, with whom he 'submitted a plan and list of contributors to William Blackwood'.[74] By Vigne's account, Pringle remembered that his eventual co-editor, 'Mr Cleghorn[,] and I . . . proposed it to Mr Blackwood'; but Pringle acknowledged that 'Hogg might have had a similar idea in his head previously, for it was a project we had been talking of in literary parties'.[75] Blackwood's magazine publishing, that is, was divided from the start.

Things got only more complicated, and are more complex than Blackwoodian tradition commonly tells. What happened next we know largely through Pringle's detractors and according to historic political and literary rivalries. The *Edinburgh Monthly Magazine* proved no adequate opposition to the *Edinburgh Review* – Blackwood found it less exciting than he had hoped and somewhat whiggish, according to Mrs. Oliphant;[76] it was duly retired, then recreated as *Blackwood's* under the young Tory Turks. But Pringle's biographer argues that the *EMM*'s circulation figures were respectable, and Hogg's biographer notes the publisher's unreasonable expectations.[77] The Blackwood archive at the National Library of Scotland further twists the tale. Here, we find Blackwood telling his London colleague, Robert Baldwin, that he regrets the *EMM*'s cessation, for 'it was doing so well'.[78] Blackwood's main complaint is that 'my Editors . . . have done little in the way of writing or procuring Contributions'. And Pringle and Cleghorn, depending on which source we credit, either decamped amid negotiations (see the letter to Baldwin) or were ousted. Whatever the case, all agree that in late 1817, they moved to the rival *Scots Magazine*, which they edited under the new name, the *Edinburgh Magazine and Literary Miscellany.*

Turnover in magazine editors was not unusual, but the Blackwood archive shows this exchange as unduly vexed, for it was entangled in friendships – exactly the context to complicate Prince's later claim on belonging. Pringle had enlisted Cleghorn, and Blackwood, feeling that neither editor was up to the task, at first sought at least to retain Pringle. To Baldwin, Blackwood insisted he sought to renegotiate with Pringle 'on account of personal friendship', and suggested only second that 'he would soon become much more useful when he had more experience and from the Editorial duty devolving upon himself alone'.[79] Moreover, the magazine subsisted thus far 'by great exertions I got from my own friends . . . friends who have in fact made the work what it is'. As for Pringle, equally caught between friendships, he argued to keep the magazine alive well beyond the point when Blackwood thought they had come to an agreement to cease publication. Thus, from June to August 1817, Blackwood's letters to Pringle seethe with frustration, as his editor could neither complete the final number nor resign himself to the journal's cessation. On 23 June, Blackwood thought he had put the *EMM* to rest. 'I have already explained to you verbally', he wrote to Pringle, 'the reasons which oblige me to put an end to our agreement'.[80] On 28 June, he invoked his 'good temper' to declare:

> You are quite correct in stating that the measure which I find myself compelled to adopt was contrary to your remonstrances, but your memory must be very treacherous indeed when you can assert that I have not hesitated to sacrifice your interests.[81]

Then, on 1 July, he retorted to another missive from Pringle by abjuring friendship; he confessed himself 'heartily sick of this correspondence. . . . I shall never open my lips to you on the subject except in the presence of a third party'.[82] Pringle replied the next day that Blackwood's was no letter to share between friends. Rather it was 'obviously intended for . . . being exhibited . . . in order to produce a certain effect'.[83] And things were only made worse by rivalries between politically opposed publishers. Blackwood and Constable, indeed, were already personal enemies. Three months earlier, Blackwood had affirmed to John Murray that 'from sad experience I have felt that [Constable] is a person who one must on all occasions avoid'.[84] Constable, he added, is a man of 'craft'. Unfortunately, the magazine that Pringle and Cleghorn contracted to edit belonged to Constable, Blackwood's arch rival.

Still, if turnover in editors was not unknown, Pringle was especially unlucky in swapping Blackwood for Constable, just as Prince would prove unlucky in attracting MacQueen's increased notice through Pringle. In the new *Blackwood's*, rivalry burgeoned under the pens of Hogg, Lockhart and Wilson. Their 'Chaldee Manuscript' pilloried Pringle and Cleghorn for their politics, publications and physical disabilities, making the change in editors a literary event.[85] The two beasts who 'touched not the ground as they went' was a sly dig at Cleghorn and Pringle for their lameness; Constable's characterisation echoed Blackwood's own language, for he reappeared as one 'crafty in counsel'.[86] And the harassment continued. As late as 1829, Hogg, that sometimes misdirected prankster, parodied Pringle's commitment to African causes in a proto-Tarzan *Blackwood's* tale of white/ape encounter that carried the title 'A Letter from Southern Africa', and that was re-released in 1832 as 'The Pongos'.[87] Worse, while Pringle had won a small settlement from Blackwood, with their accounts finally closed in 1820, his suit after the Chaldee shows the damage as irretrievable.[88] Although Blackwood's letters of 1817 imply well-intentioned efforts to retain Pringle, Pringle saw things differently. Blackwood, he claims, did

> everything in his power to . . . ridicule those personal infirmities under which . . . the pursuer has the unhappiness to labour; to degrade and vilify his character . . . to . . . injure him in private and public esteem; and to deprive him of that reputation to which alone he must be indebted for the means of his subsistence, and that of his family.[89]

Pringle felt himself ejected, his pathway back to Scotland blocked, his literary home corrupted. This *Blackwood's* experience would block Mary Prince's way home, too.

Mary Prince and the Unhomeliness of *Blackwood's*

Such was the *Blackwood's* background lurking just out of the foreground in MacQueen's response to Mary Prince. MacQueen, that avid campaigner for colonial rights, knew just as well as Pringle the history of Scottish in-fights, for although not a member of the *Blackwood's* clique, he became embroiled in Maga's issues from early on. It was even as the 'Chaldee Manuscript' echoed across Edinburgh that Blackwood and MacQueen established their partnership. In the years since then, MacQueen had kept up his commercial reports. Now, in the months leading up to his intervention in the *History of Mary Prince*, he was arguing persistently to Blackwood for additional pages in which to elaborate his arguments.[90] On 29 May 1831, he cheered on the magazine for its ability to 'gall the Whigs and Revolutionists'.[91] With Parliament debating slavery, and with abolition ever more likely, this same letter worried that even *Blackwood's* could not 'restore to their senses before it is too late the deluded and maddened people of this Country'. Some 'terrible calamity' was coming, a 'calamity which will dismember and destroy our Empire'. The problem lay in 'The Public Press [that] has become so prostituted &

degraded'. It lay, in other words, in writers like Pringle. Especially Pringle, in fact, for as we have seen, MacQueen directed his attack against '"*the well known*" Mr. Pringle' – well known to MacQueen not just as abolitionist but as ur-Blackwoodian, now outrageously contending for the present.[92]

And MacQueen's fraught circumstances produce overwrought discourse that contends with Pringle as much for origins and authenticity as for principles and politics. Pringle is a multiplier of 'anti-colonial vermin'.[93] He has made himself a slave, for Wood should 'come and take Pringle by the neck, and with a good rattan or Mauritius *ox* whip, lash him through London'.[94] MacQueen's anger had staying power, too. In 1832, he was still arguing the cause in the *Glasgow Courier*, fulminating that '*Thomas Pringle*, the Secretary of the Anti-Slavery Society, and the Editor . . . of that vile publication . . . the *Anti-Slavery Reporter* . . . made up the history of an *ex black slave*'.[95] Pringle is the distanced associate of execrable London societies. MacQueen could hardly push him further from 'home', and from Scotland. By contrast, MacQueen touts himself as '*Mr. M'Queen* of this city' (Glasgow), who 'took to pieces, and', as a superior editor, 'from authentic documents . . . exposed and refuted . . . Mr. Pringle's conduct'.[96] But MacQueen protests too much. He was caught in a particular past. Even as he cast himself as Pringle's nemesis, he felt less and less at ease in a Britain that found little of home in a plantation house.

Mary Prince's *History*, then, certainly came at a crucial moment in the campaign against slavery. Yet in a way we have not fully recognised, it comes into contention and comes alive through its discourse of homecoming, too. Ironically, however, for MacQueen and Pringle, it thus echoed loudly to a past that held them in thrall: the scandal of 1817 that played out between *Blackwood's* successive editorial teams. And with battle joined again in 1831, MacQueen proved the unluckier of the two men. Early in the dissension generated by Prince, *Blackwood's* London publisher, Thomas Cadell, had proved an anxious partner. He quavered, 'I have been served with a Writ threatening me with an Action as the publisher of a Libel upon Mr Pringle, who is alluded to so violently & personally in that Article'.[97] Cadell required MacQueen to avow his authorship so that the case could be lodged against him, instead. Blackwood himself hinted to MacQueen that 'The expenses . . . will be heavy, but I hope you will be saved from all loss by your West Indian friends.'[98] But MacQueen's faith that the 'Colonies & those connected with them will not . . . allow me to suffer . . . by expenses in what is in reality their cause' was overconfident.[99] And though continuing to rage to Blackwood about the battles he was fighting for the colonies and against Pringle, he became increasingly adrift. He was delinquent in providing materials for the London attorney Edward Foss, retained in his defence, claiming 'the documents & references . . . are so numerous . . . that . . . I know not what to send'.[100] Perhaps he sensed the trend of events outside the court, for after the libel suit and its loss to Pringle, and despite Pringle's loss in turn to Wood,[101] Foss, who really worked for Cadell and Blackwood, lobbied to vet MacQueen's future articles for publication.[102] To add insult to injury, friend Blackwood dunned his contributor for fees to pay the lawyer.[103] Indeed, after placing twelve featured articles in *Blackwood's* between 1826 and 1833, MacQueen seems to have published only one such piece, the 1844 essay 'Africa – Slave Trade – Tropical Colonies', thereafter.[104] The pressures of prosecution, that is, fed MacQueen's tribalism with his Scottish Tory publishers, but it drove them apart, too.

While MacQueen's rivalries persisted, his battle was already lost – whether in support of slavery, against Pringle, or for *Blackwood's*. In February 1831, MacQueen applauded Blackwood, remarking, 'Your pages are the weapon [the abolitionists – whom MacQueen mocks as 'the Saints'] and the Government above all others dread'.[105] By late 1833, he was no longer at home in those same pages. With a manuscript in hand, he wrote in perplexity to Blackwood on 29 November, Pringle still on his mind: 'I am somewhat at a loss what to strike out in what is considered objectionable . . . I have no wish that either you or myself should get any trouble from Pringle.'[106] In 1831, MacQueen's febrile discourse perhaps expressed his anxiety over an outmoded cause, coupled with a last-ditch opportunity to argue across distant but deeply disliked personalities and histories. Now, MacQueen's contempt for Pringle remained, but even *Blackwood's* recognised that time had moved on. In August 1833, the Slavery Abolition Act outlawed slavery throughout the empire. And in November, as MacQueen attempted confusedly to belabour his points one more time, Pringle wrote to Blackwood that with 'the great question of negro emancipation . . . settled, James MacQueen . . . must soon cease from his loud and foolish barking'.[107] Time and the courts had refigured MacQueen as Blackwood's unruly house dog, subject to discipline.

The History of Mary Prince, then, gains additional significance when viewed from a Scottish perspective. Indeed, seeing Prince's book in the context of its production (through Pringle) and reception (through MacQueen) accomplishes important work to re-engage Scotland with the under-acknowledged history of slavery that haunts its past. In this context, Prince's narrative exposes the disturbingly narrow and self-referential view of a *Blackwood's* supposedly engaged in a crucial human debate. Prince, in *Blackwood's* pages, was not the only issue – perhaps not even the main issue. MacQueen's obsessive resistance to her quest pointed back to the magazine's formative moments as much as it challenged the merits of her cause. Set to deny Mary a home, MacQueen simultaneously and even more strenuously contested with Thomas Pringle the space that was *Blackwood's*. The year 1831, that prismatic moment for the abolition campaign, threw up shadows of *Blackwood's* doubled and troubled origin myth and Pringle's expulsion. As *Blackwood's* numbers and behind-the-scenes exchanges show, home, insofar as it was Maga, was an uncanny place. They show, indeed, that, unconscionably, *Blackwood's* own anxiety of origins compromised Mary Prince's quest for a home. It seems just, then, that MacQueen's obsession with personalities and the past ejected him, if only temporarily, from Maga's present.

Notes

1. Prince's narrative appeared 42 years after Olaudah Equiano's *The Interesting Narrative of the Life of Olaudah Equiano, or Gustavus Vassa, the African* (London: 1789); Madison-MacFadyen calls Prince 'the earliest known black woman writer from the West Indies to author a slave narrative' ('Mary Prince', p. 654).
2. Prince, *History*, p. x.
3. Baumgartner, 'The Body as Evidence', p. 259.
4. Vigne, *Thomas Pringle*, p. 218.
5. See Dumas, '*The Edinburgh Review*', pp. 562–3, 570–1.
6. Anon., Review of *Sunny Memories*, p. 303.
7. Todorova, '"I Will Say the Truth"', p. 286.
8. Brown, '"Guid black prent"', p. 81.
9. Anon., Review of *An Inquiry*, pp. 62–3.
10. Anon., 'Report of the Select Committee', p. 442.

11. [Lockhart], 'Noctes XLVI', pp. 399–400.
12. North's 'Canadian Boat-Song' is variously attributed to William Dunlop, John Galt, David Macbeth Moir and John Wilson.
13. Scott, *Hints Addressed to the Inhabitants*, pp. 6–7.
14. Anon., 'The King's Visit', p. 244.
15. [Wilson], 'The King', pp. 257, 264 (see also p. 253).
16. Ibid. p. 263.
17. Ibid. p. 258.
18. Lockhart, *Memoirs*, vol. 5 (Edinburgh), p. 204.
19. Prince, *History*, pp. 7–8.
20. Ibid. p. 8.
21. Baumgartner, 'The Body as Evidence', p. 256.
22. Prince, *History*, pp. 7–8, 12, 13, 34–5.
23. Ibid. pp. 17, 23.
24. Pringle, *Poetical Works*, pp. 5, 4, 46.
25. Pringle, 'Supplement', p. 24.
26. Ibid. p. 32.
27. Ibid. pp. 26, 35.
28. Pringle reproduces this letter in ibid. pp. 27–8.
29. Ibid. p. 27.
30. Ibid. p. 37.
31. See Lambert, '"Glasgow King"', pp. 391–5, for MacQueen's Grenada experiences.
32. Ibid. p. 394.
33. MacQueen, 'Colonial Empire', p. 755. Through MacQueen, the 'West Indian interest in Scotland, always strong, became increasingly organized' (Whyte, *Scotland and the Abolition*, p. 140).
34. Blackwood, Letter to MacQueen, 20 November 1817.
35. Blackwood, Letter to MacQueen, 25 July 1826.
36. MacQueen, 'The British Colonies', p. 203.
37. MacQueen, 'Colonial Empire', p. 744.
38. Ibid. p. 744.
39. Ibid. p. 748.
40. Ibid. p. 750.
41. Ibid. pp. 744–5.
42. Ibid. pp. 752, 747.
43. Ibid. p. 745.
44. Documented in *The Times*, 1 March 1833. See Prince, *History*, pp. 100–3.
45. Davis, 'Reflections', pp. 2–15, and Madison-MacFadyen, 'Mary Prince, Grand Turk', n. 15 and 18.
46. Wilson's stories were collected as *Lights and Shadows of Scottish Life*. He married Jane Penny in 1809.

47. MacQueen, 'Colonial Empire', p. 745.
48. Ibid. p. 745.
49. Ibid. p. 750.
50. Ibid. p. 751, and Prince, *History*, p. 55.
51. MacQueen, 'Colonial Empire', p. 751.
52. Allain, *The Legal Understanding of Slavery*, pp. 78–81.
53. Tytler, *The Decisions of the Court*, p. 282.
54. Allain, *The Legal Understanding of Slavery*, p. 79.
55. Ibid. p. 80.
56. Whyte, *Scotland and the Abolition*, p. 62.
57. Lambert, '"Glasgow King"', p. 391.
58. Ibid. p. 395.
59. Whyte, *Scotland and the Abolition*, pp. 185, 187, 190–2.
60. Lambert, '"Glasgow King"', p. 385.
61. MacQueen's 'The River Niger' was followed by an excerpt from the *Literary Gazette* that finds 'the greatest obstacles' to civilisation and trade in 'the still existing slave-trade near the mouth of the river', p. 136; see also note and commentary pp. 135–6.
62. MacQueen, 'Colonial Empire', p. 744.
63. Ibid. p. 755.
64. Ibid. p. 754.
65. Ibid. p. 755.
66. Ibid. p. 758.
67. Pringle, *Narrative*, p. 3.
68. Vigne, *Thomas Pringle*, pp. 84–5.
69. Pringle, *Narrative*, p. xxxvii.
70. Vigne, *Thomas Pringle*, p. 83.
71. Ibid. pp. 121–5.
72. Pringle, Letter to Scott, 1821.
73. See Freud, 'The Uncanny,' pp. 217–56, and Wolfe, *You Can't Go Home Again*.
74. Hughes, *James Hogg*, p. 146.
75. Vigne, *Thomas Pringle*, p. 30.
76. Oliphant, *Annals*, vol. 1, p. 100.
77. Vigne, *Thomas Pringle*, p. 30; Hughes, *James Hogg*, p. 147.
78. Blackwood, Letter to Baldwin et al., 23 July 1817, NLS MS 30001.
79. Ibid.
80. Blackwood, Letter to Pringle, 23 June 1817.
81. Blackwood, Letter to Pringle, 28 June 1817.
82. Blackwood, Letter to Pringle, 1 July 1817.
83. Pringle, Letter to Blackwood, 2 July 1817.
84. Blackwood to John Murray, March 1817.

85. [Hogg, Lockhart and Wilson], 'Chaldee Manuscript', pp. 89–96.
86. Ibid., pp. 89–90.
87. [Hogg], 'A Singular Letter', pp. 809–16.
88. Vigne, *Thomas Pringle*, pp. 35, 40.
89. Qtd. Vigne, *Thomas Pringle*, p. 35.
90. MacQueen, Letters to Blackwood, 3 February and 6 February 1831.
91. MacQueen, Letter to Blackwood, 29 May 1831.
92. MacQueen, 'Colonial Empire', p. 744.
93. Ibid. p. 748n.
94. Ibid. p. 752.
95. Quoted in Thomas, 'Pringle v. Cadell', p. 122.
96. Ibid. p. 122.
97. Cadell, Letter to Blackwood, 19 November 1831.
98. Blackwood, Letter to MacQueen, 23 February 1832.
99. MacQueen, Letter to Blackwood, 22 November 1831.
100. MacQueen, Letter to Blackwood, 20 December 1831.
101. The cases were heard back-to-back in February 1833.
102. Blackwood, Letter to MacQueen, 21 November 1831; MacQueen, Letter to Blackwood, 12 December 1833.
103. Robert Blackwood, Letter to MacQueen, 12 May 1834.
104. Lambert, '"Glasgow King"', p. 402.
105. MacQueen, Letter to Blackwood, 3 February 1831.
106. MacQueen, Letter to Blackwood, 29 November 1833.
107. Pringle, Letter to Blackwood, 8 November 1833.

Part V

Blackwoodian Genealogies

Chapter 10

The Politics and Aesthetics of Extraction: Cultural Interventions in *Blackwood's* and the *Imperial*

Kristin Flieger Samuelian

For *Blackwood's* and other magazines of the early 1820s, extraction – selecting or repurposing excerpts from longer texts, often with strategically inserted glosses or commentary – was a method of establishing cultural authority. Selection, extraction and translation are elements of *Blackwood's* allusiveness, means by which the magazine, as David Stewart puts it, engaged in 'a productive, but never unreflective dialogue with a miscellaneous age'.[1] Selections, especially from older works, were a characteristic mode of *Blackwood's* reconstruction of history and declaration of aesthetic values. Mark Schoenfield has identified the system of 'calculated antiquarianism' evident in segments such as the 'Antiquarian Repertory', in which extracts from medieval texts engaged in a 'system of authentication' that included relevant articles elsewhere in an issue and corrective letters in subsequent issues, allowing the magazine to claim precedence over other periodicals by asserting 'a sufficiently nuanced understanding of history as it was'.[2] The 'Antiquarian Repertory' was a feature of the early issues and had 'vanished as a distinct category' by the time the *Edinburgh Monthly Magazine* became *Blackwood's Edinburgh Magazine* in October 1817. Yet, as Schoenfield notes, 'a dialectic between the contemporary moment and the medieval period' continued to be a distinguishing feature of Maga well beyond its early numbers.[3] And the miscellaneous, disingenuously haphazard ordering of the newly reimagined magazine, which made reading, in Philip Flynn's words, 'an exercise in the unexpected', replicated and remediated the very medieval and early modern encyclopaedic genres Blackwood's continued to draw from.[4]

The complex relationship between periodicals and volume miscellanies is traced by Barbara Benedict in *Making the Modern Reader*. Benedict argues that the periodical had been in the process of supplanting the miscellany since the beginning of its ascendancy in the middle of the eighteenth century.[5] Through strategic moves like extraction, *Blackwood's* and other journals signal a relationship that is as much accretive as substitutive. Miscellaneity recurs, tied to the rise of Tory historiography, suggesting that the encyclopaedic mode is not simply a precursor to the periodical but its model and sometimes its source.

In this chapter, I explore instances of strategic extraction in two periodicals, *Blackwood's* and the evangelical *Imperial Magazine*, which was launched just after *Blackwood's* and ran until 1834. The case studies I will highlight from Maga and its lesser-known imitator exemplify how Romantic-era periodicals established their own authority via strategic extraction from miscellanies of the medieval and early modern eras. As I will show, both *Blackwood's* and the *Imperial* employed ludic and authoritative antiquarianism to assert a modern, rational and Protestant British supremacy.[6]

Miscellaneity and Violence in *Blackwood's*, 1819

The *Blackwood's* articles at the heart of this chapter appeared, respectively, in April and October of 1819 as 'Catholic Legends' and 'Extracts from the "Prato Fiorito" on the Vice of Dancing'. Both consist of selections from the seventeenth-century Italian miscellany *Prato Fiorito di Varii Essempi* ('Various Examples from the Field of Flowers'). The Italian title plays on the early modern term for a literary anthology, florilegium: literally a gathering of flowers. The selections and translations are by J. H. Merivale, a highly regarded scholar, translator, poet and sometime contributor to *Blackwood's* and the *Quarterly Review*. Merivale offers these excerpts as 'a tolerable specimen of a multitude of works devoted to similar purposes':

> to those who derive any gratification from contemplating the various modes in which the follies of mankind have, from time to time displayed themselves, and who are not well read in that description of lore which is here unfolded to them, it may be not unamusing, nor

altogether uninstructive, to display a few of the flowers that are to be found together in this field of variegated allurement.[7]

Prato Fiorito was a vernacular work, published in 1608 by Giuseppe Ballardini. It is available in English still only through Merivale's selections in *Blackwood's*. As a florilegium, the *Prato* consisted of extracts – examples – drawn primarily from medieval texts, many of which were themselves miscellanies. Ballardini selects, for instance, from the well-known thirteenth-century encyclopaedia *Speculum Historiale*, compiled by Vincent of Beauvais. Merivale's extracts in *Blackwood's*, then, are quotations of quotations: medieval selections nested within early modern selections framed by a Romantic-era periodical historicism that was, in Schoenfield's phrasing, '*Maga's* foundational discourse'.[8] Mary Franklin-Brown has pointed to what she calls an 'epistemic heterogeneity' in the encyclopaedias of the later Middle Ages.[9] If 'the scholastic encyclopedia compensated for . . . the heteroglot murmur of discourses circulating through the halls of the monastery, the school, the university, and the castle, by gathering them all into a single space', it nonetheless drew 'dissonant discourses, into contact with each other'.[10] One factor of this 'radical heteroglossia' is a certain transfer of agency: the encyclopaedist selects but does not interpret, and 'the liberty and responsibility' of the reader 'increases as the compiler renounces his own'.[11]

Merivale's trick in these two articles is to model the very heteroglossia on display in the sources he cites. His framing in *Blackwood's* replicates the premise of his originals, linking instruction and amusement in an apparently haphazard way: a field of wildflowers rather than a cultivated garden. Merivale's deprecating double negatives – not altogether uninstructive or unamusing – stress this accidental value. As there is no system for gathering the flowers together, so there is no deliberate, coherent meaning to be derived from them. But they might just happen to instruct and amuse anyway. He declares, for instance, that the October article focuses on dance because it was 'the first subject which I happen[ed] to hit upon', then reverses himself by asserting that the topic 'is one which appears to me, of all others, to afford an useful field for reflection at the termination of a London season'.[12]

This seemingly unsystematic system of selection – at once casual and reasoned, random yet on point – was emerging as a favourite Blackwoodian device. An ostensibly chance selection from a text under review could demonstrate the reviewer's confidence in his argument and the text's endorsement of that confidence, as if the reviewer has said, 'I have selected this passage at random, and you can see how excellent – or how dreadful – it is; you can take it from me that the entire text is equally excellent or dreadful.'[13] In the two articles from April and October of 1819, Merivale as translator asserts an implicit authority that undercuts this casualness – sometimes creatively paraphrasing or strategically misquoting, sometimes inserting ironic glosses or wry asides, or framing his selections in ways that shape readerly expectations. The April instalment, 'Catholic Legends', quotes from 'Della usura', the eighth chapter of the *Prato Fiorito*'s first book.[14] The examples here consist primarily of lurid tales of moneylenders at the point of death being dragged to hell by devils; abandoned after death by greedy widows and children; and, in instances of Dantesque *contrapasso*, devoured by dogs or tortured after death by devils thrusting red-hot gold pieces into their vitals. This cabinet of curiosities affords *Blackwood's* primarily Protestant readership the gratification of observing from a distance the violence and absurdity of an unenlightened Catholic and European past. The compression in the title, 'Catholic Legends', stresses this difference and instructs Merivale's readers how to receive the examples. Are they legends – and therefore false – because they are Catholic: in other words, superstitions? Or are they Catholic legends: cautionary tales told within the framework and with the sanction of Catholic doctrine? Either and both, the title suggests: they are not to be taken seriously.

Such sceptical antiquarianism is a legacy from older series, recurring occasionally but persistently in the restructured *Blackwood's*.[15] The pseudo-antiquarianism of the satirical 'Chaldee Manuscript' of October 1817 is an extreme instance, Merivale's deflating editorship a more tempered version.[16] Of the eighteen examples in the *Prato* chapter, he selects the first twelve, often summarising or mixing translation with summary. Like the dancing excerpts, the occasion claimed for these extracts has its own historical particularity, noted in Merivale's hope that their 'fearful examples', along with 'the admirable train of reasoning and reflection by which they are preceded', might 'induce some members of our British legislature to pause before they give their sanction to the sweeping indemnity to usurers, intended by Sergeant Onslow's bill'.[17] The bill he references did not promise sweeping indemnity to usurers, although the claim that it did was used to defeat it politically. Arthur Onslow, Serjeant-at-law and legal adviser to the Crown, sponsored a bill in 1816 to repeal an early eighteenth-century law restricting the rate of interest on loans to five per cent. Onslow's bill had support from both parties, in part because the original restriction was rarely enforced; but despite repeated introductions in 1817, 1818 and multiple times thereafter, it was not passed until 1833. *Blackwood's* appears to have favoured repeal on the grounds that the bill would effectively regulate what was regularly abused. John Galt's September 1821 instalment of 'The Steam-Boat', for instance, contains the anecdote of 'old Joe Brianson', a usurer whose family's refusal to mourn his death recalls the milder of the *Prato* examples.[18] Merivale's prefatory text to the 'Catholic Legends' draws attention to the legends' incoherence – and hence to the incoherence of arguments against the bill. Neither is guided by an admirable train of reasoning and reflection. He concludes by ironically expressing the hope that his examples 'will prove sufficient to deter sinners from the commission of this damnable crime of "teaching money to procreate," and substitute the more effectual terrors of hell in the room of the weak and impotent sanction of legislative enactments'.[19]

If the examples quoted in 'Catholic Legends' highlight the 'unaccountable terrors and apprehensions' of superstition, Merivale's October extracts 'on the Vice of Dancing' seem more concerned with connecting medieval Catholicism to contemporary low-church Protestant enthusiasm.[20] These selections condemn dancing as 'the head and fountain of all sins and wickedness' and describe instances of religious mania, such as the story of the fourteenth-century villagers who, 'like to people possessed with phrenzy, or idiots', danced until they collapsed from exhaustion.[21] Merivale's interruptions and ironic commentary are more frequent here than in the earlier instalment. He begins with a translation from the opening of Book I, Chapter 10, 'Del Ballare', but his editorial intrusions disrupt and break apart the original, calling attention to its disjointedness and illogic:

> 'Truly', observes our pious and eloquent author, 'one of the most singular follies committed by man and woman among the vanities of this world, is light and dishonest dancing; which (as a learned doctor writes) it may well be said, is the head and fountain of all sins and wickedness – or, *at least*' – (and here we may well admire the scrupulous spirit of candour and moderation in argument which distinguishes our author, and forbids him from asserting even so obvious a truism as this, without adding the due qualification,) – 'or, *at least*, of the greater part'.[22]

Merivale parodies the *Prato* author's parenthetical glosses and qualifications (the italics are Merivale's) with an interruption of his own, which is twice as long as those in the original. He then extends his gloss beyond the parenthesis so that his commentary dwarfs the original qualification, taking up most of the remainder of the paragraph:

> To have stated that the sin of dancing is the root and foundation of *all* other sins without exception, few persons would have carried their criticisms so far as to condemn for being hyperbolical; but our author is too conscientious to assert, even as a general proposition, what may be liable to be disproved in particular instances, and I must confess that, in my opinion, he has rather strengthened than detracted ought from his argument by the modest sobriety of the subsequent qualification.[23]

Merivale then follows his own elaborately qualified commentary with an analogy; the qualification that strengthens rather than detracts resembles a well-known exchange between two 'talking statues' during the French occupation of Rome:

> Thus, 'Tutti i Francesi sono ladri' is a national remark, the justness of which no true Englishman could dispute even in this bold uncompromising way of stating it – but how much more forcible is it rendered by the qualifying clause – "Non tutti – ma *Buona Parte*". But to proceed.[24]

Roman talking statues are stone figures plastered with handwritten notes, a practice begun in the sixteenth century as a form of anonymous street political discourse. The pretence is that the notes are statements made by the statues, who have been given names. Merivale references a dialogue staged in 1808 between one of the most famous talking statues, an armless torso named Pasquino, and another statue located about a mile away. The story was recounted in Willem Lodewyk Van-Ess's 1809 biography of Napoleon, and versions of it appear in periodicals and travelogues throughout the nineteenth century. One statue claims, 'All Frenchmen are thieves', and the other responds, punning on Napoleon's name, 'Not all, but the greater part' ('*Buona Parte*').[25] Like the statue's 'not all', the conscientious writer's 'at least' is a qualification that reinforces the original claim, allowing Merivale to endorse both the generalisation and its correction. The style of the paragraph in *Blackwood's* critiques the complex style of the original by replicating it.

Merivale concludes this section with a calculated misrepresentation:

> But to proceed, 'Inasmuch as', adds our author, still following up the same sentence, 'it is impossible ever sufficiently to express how many and great are the evils which spring from dancing; seeing that by it all human feelings are vitiated; the heart itself grows corrupt and hardened; and, finally, the poor and miserable soul utterly perisheth'.[26]

The sentence in the original Italian begins '*Imperoche*', which Merivale translates 'Inasmuch as'. *Imperoche* is an archaic and rarely used conjunction with no direct English equivalent. In Merivale's translation, 'inasmuch as' appears to introduce a dependent clause: dancing is the head and fountain of sins and wickedness, *inasmuch as* it is impossible to sufficiently enumerate its many evils. In the original, '*non si potrebbe*' is the main verb.[27] Merivale obscures the sentence break to increase the appearance of prolixity in his source. Such moves highlight the religious excess in this Counter-Reformation miscellany by connecting it to rhetorical excess. As both translator and editor, Merivale subtly manipulates his materials. Appearing to cede liberty and responsibility to his readers, he retains control.

The notion that a discourse composed of extracts can be fragmentary and yet coherent is central to the structuring of *Blackwood's*, especially as it was reimagined in the years following its 1817 relaunch. In an instance of casual cross-referencing, both of Merivale's pieces on the *Prato Fiorito* appear adjacent to articles that reinforce the British supremacism on display in his editing. The 'Catholic Legends' extracts are followed by a still-unattributed essay 'On the Study of Language, as Essential to the Successful Cultivation of Literature', which begins by arguing that literature, and poetry in particular, is crucial in forming the British character. As 'marble' is to the Greeks and 'the colours of the pencil, and the modulation of sound' to the Italians, so 'the mind of this country has habitually resorted to language for the permanent expression of its power'.[28] What is habitual, however, is also natural: in pursuing any art, nations 'are merely giving more complete developement to the principles of power which Nature has implanted in them in an especial manner; a purpose which may be important to the intellectual and even moral character of a nation'.[29] This issue of *Blackwood's* has already introduced the usury extracts as both ephemeral and keyed to a contemporary political debate. The meditation on language and national character that follows them refashions this tension between the whimsical and the meaningful, between amusement and instruction, into a tension between idiosyncrasy and supremacy. Sculpture, painting and music are all very well as arts go, but only writers 'hold in their hands a power which the mind of the whole people acknowledges, and by which, therefore, they are able to sway the minds of a whole people'.[30] This awesome power belongs properly to the British. The two articles side by side mix a careful non-evaluation of national and natural difference with an assertion of British Protestant superiority.

Merivale's October article is placed alongside similarly nationalist pieces, once again highlighting a dialectic between the topical and the artefactual and enforcing relevance through what appears casual. The 'Vice of Dancing' excerpts are bracketed by two articles, also attributed to Merivale, that offer reminders of European political instability – subtle and not-so-subtle warnings that the recent past might be at once index and shaper of the future.[31] Directly preceding Merivale's contribution, an essay on 'Louis XVIII. and the French Royalists' links the Restoration monarch's 'low' manners, lower tastes and 'sensuality and selfishness' to his early support of the Revolution. After offering the half-hearted disclaimer, 'Observe, we speak of thirty years ago', Merivale asserts, 'it is surely not too much to say, that somewhat of his original and natural indolence and selfishness is likely still to adhere to him.'[32]

The Merivale essay placed on the other side of his *Prato* extracts, titled, 'A European National Tribunal', completes a triad of articles in which European madness is both removed from the post-Waterloo moment – set apart as an artefact or a curiosity – and presented as a continuing threat needing to be offset by British Tory Protestantism. This third article begins by applauding the global alliances of the past 70 years, 'in which the four great powers, Austria, England, Prussia, and Russia, (France being admitted latterly to the conferences,) settled all the questions relative to the division and policy of the great European family'.[33] The parenthetical qualification serves as a backhanded transition to the real aim of the piece, which is not to laud 'the happy result . . . of a general and lasting peace' throughout Europe but to note its precariousness, the result of the French wars themselves and the continuing threat of their re-emergence.

The 'load of expense and financial pressure' placed on Europe in consequence of the Revolutionary and Napoleonic Wars 'may, perhaps, be the germ of new troubles', especially given that both 'have unfortunately concluded with consolidating the triumph of their mischievous principles, by the *impunity* which has been extended to *all*, and the *rewards* which have been lavished on *most* of the surviving criminals of that atrocious revolution'.[34] The essay ends by reversing the complacent optimism of its opening. Europe is not stable, as the Revolution still extends its pernicious influence, and the threat remains that a 'judicial union of . . . sovereigns may' not 'continue to decide upon all national differences, and thus deliver mankind from internal wars for the future'.[35]

This kind of bracketing and cross-referencing was a core feature of a magazine that, in David Stewart's phrase, 'made mixture a principle'.[36] Merivale's allusion to the Napoleonic pun in the dancing article is an instance of seemingly chance cohesiveness, a moment of implicit meta-commentary that draws attention to the work of his article. Talking statues were often placed in squares and urban centres far from their original location; some were artefacts, so old their intended placement and significance were unknown; many were missing limbs or were mere torsos. This geographic and historical decontextualisation, together with their bodily fragmentariness, replicates the studied randomness of extraction and is belied by the intra-urban conversations produced upon them. Merivale's *Blackwood's* articles of April and October 1819 and the miscellanies they draw from are likewise conversations produced upon bodies: bodies torn, desecrated or violated in the usury excerpts, bodies afflicted, enervated or reduced to parts in the dancing excerpts. In this way the two essays on the *Prato Fiorito* help to consolidate *Blackwood's* historical authority by strategically deploying the incoherence, the structural violence, in extraction.

Unearthing Fragments in *The Imperial Magazine*

If the *Blackwood's* phenomenon instantiated the periodical's relationship to older forms of miscellaneity, the example of *The Imperial Magazine* suggests the extent to which that relationship became fixed in print culture as the eighteenth century merged into the nineteenth.

Without the reach or heft of *Blackwood's*, the *Imperial* nevertheless deployed miscellaneity in similar ways, producing meanings not immediately apparent when articles are read separately – tracing, in Benedict's words, 'value in the dynamic comparison'.[37] The *Imperial* was founded in Liverpool in 1819 and was typical of smaller periodicals that imitated the organisational structures of powerhouse miscellanies like *Blackwood's*. Although it was politically and religiously unaffiliated, Charles Brooks Dodson points out that the magazine 'clearly expresses the Dissenters' position'.[38] Its founder and chief editor from 1819 until his death in 1833 was the well-known Methodist theologian Samuel Drew, and the periodical's full title was *The Imperial Magazine or, Compendium of Religious, Moral, and Philosophical Knowledge: Comprehending Religion, Literature, Moral Philosophy, or Ethics, Natural Philosophy, Chemistry, Review of Books, Historical Narrative, Antiquities, Domestic Economy, Trade, Miscellaneous Articles, Poetry*. Foreign missionary reports were a consistent feature and made up roughly 10 per cent of each issue, although Dodson notes that, like other religious periodicals, the journal emphasised what Patrick Scott calls '"timeless" religious articles rather than the topicality of the more famous quarterlies of the time'.[39]

As in *Blackwood's*, history and topicality are co-operating elements in the *Imperial*. Its missionary reports – typically extracts of letters from the Far East or Global South – were often followed by or linked by reference or allusion to travelogue-style accounts of the geography, people and cultures of those places.[40] Both features were also occasionally placed in apparently accidental conversation with medieval and early modern fragments. An 1821 unsigned letter to the editor discussing Bishop John Earle's seventeenth-century miscellany *Microcosmographie* implicitly recognises this linkage as part of the magazine's project. The second to last paragraph ends with the following:

> It is scarcely possible that a work like the Imperial Magazine can render more service to the literary world, than by occasionally publishing extracts from meritorious works, which . . . are not generally known . . . I therefore hope to see many such extracts in the Imperial Magazine.

The paragraph that follows begins without transition:

> I have been informed that you number among your readers, several who have resided at, or visited New Zealand, or who are in possession of

information relating to that interesting country. If so, I hope they will seize this opportunity to lay their information before the public through the medium of your Magazine. So little, comparatively speaking, is known in England respecting these fertile and beautiful islands, that I am certain any remarks upon their climate, soil, animal and vegetable productions, hydrography, minerals, harbours, or inhabitants, will excite much interest, and greatly gratify many of your readers.[41]

This juxtaposition – history and geography casually joined as journalistic aims – was often replicated in the magazine's layout. The *Imperial* had a narrower aim and audience than *Blackwood's*. Its poetry is devotional, and many of its articles are homiletic. Because its travel writing often focused on the newest worlds of Australia and New Zealand, the magazine located evangelicalism within a project of British Protestant imperialism, illustrating what David Hempton calls Methodists' 'conviction that they were marching in tandem with the unstoppable progress of a superior Western civilization'.[42] Nonetheless, the ordering of contributions seems more purposeful than their titles alone would suggest. An 1820 article on 'The Wisdom of God in the Formation of Man', for instance, is followed by a series of entries on science, mathematics and grammar, the first and longest of which, 'Animadversions on "A Dissertation on Geology"', promises 'a connected view of physical with revealed Truth; which ought never to have been separated'.[43]

Sometimes an apparently random sequence of articles will highlight ideas or tropes in the magazine's project. One instance is the February 1820 juxtaposition of two extracts: one from a missionary's letter and one recounting the story of a supposed illegitimate Plantagenet prince. The first reports enthusiastically that the newly built chapels on the island 'of Hueine [Huahine], in the South Seas' cannot house all interested followers. After an overflow congregation caused one sermon to be preached outside the church 'under a grove of cocoa-nut trees', the native king reminded his people 'of their former idolatry', 'what numbers of them fell as sacrifices' and 'how all the poor lived in perpetual fear'.[44] The correspondent who shares this anecdote then supplies the happy conclusion, the 'after' to the king's recollection: 'The morais [sacred sites] are all thrown down, and the gods destroyed; nor do we hear any express a desire after them, but many look back on them with shame.' Among the converts are those who 'were formerly cannibals, and exceedingly savage'.⁴⁵ The work of conversion is ongoing, but the tone of both letter and sermon is complacent, and the most consistent expression of that complacency is through comparative historicising.

That the past is past is essential to the project of missionary work, but, once again, sequencing produces a more complex aggregate meaning. The article following the missionary letters in the February 1820 number of the *Imperial* offers a historical perspective more aligned with *Blackwood's* understanding of the past as, in Schoenfield's terms, 'precursor and uncanny model for the contemporary moment'.⁴⁶ Titled 'Singular Piece of History', this anonymous article consists largely of extracts from Volume II of Francis Peck's miscellany *Desiderata Curiosa* (1732–5). At its core is a section titled 'Richard Plantagenet', which recounts the life of a bricklayer reputed to be the illegitimate son of Richard III. It begins with a description of this royal bricklayer's supposed tomb:

> *Richard Plantagenet.*
> On the north side of the chancel in Eastwell Church, Kent, is an ancient tomb, which has been assigned to Richard Plantagenet, whom a traditional tale represents as having been a natural son of Richard the Third, and whose burial is thus recorded in the register of Eastwell, under the date 1550, 'Richard Plantagenet was buried the 22ij[th] daye of Desember. Anno di supra'.⁴⁷

This article cites documentary evidence: the tomb, the register and the information that the prefixed check mark 'occurs before every subsequent entry in the old register, where the person recorded was of *noble blood*'.⁴⁸ But the connections among these are attenuated or arbitrary. The tomb is linked to the register only by 'a traditional tale', the same one recorded in Peck. The next section, which gives the introduction to Peck's account, is prefaced by the phrase 'in a note under', set off from the main body of the text in a separate paragraph:

> In a note under –
> 'The story of Richard Plantagenet has exercised the pen of several writers: . . .'⁴⁹

'In a note under' are the only words not in quotation marks, but this detail is easy to miss. The fragment, with its dangling preposition, raises the question of what exactly this note is under. The correct answer is under the opening paragraph of the unidentified source, but that preposition directs readerly imagination towards other possibilities. The phrase's proximity to the quote from the register can suggest that the note was pencilled in under the entry, which would offer further evidence of Richard's history and a stylistic link to the tales and legends that have exercised the pens of other writers. The word also mingles rhetorical and ecclesiastical architecture, echoing the possibility that Richard's remains are 'under' the anonymous tomb in the chancel. Architecture is central to this story, which recounts Richard's discovery by Sir Thomas Moyle, whose house he was building and who noticed him sitting apart reading Latin and induced him to tell his story. The editorial insertion – the only one in an article otherwise entirely composed of quotations and extracts – functions not so much to contextualise as to share in the production and dissemination of this secret history. If Merivale's insertions drew attention to the incoherence of his source texts, this one, in its unobtrusiveness, obscures the editor function in a way similar to pseudo 'found manuscripts' like Chatterton's Rowley poems. Absent the introduction and ironic glosses of the *Prato* excerpts, 'A Singular Piece of History' evokes and reproduces popular antiquarianism – offering its seamless singularity as a counter to the fractured present, which for the *Imperial* is emblematised in the chaotic but convertible New World.

The *Imperial*'s emphasis on preservation in 'A Singular Piece of History' offsets the conversion narrative of the missionary letter immediately preceding it. There the morais have been torn down; here the church remains. If the focus in 'Missionary Intelligence' is on how what formerly obtained no longer obtains – superstition, idolatry, cannibalism – the focus here is on a continuity with the past, established by what is – or may be – 'under'. Richard's actual remains, like the note that introduces the excerpt, are ambiguously located: 'We cannot say, whether he was buried in the church, or churchyard'.[50] The question of where the illegitimate prince lies moves this extract towards contemporary debates about interment. In keeping with its Nonconformist character, the *Imperial* published articles and letters advocating the replacement of chancel and churchyard burial sites with cemeteries as a public health measure. A June 1819 letter to the editor from a 'Friend to Decency' condemns 'the manner in which the living are annoyed by the interment of the dead'.[51] Bodies stacked with bodies in crowded churchyards and churches '"grossly familiar" ... consume, side by side' or 'are torn from their graves' with 'brutal indifference'.[52] The attendant 'putrid fumes' that 'cannot but pollute the atmosphere' are the putative health hazard, but Thomas Laqueur points out that science already knew better.[53] 'Rotting bodies, however smelly', Laqueur notes in *The Work of the Dead*, 'did not create a public health crisis.'[54] The focus in this letter is therefore not so much infection as incoherence. The simultaneous dumping and disturbing of so many bodies and body parts is the clear attention-getter and the rhetorical core of the piece. Corpses are at once mangled and mingled, decaying past recognition as human forms and forced into a ghastly intimacy, 'grossly familiar'. The allusion to Robert Blair's 1743 poem 'The Grave' emphasises that it is interment rather than death that is the eraser of rank and the leveller of all.[55] For the *Imperial*'s correspondent, however, such intimacy is more horrifying than consolatory. The notion of an indiscriminate congress of multiple bodies, limbs and organs carries a whiff of licentiousness, suggesting that the pollution of communal space is of more than one kind.

Conversion, preservation and decomposition all constitute ways in which understandings of the past merge with understandings of the present (even conversion's corrective narrative must continually evoke what is past in order to applaud its passing). Their coexistence in these sequential pieces in the *Imperial* enables a dialogism without appearance or declaration of project, allowing the magazine, like *Blackwood's*, to replicate and engage with its era's miscellaneity. A sequence published in May 1821 is another instance of this dialogism. 'Answer to a Query on Burying in Churches' consists primarily of an extract from Charles Wheatly's 1710 *Rational Illustration of the Book of Common Prayer* and offers none of the prurient details of the 1819 letter, commenting only that 'the interment within the shrines of our sanctuaries is detrimental to the health of mankind'.[56] If this letter sidesteps the materiality of death, however, the article immediately preceding it does not. 'An Extract from a Paper concerning the Customs of the New-Zealanders' (subtitled 'New-Zealandman's Head') describes the preserved head 'of a person of the most exalted rank', currently 'in the possession of a gentleman in the city (London)'.[57] Markings visible on the head attest to its original owner's status: 'every step in dignity is marked by a fresh scratch on the face', indicating that the owner 'must have arrived at the *ne plus ultra* of elevation' before losing it.[58] Unlike the mass of bodies decomposing in Christian burial, the head retains not only its form but also its rank and is, moreover, 'much less disgusting than such a preparation might be conceived to be'.[59] In other words, the head is the physical and rhetorical opposite of these English bodies. While its materiality aligns it with the grossly familiar corpses, its singularity and putative royalty connects it with Richard Plantagenet's elusive remains. It may be that Richard's bones mix with those of centuries of parishioners, but they are nowhere in the extract. Instead they are metonymised in the structures with which he is identified – 'the ruins of a building' and 'a well, now filled up', both named for him – that reiterate his exceptionality: a scholar among bricklayers who kept to himself.[60]

The New-Zealandman's head is both synecdoche and artefact. Even as it violates the Protestant norms that undergird the *Imperial*'s project, its disarticulation from its owner's body is cause not for horror but for curiosity. In its partiality and geographic displacement, it resembles talking statues, whose meaning depends in part on their alienation from their original contexts. In other words, the head is an extract – dislocated from its source and put to a new sort of cultural work. Unlike the holy relics of medieval and Counter-Reformation religious practice, the head is valuable not for its intrinsic connection to 'the special dead' but for its utility, for what it can teach Westerners about a culture to be both studied and obliterated.[61] Shrunken heads took their place with ritual sacrifice and cannibalism as cultural practices that illustrated the need for conversion even as they provided matter for scientific enquiry: the 'befores' in the narrative of inevitable Westernisation. Like the former cannibals, the head is shorthand for a savagery safely in the past.

Regular subscribers to the *Imperial*, however, would have already encountered the January 1821 article 'Shocking Instance of Cannibalism, in New Zealand', which supplies the missing middle to the story of Protestant colonisation, infused with all the frisson of the *Prato*'s torture anecdotes or the interment debate's open graves. Tales of cannibalism in the Global South were common throughout the nineteenth century, although substantiation was sketchy. In 'Shocking Instance', typical of such accounts, the eyewitness records a fire, a gathering of Maori and the dismembered body of a boy, 'half roasted' and held by 'a savage-looking man, of gigantic stature, entirely naked, and armed with an axe'.[62] He draws his own conclusions as to the 'melancholy fact', expecting his readers to draw the same.[63] As Gananath Obeysekere points out, anthropophagy as a sign of difference was not only 'justification for . . . conquest' from the sixteenth century onward but was also in the nineteenth century 'what the English reading public relished'.[64] Cannibalism in 'Shocking Instance' is not only a way of othering the South Sea islanders. In its representation, which focuses more on the mangled body than on its consumption, it is a violation that produces its own redemption. Because the missionary convinces the Maori to reassemble and bury the remains instead of eating them, the shocking instance becomes a teachable moment.

The re-membered boy is still missing one arm, and the missionary presumes, on fairly insubstantial evidence, that it has been consumed. When asked, the Maori 'put their fingers to their open mouths, to signify that this part had been already eaten'.[65] Obeyesekere points out that accounts of cannibalism were often shaped by mutual suspicion and confirmation bias. The British assume the Maori are cannibals because cannibalism 'defines the savage'.[66] That assumption dictates the framing of their enquiries, which then leads the Maori to assume that the British practise cannibalism. It is as if, with limited access to each other's culture and language, one side asks, 'Are you cannibals?' and the other side responds, 'Why? Are you?' Each assumes the answer is yes, and subsequent actions confirm their assumptions. As Obeyesekere notes, even the oft-repeated anecdote of Maori pantomiming cannibalism 'is a reaction to the British inquiry that elicited information through similar performative actions'.[67]

An article published in the next number of the *Imperial*, 'Interesting Particulars Respecting New Zealand. – By an Eyewitness', instances the account of 'the roasted youth' as 'most unequivocal' evidence for cannibalism.[68] But this eyewitness adds that the Maori 'discover a surprising willingness to receive information', proof 'that God is preparing them to receive the ever-blessed gospel of peace'.[69] In other words, the boy, like the head, is evidence. His reassembly and burial is an intervention: the substitution of interment for consumption, consigned to the shameful past. What remains of Richard Plantagenet is scattered over a variety of markers both structural and textual. His fragmentation is figurative and discursive, but the literal maintains an atavistic presence in its coincidence with contemporary debates. We do not know if Richard is buried in Eastwell at all, but we also do not know if he is buried in the church or churchyard, or if his bones have been displaced so often over the centuries that they no longer cohere in anything but dust. At the same time, he, along with the boy and the head, is singular, an exception that, like extracts within miscellanies, works long and recent past into current conversations.

Conclusion

In all of the variations and experiments outlined here, extracts, whether in giants like *Blackwood's* or in their lesser imitators, are a sustaining unit of Romantic periodicals. Essentially contractions – the part for the whole – they are also instruments of expansion, helpful when pages are needed or production deadlines are tight. Extracts are both legitimating and dialogic: as artefacts, they work to produce historical authority; within issues, they corroborate and authenticate, but they can also reframe or complicate what had seemed univocal. Their insubstantiality authorises the compiler who selects, excises, translates, interpolates and organises. This authority distinguishes Romantic miscellanies, in their very antiquarianism, from some of their key source material. Franklin-Brown points out that bound medieval encyclopaedias homogenised their content, 'implying that there are no fissures between all these juxtaposed quotations, that the masonry wall is constructed all of a single block'.[70] When extracts are reinserted into monthly magazines – introduced, emended, explained, arranged – they no longer elude the cultural work of their new contexts. The *Blackwood's* extracts in April and October 1819 and those in the *Imperial* offer the distant past as a way of recognising the problematic present. Through them, both journals worked to disarticulate British Protestantism from the enthusiasm and superstition of other worlds and times and to naturalise its supremacy.

Notes

1. Stewart, 'Blackwoodian Allusion', p. 116.
2. Schoenfield, *British Periodicals*, pp. 106, 108.
3. Ibid. p. 107.
4. Flynn, 'Beginning *Blackwood's*', p. 25.
5. Benedict, *Making the Modern Reader*, p. 17. Benedict charts the shift throughout the second half of the eighteenth century from an

understanding of the miscellany as a heteroglossic text in which the reader is 'a collaborative participant in forging literary culture' to the 'seamless' anthology, which structures the reader as 'a recipient of commodified literature' that is 'dehistoricized, depoliticized and hence "timeless", immortal or, in other words, eternally contemporary' (pp. 6–7).

6. 'Ludic' is David Stewart's term for *Blackwood's* allusiveness and its mixture of 'the topical and the canonical' ('Blackwoodian Allusion', p. 116).
7. 'Catholic Legends', p. 52. Alan Lang Strout attributed the article to Merivale, adding a '?' in parentheses (p. 51). In 1965, Brian Murray ('The Authorship') confirmed Merivale's authorship, noting that Blackwood had signalled his approval in a letter to Merivale: 'Confirmed by letter of Blackwood to Merivale (13/4/19). Blackwood is delighted with the Popish Legends which will appear in this number' (p. 144).
8. Schoenfield, *British Periodicals*, p. 100.
9. Franklin-Brown, *Reading the World*, p. 215.
10. Ibid. pp. 216–17.
11. Ibid. pp. 216, 266.
12. 'Extracts', p. 43.
13. 'We shall do little more than select a few passages of the most decisive character – nothing doubting that these will be more than enough to induce our readers to follow the whole argument through the luminous exposition of the book itself' ([Lockhart?], 'Remarks on Mr Mitford's View', p. 445). On Watt's *Bibliotheca Britannica*: 'we shall select two articles, from which they may be able to form an accurate notion of the execution of the Bibliotheca Britannica; – and we shall make our selections almost entirely at random' ([Lockhart?], 'Remarks on Dr Watt's Bibliotheca Britannica', p. 554).
14. This chapter draws in part upon Thomas of Cantimpré's thirteenth-century bestiary *Bonum universale de apibus*.
15. The number for August 1818 includes a reproduction of a letter from Nell Gwynn, dated 1684 (p. 547); the September 1818 number includes 'Selections from Athenaeus' in an anonymous translation edited by Murray (p. 650).
16. The thinly veiled attack on Archibald Constable and the *Edinburgh Review* begins by declaring that the 'present age seems destined to witness the recovery of many admirable pieces of writing, which had been supposed to be lost for ever' ([Hogg et al.], 'Chaldee Manuscript', p. 89). In the *Prato* articles, the dialectical non-opposite to the present is not the medieval period but the Counter-Reformation of the sixteenth and seventeenth centuries.
17. 'Catholic Legends', p. 52.

18. 'The Steam-Boat, No. VII', pp. 169–70. John Wilson's review of John Bull's 'Letter to Lord Byron' calls Bentham's defence of the bill 'a work bearing marks of intellect far superior to the production of an average Edinburgh Reviewer' (p. 421).
19. 'Catholic Legends', p. 54.
20. Hume, 'Of Superstition and Enthusiasm', p. 73. Ann Taves argues that Hume 'associated superstition with Catholicism, High Church Anglicanism, old-fashioned Toryism, absolutism, and divine-right monarchism, and enthusiasm with Puritanism, personal autonomy, individual rights, and the absence of mediating factors between God and man' (*Fits, Trances, and Visions*, p. 43).
21. 'Extracts', p. 44.
22. Ibid. pp. 43–4.
23. Ibid. p. 44.
24. Ibid.
25. Van-Ess, *The Life*, p. 79. Van-Ess translates 'thieves' as 'rascals', but in most references, including Merivale's, it is 'thieves'.
26. 'Extracts', p. 44.
27. '*Imperoche non si potrebbe mai à bastanza esprimere quanti mali di quì ne avvengono*' (*Prato Fiorito*, p. 64). I am indebted to my colleague at George Mason University, Kristina Olson, for pointing out this detail.
28. Anon., 'On the Study', pp. 55–6.
29. Ibid. p. 55.
30. Ibid. p. 56.
31. The articles are both signed 'M'. Strout tentatively attributes them to Merivale (*Bibliography*, pp. 59–60).
32. [Merivale?], 'Louis XVIII', pp. 42–3.
33. [Merivale?], 'A European National Tribunal', p. 45.
34. Ibid. p. 46.
35. Ibid.
36. Stewart, 'Blackwoodian Allusion', p. 116.
37. Benedict, *Making the Modern Reader*, p. 12.
38. Dodson, 'The Imperial Magazine', p. 186.
39. Ibid. Dodson is quoting Scott, 'Victorian Religious Periodicals', p. 327.
40. See, for example, the articles 'Missionary Intelligence. – Return of Mr. Brown from St. Domingo' and 'Character and Manners which Prevail in the Republican Part of St. Domingo: Drawn from Recent Observation', which appeared back to back in the first issue of March 1819.
41. Anon., 'Observations', col. 844.
42. Hempton, *Methodism*, p. 208. The *Imperial*'s focus on the 'uncivilised' Pacific islanders allows it to sidestep scepticism about liberal Whiggish colonial expansion, particularly in Asia, driven by commercial interests

and that, for *Blackwood's*, too often entailed a 'lack of respect for antiquity' (Jarrells, 'Tales of the Colonies', p. 270).
43. Anon., 'Animadversions', col. 19.
44. Borff, 'Extract of a Letter', cols 59–60.
45. Ibid. col. 61.
46. Schoenfield, *British Periodicals*, p. 100.
47. Anon., 'Singular Piece', col. 62.
48. Ibid. col. 62.
49. Ibid.
50. Ibid.
51. Anon., 'Bad Effects', col. 453.
52. Ibid. col. 453.
53. Ibid. col. 454.
54. Laqueur, *Work of the Dead*, p. 227. Laqueur argues that the 'main reason why the old regime of the dead could not sustain itself' had less to do with overcrowding and public hygiene than with the influence of dissenting religious groups like Congregationalists, Baptists and Methodists: 'Nonconformists sitting on parish vestries opposed using public money to support an established Church in which they did not worship and churchyards in which their dead were often made to feel unwelcome' (p. 228).
55. Lines in Blair's poem read, 'Under ground / *Precedency's* a Jest; Vassal and Lord / Grossly familiar, Side by Side consume' (lines 229–31), highlighting, as Christopher Hamlin notes, the 'egalitarianism' in 'eighteenth-century expressions of postmortem consumption'. 'Even more than death, rot is the great leveler' ('Good and Intimate Filth', p. 11).
56. Anon., 'Answer to a Query', col. 416.
57. 'Extract from a Paper', cols 413–14.
58. Ibid. col. 414.
59. Ibid. col. 413.
60. Anon., 'Singular Piece', col. 65.
61. Laqueur, *Work of the Dead*, p. 47. Laqueur notes that, after the Reformation, 'Catholics embraced bones as never before' (p. 48).
62. Anon., 'Shocking Instance', cols 27–8.
63. Ibid. col. 27.
64. Obeyesekere, *Cannibal Talk*, pp. 1, 28.
65. Anon., 'Shocking Instance', col. 28.
66. Obeyesekere, *Cannibal Talk*, p. 34.
67. Ibid. p. 53.
68. Anon., 'Interesting Particulars', col. 132.
69. Ibid. cols 132–3.
70. Franklin-Brown, *Reading the World*, p. 236.

Chapter 11

The Challenge of Longevity: *Blackwood's* as a Post-Romantic Periodical

Joanne Shattock

Let us thank Heaven, whatever may be the uncertainties of modern times, no one can entertain any doubt as to the principles of Maga. *Our trumpet has never given forth an uncertain sound:* and from our golden age, with its Ambrosial Nights, unto this ordinary to-day, which has only political articles, and knows not the inspiration either of Christopher or his Shepherd, our worst enemy cannot accuse us of indifference to the affairs of the State.[1]

Time spared not Tickler, nor the Shepherd, nor O'Doherty, nor North himself; and Time took me one day by the ear, and, showing me the dun-coloured monthly pamphlet, said to me, 'Behold how stupid *Blackwood's Magazine* has grown!' The present number is marked DCXXIII. A ripe old age; but how desperately dull is that six hundred and twenty-third number! I suppose it is rank sedition to say so; but the time is sure to come, sooner or later, when it becomes a duty to talk sedition, and when sedition is merely the truth.[2]

Both of these quotations from mid-nineteenth-century articles could be interpreted as supporting a popular narrative of the gradual decline of *Blackwood's Edinburgh Magazine* after its golden age. It is a narrative implicit in David Finkelstein's carefully researched and well-documented *The House of Blackwood: Author–Publisher Relations in the Victorian Era* (2002) and in some of the essays in his collection *Print Culture and the Blackwood Tradition 1805–1930* (2006). The idea that *Blackwood's* had had a glorious period and that the present was different was in the minds of insiders, at least, at mid-century. Exactly when the golden age ended was less clear – perhaps after its first decade, with the transition to a Victorian *Blackwood's* signalled in the 1826 preface, as David Latané and others have argued.[3] Another natural break occurred after the death of William Blackwood I in October 1834, which in turn brought to a close the *Noctes Ambrosianae*, which Margaret Oliphant later described as 'one of the most admirable mediums for the "criticism of life" that the world has ever known – as well as, perhaps, the most popular and living series of periodical literary sketches ever given to the world'.[4]

Whenever this golden age ended, there is no doubt that William Blackwood I (1776–1834) had been in the enviable position of having created a magazine that new ones sought to emulate – the *London Magazine* (1820–9) and *Fraser's Magazine* (1830–82) are the obvious examples – whereas his successors, particularly John Blackwood (1818–79), who took over in 1845, had the more difficult task of sustaining a by now well-known brand in a very different and volatile market. Rather than setting the agenda, as his father had done, John Blackwood had to withstand and respond to challenges from new house magazines, notably *Macmillan's Magazine* (1859–1907) and the phenomenally successful *Cornhill* (1860–1975), the magazine of publishers Smith Elder. They were soon followed by a raft of others, many of whom now sought to emulate not *Blackwood's* but the *Cornhill*.

John Blackwood produced the magazine in an era when the number of potential readers had vastly increased, production and transportation costs had fallen, and the so-called Taxes on Knowledge were in the process of being repealed.[5] Competition came not only from the magazines established by rival publishing houses but potentially from other directions. Laurel Brake has noted dips in circulation in the 1860s and has argued that *Blackwood's* lost readers first to the more lively, market-savvy *Cornhill* and *Macmillan's* and then to new-style monthly reviews, including the *Fortnightly* (1865–1954), the *Contemporary Review* (1866–1988) and the *Nineteenth Century* (1877–1901).[6] It is also possible that Dickens's new weekly, *Household Words* (1850–9), and its successor, *All the Year Round* (1859–95), made inroads on *Blackwood's* circulation due to the high quality of the original fiction they serialised.

In this chapter I want to look closely at the contents and the management of the magazine in the decades following William Blackwood I's death in 1834 and to plot the transition of *Blackwood's* from a Romantic to a Victorian periodical. In doing this I will be addressing one of the questions posed by the essays in this collection: whether a distinctive approach is needed for the study of Romantic-era periodicals rather than regarding them as a subset of the nineteenth-century periodical press as a whole. The 'challenge of longevity' of my title is also a challenge that confronts scholars of Romantic-era periodicals: whether it is legitimate or practicable to study them as a discrete and distinctive field or whether they must be considered in the context of their wider histories, many of which, like *Blackwood's,* extended into the next century.

Maga after William Blackwood I

To return to the quotations at the beginning of this chapter: the first is from Margaret Oliphant's anonymous review of the third and fourth volumes of Macaulay's *History of England*, a review in which she had been guided by John Blackwood, who was keen to give the Whig historian, once a Member of Parliament for Edinburgh, his just deserts in his staunchly Tory magazine. The young Oliphant was no doubt anxious to please but she also articulated what others felt, that if Maga was less illustrious than it had been, at least its political principles were intact. And the political dimension of *Blackwood's* would distinguish it from its new competitors.[7]

The second quotation comes from an essay by G. A. Sala written in response to an attack on sensation fiction, and on Mary Elizabeth Braddon in particular, in an anonymous review in *Blackwood's* in September 1867. The review was by Margaret Oliphant, although Sala seems not to have been aware of this at the time. His purpose was to defend Braddon against what he saw as a dishonest argument that English fiction had always been written for a family readership and that the new vogue for sensation, with its dubious morality, showed the pernicious influence of French fiction. Oliphant's argument and Sala's response are less important here than the fact that an anonymous article in *Blackwood's* in 1867 was judged to have delivered a serious blow to a popular writer's reputation, one that required a public response. Clearly, then, in the 1860s the magazine still retained its critical clout and its power to offend, provoke and spark controversy, albeit in a very different climate to that of 1817 and the decade that followed. Oliphant's January 1896 review of *Jude the Obscure*, 'The Anti-Marriage League', could be regarded as a later example of Maga's continuing power to generate controversy. On this occasion Oliphant feared she might be accused of libel, having added her initials at the end of her review.[8]

Alexander Blackwood (1806–45), William Blackwood's eldest son, took over the magazine in October 1834 with no outward sign of change. The succession was seamless. Although anonymity remained the magazine's policy, the regular contributors were familiar names to those in the know: Wilson, De Quincey, Maginn, Archibald Alison, Douglas Jerrold, David Macbeth Moir, George Moir, Charles Neaves, William Henry Smith, George Croly and Frederick Hardman. Alexander recruited two newcomers: the poet and critic W. E. Aytoun and the Rev. William Lucas Collins, both of whom would become prolific contributors over many years. There was new serial fiction: Samuel Warren's highly successful *Ten Thousand a Year* (October 1839–August 1841) and Samuel Phillips's novel *Caleb Stukeley* (February 1842–May 1843) and his tale *The Banking House* (November 1843–January 1844).

De Quincey's second paper on 'Murder as One of the Fine Arts' (November 1839) and Part I of 'Suspiria de Profundis' (a sequel to the *Confessions of an English Opium Eater*, March 1845) plus Wilson's essays 'Christopher in his Cave' (August 1838), 'Christopher among the Mountains' (September 1838) and 'Christopher in his Alcove' (April 1839) could be interpreted as offering a homage to the past but also reassurance, a positive indication of the continuation of the miscellany tradition and of the healthy proportion of creative writing in the magazine. It is also worth noting the number of women who wrote for *Blackwood's* during Alexander's 10-year editorship: the poets Caroline Bowles Southey and the young Elizabeth Barrett (later Browning); the novelists Anna Elizabeth Bray, Catherine Gore and Caroline Clive; and two formidable reviewers Mary Margaret Busk and Hannah Lawrance. Alexander added two major recruits at the end of his term, the novelist Edward Bulwer-Lytton and the journalist George Henry Lewes, both of whom would become crucial to John Blackwood's editorship.

John Blackwood's Magazine (1845–79)

The transition from Alexander to John Blackwood in 1845 was equally seamless. Like Alexander, John had been in training for a role in the publishing house from an early age. He used the period from 1840, when he was in charge of the firm's new London office, to make contacts in the political world, the most important of which was J. T. Delane, editor of *The Times*, and in literary London, the most significant of whom was Thackeray. John was good-looking, genial, gregarious and at home in the predominantly masculine world of the magazine and the publishing house. He would soon prove equally at ease with women authors and contributors. He was not an intellectual, but he became an astute judge of what constituted a Blackwood book, what would sell and in which format, and what would, and would not, work in *Blackwood's Magazine*. Much later, Margaret Oliphant was to say of him, 'his excellent judgment had the additional advantage of being unprofessional, not that of a competitor and fellow-craftsman, but of a man of the world, living in the atmosphere of the reader rather than of the writer'. 'Few better or bolder critics ever existed', she added.[9] George Eliot's reference to 'my dear lost Friend' on learning of his death in 1879 was heartfelt and genuine.[10] He had earned her respect.

John Blackwood's attempts to sustain the magazine's reputation as a fiction-bearing miscellany and a showcase for Blackwood authors, a reputation which William Blackwood had built, met with varying degrees of success. On taking over the editorship and then the firm in 1852, he continued his brothers' practice of making regular visits to London to oversee the London office and to keep in touch with Blackwood authors and contributors as well as to recruit new ones. Sociability was a key to his style of editorship, as it had been to his father's. He entertained male colleagues to dinner at the Burlington Hotel in Cork Street and visited women authors at their homes. But equally significant was the fact that although he had a toehold in London literary and political circles he was not really a part of those worlds.

Nevertheless, the contacts he established among writers and in the Conservative Party were crucial to the success of the publishing house and magazine. One of the most important was Bulwer-Lytton, whose political career was in the ascendant in the 1850s and who rivalled Dickens as the nation's most popular novelist. The serialisation of his domestic novel *The Caxtons* (April 1848–October 1849) was followed by *My Novel* (September 1850–January 1853), a lengthy saga of English provincial life, and then *What Will He Do with It* (June 1857–January 1859). In 1852 Blackwood recruited Margaret Oliphant, inaugurating a 45-year association with the firm during the course of which she became increasingly influential.

But the most important recruit in the 1850s was undoubtedly the author of *Scenes of Clerical Life*, introduced by her partner, G. H. Lewes, as his anonymous 'friend'. As the broker of what became a 20-year relationship between George Eliot and Blackwood and Sons, Lewes was extremely important to the publishing house and for a short period to the magazine. He and John Blackwood were to become the two most influential agents in Eliot's writing career. As David Finkelstein has demonstrated, George Eliot was quite simply the House of Blackwood's most important acquisition in the mid-nineteenth century. But, apart from *Scenes of Clerical Life* (serialised in 1857), her story 'The Lifted Veil' (July 1859) and the curious 'Address to Working Men by Felix Holt' (January 1868), she was of little help to the magazine. Had things worked out differently, the serialisation of *Adam Bede* in 1859, followed by *The Mill on the Floss* in 1860, might have transformed the fortunes of *Blackwood's Magazine* at a crucial point in its history.

The delicate relationship between the sensitive but determined novelist and the discerning but pragmatic publisher evolved through their regular correspondence, which began in the autumn of 1856. Blackwood's nervousness over the subject matter of 'Janet's Repentance', the third of the 'Scenes', led Eliot to bring the series to a premature conclusion. Yet she began *Adam Bede* in the full expectation that it would be serialised in Maga. It was Blackwood's squeamishness over the plot surrounding the seduction of Hetty Sorrel and possibly Eliot's treatment of Methodism, both of which he thought might offend the magazine's readers, that led to the decision to publish the novel in three volumes, with spectacular critical and commercial success. The question of serialisation was raised with *The Mill on the Floss* but, conscious of Eliot's dislike of its pressures, Blackwood deferred to her wishes and published it in the conventional format.[11]

It was all the more ironic that Eliot should then be poached by George Smith to serialise *Romola* in the *Cornhill* in 1862–3. Blackwood, although inwardly furious, resolved not to pick a quarrel, which paid off in the long run because she returned to Blackwood and Sons for the rest of her writing career. But in the early 1860s he must have viewed the contents of both the *Cornhill* and *Macmillan's* magazines, in contrast to *Blackwood's*, with dismay. By any measure these two new 'shilling monthlies' – so called because of their competitive price compared with the two shillings and sixpence charged by traditional magazines – outflanked and outshone *Blackwood's*. They also outsold it. George Smith appointed Thackeray as his editor so that his name would attract talent, which it did. The list of serial fiction in the first five years of the *Cornhill* was stellar: Trollope's *Framley Parsonage*, *The Small House at Allington* and *The Struggles of Brown, Jones and Robinson*; Thackeray's *Lovel the Widower*, *Denis Duval* and *The Adventures of Philip*; Elizabeth Gaskell's *Cousin Phillis* and *Wives and Daughters*; Eliot's *Romola* (which was not the success Smith had hoped for); and Wilkie Collins's *Armadale*. In addition to these novels and stories, the *Cornhill* published essays by Matthew Arnold and serialised Thackeray's *Roundabout Papers* and *The Four Georges* and Ruskin's *Unto This Last*.

Initially *Macmillan's* did not give fiction the high priority it received in the *Cornhill*. The firm's fiction list was less impressive than it would become. The magazine did, however, serialise novels by Thomas Hughes, Henry and Charles Kingsley, Charlotte Yonge, Margaret Oliphant and R. D. Blackmore. Where *Macmillan's* outperformed *Blackwood's* was in the high-profile contributors it engaged in other fields, a feature made all the more significant because contributions were signed. *Macmillan's* articles in the first five years were written by, among others, T. H. Huxley, Herbert Spencer, Matthew Arnold, Coventry Patmore, Leslie Stephen, W. M. Rossetti, the theologian and mathematician William Whewell, the historian G. O. Trevelyan and its Christian Socialist supporters F. D. Maurice, J. M. Ludlow and the Kingsleys. It also engaged a number of eminent women writers in these years, including Frances Power Cobbe, Harriet Martineau, Dinah Craik, Caroline Norton and the poet Augusta Webster.

Blackwood's serial fiction for the same period could not compete. Of the novelists, only Charles Lever was a major figure, and by the 1860s, as John Sutherland has shown, the sums he could command for a novel were in decline.[12] Laurence Oliphant's *Piccadilly* was serialised in 1865 and Margaret Oliphant's the 'Chronicles of Carlingford', a series of short stories and novels that would make her reputation, between 1861 and 1866. John Blackwood secured Trollope's *Nina Balatka* for serialisation in 1866–7 and *Linda Tressell* in 1867–8, but Trollope's going rate, like Lever's, had fallen, and the two novels, which at Blackwood's suggestion were published anonymously, were not a success.[13] R. D. Blackmore and Charles Reade became *Blackwood's* authors in the 1870s, John Blackwood's last decade. He accepted Trollope's *John*

Caldigate (serialised April 1878–June 1879) and *Dr Wortle's School* (May–December 1880) but rejected *Ayala's Angel* (1881), much to Trollope's mortification.[14] Bulwer-Lytton's last unfinished novel, *The Parisians*, was serialised in 1873. Compared with the contents of rival magazines, *Blackwood's* serial fiction in the 1860s and 1870s consisted of novels in the 'second division' of contemporary fiction.

For reviews and articles, John Blackwood drew on a small group of regular contributors each of whom had a range of expertise. It was an extension of the way his father had conducted the magazine. In addition to Lewes, he recruited the critic E. S. Dallas, the historian John Hill Burton and the economist Bonany Price. They couldn't, however, match the talent produced by Macmillan; moreover, *Blackwood's* articles were still published anonymously. The all-important political articles, usually one in each number, were assigned to a small group of writers, none of whom were national figures, although their political sources, within the government and the Conservative Party, were at a high level.[15]

Meanwhile, the competition had intensified. New monthlies, many of them publishers' house magazines, were springing up almost annually: *Temple Bar* (1860–1906), the project of John Maxwell, was edited by G. A Sala and sub-edited by Edmund Yates. It was not illustrated, but in other respects sought to compete with the *Cornhill* in eschewing politics and specialising in fiction. *St James's Magazine* (1861–1900), also promoted by John Maxwell, the partner of Mary Elizabeth Braddon, sought to rival the *Cornhill*, but it included articles on foreign affairs and social questions although it was not party political. *Belgravia* (1867–99), edited by Braddon, serialised her own novels and also those of Thomas Hardy, Wilkie Collins, Mark Twain and Charles Reade. *Saint Paul's* (1867–74) was edited briefly by Trollope, during which period it serialised his political novel *Phineas Finn* (1867–9). But, despite its celebrity editor, *Saint Paul's* could not withstand the competition and failed after seven years. *Tinsley's Magazine* (1867–92) was the house magazine of Tinsley Brothers, newcomers to fiction publishing and a firm that Blackwood and Sons considered downmarket. In addition, *London Society* (1862–98), the *Victoria Magazine* (1863–80) and *Argosy* (1865–1901) were all potential competitors for *Blackwood's*.

Contrary to Laurel Brake's argument, there is no incontrovertible evidence that the new monthly reviews, the *Fortnightly*, the

Contemporary and the *Nineteenth Century* –powerful as they were, and game changers in the development of the review as a genre – made serious dents in *Blackwood's* reader base in the 1860s. *Blackwood's Magazine* remained a miscellany, but in a Victorian mode, the house journal of William Blackwood and Sons, whose priority was to promote Blackwood authors and Blackwood books. Its political articles, which ended each number, were important and distinguished *Blackwood's* from the new generation of monthly magazines, but John Blackwood's aspirations for his magazine were modest. He showed no inclination to ape the new monthly reviews by turning it into a wide-ranging organ of opinion. Book reviews now featured prominently, covering a spectrum of subjects but without a commitment to review books in all categories regularly, as was the usual practice of reviews. The one new monthly review which seriously damaged *Blackwood's* circulation was the *National Review*, established in 1883, four years after John Blackwood's death. The *National* attracted some of *Blackwood's* contributors, both political and literary, and, more significantly, eroded its position as a key Conservative Party organ.

A much better comparator for *Blackwood's*, from the mid-century onward, was *Fraser's Magazine*, an old-style monthly miscellany, which had, after all, been modelled on its Scottish predecessor in its political agenda and its penchant for wit, controversy and, at times, scurrility.[16] As the editors of the *Wellesley Index* point out, *Fraser's* effected the transition from a Regency magazine to a Victorian one in 1847, when the ownership passed to J. W. Parker and Son. Its political stance changed along with its personnel and its polemical style. *Fraser's* carried on until 1882, but it was in effect two different publications before and after 1847.[17] Although it was owned by J. W. Parker from 1847 to 1863, and after that by Longman, it was never a house magazine.

How then did *Blackwood's* survive first the transition from the Romantic to the Victorian era and then the remorseless competition of newer monthlies? As I noted earlier, John Blackwood saw the magazine's role as showcasing the firm's authors and books, serialising novels and tales first in the magazine and then ringing the changes by a well-tested sequence of three-, two- and one-volume reprints.[18] His often-quoted comment in response to George Smith's offer of £10,000 for *Romola*, that he did not believe in paying 'wild sums' for books, summed up his attitude.¹⁹ Under his direction Blackwood and Sons became a leading publishing house.²⁰ The magazine was an extension of the publishing firm; the two ran in tandem rather than as separate enterprises. John Blackwood had no desire to create a sensation with *Blackwood's Magazine*; it was sufficient that it promoted the firm's publications. This is borne out in the correspondence with his brother, Major William Blackwood (1810–61), and in the letters that passed between them and the London and Edinburgh office managers. Blackwood books were promoted in the magazine by carefully timed reviews. A select group of regular contributors were pressed into service to review one another's books and were also encouraged to place reviews of Blackwood books in other journals. And here the firm's policy of anonymity was extremely helpful.

As John Blackwood saw it, the Blackwood brand may have been in need of refreshing, but it was essentially sound. Compared to the large number of contributors recruited by other magazines, Maga's regular contributors were a kind of extended family, a Victorian version of William Blackwood's original cohort. The House of Blackwood in return was loyal to its contributors. One unusual feature of the magazine was the number of obituaries it published. In marking the passing of its faithful servants, the magazine tacitly acknowledged that an old order was giving way to the new. John Wilson's death in 1854 was marked by two commemorative articles, George Moir's 'The Death of Professor Wilson' (April 1854) and Samuel Warren's 'A Few Personal Recollections of Christopher North' (December 1854), an early sign that the magazine would seek to keep the legendary years alive, and to capitalise on them. There were obituaries of 'Delta' (David Macbeth Moir) in 1851, W. E. Aytoun in 1865, the elder Archibald Alison in 1867, George Moir in 1871, Charles Neaves in 1873 and Samuel Warren in 1877. The deaths of current distinguished contributors, Lever in 1872, Bulwer-Lytton in 1873, George Eliot in 1880 and Trollope in 1882, the last two after John Blackwood's own death, were marked by detailed and appreciative tributes.

One modern publishing practice which neither John Blackwood nor his successor encouraged was that of collecting and republishing articles from the magazine in volume format. One exception was the republication of a collection of the *Noctes Ambrosianae* in 1855, but this was exclusively of John Wilson's contributions, and only those written after 1826. G. H. Lewes's *Sea-Side Studies* (1858) and *The Physiology of Common Life* (1859–60) consisted of articles first published in the magazine and were enthusiastically promoted by Blackwood, but in general he resisted the trend to republication which was practised elsewhere by high-profile reviewers and essayists like Leslie Stephen, Matthew Arnold and T. H. Huxley.[21] Margaret Oliphant, whose series of biographical essays, *Historical Sketches of the Reign of George II* (1869), had been planned and written with volume publication in mind, distinguished between the republication of significant essays and what she regarded as opportunistic 'bookmaking' by her fellow reviewers. She lambasted Grant Allen, Robert Buchanan, Walter Pater and Arnold among others for their practice of republishing book reviews, arguing memorably in a July 1879 review of Arnold's *Mixed Essays* that a magazine was a 'half-way house between the ephemeral and the permanent'.[22] The words were hers, but they became enshrined as the firm's policy.

The Next Generation: William Blackwood III (1879–1912)

Although it took some time to sink in, John Blackwood's death in 1879 was the end of an era. Margaret Oliphant rightly identified him as 'perhaps the most gifted of Mr Blackwood's sons'.[23] His successor, William Blackwood III (1836–1912), the son of Major William Blackwood, had joined the firm in 1857 but inherited neither his grandfather's nor his uncle's commercial instincts, nor, it soon became apparent, their judgement when it came to spotting and nurturing winners. He struggled initially in taking control of the magazine, relying on 'old Langford', Joseph Langford, the long-serving manager of the London office, and wondering aloud as to what 'my uncle' would have done as problems arose or decisions had to be made. His emotional response to the news of George Eliot's death in 1880, a year after John Blackwood's, was a palpable indication of his vulnerability and his sense of inadequacy in his new role.[24]

Despite his initial anxieties, William Blackwood III saw the magazine and the firm through to 1912, his term just a year short of John Blackwood's 34 years at the helm. His lapses in judgement during his long directorship have been well documented. Having engaged

Wilde, Hardy and Conan Doyle for the magazine, he then did not encourage them. He turned down Stevenson's last novel because the asking price was too high. His greatest coup was Conrad, but, having serialised *Heart of Darkness* and *Lord Jim*, he was not able to keep him.

Yet for all his shortcomings, there were several important developments over which William Blackwood III presided as an editor and manager. First, the magazine moved gradually to a policy of signature, belatedly catching up with the times. Second, under his watch *Blackwood's* engaged a phenomenal number of women writers. In the opening number of her book review series 'The Old Saloon', in January 1887, Margaret Oliphant had called up the shades of the magazine's past, musing on the portraits on the walls of the saloon at 45 George Street, the firm's Edinburgh premises since 1830. She then alluded to the magazine's present. 'We are not formed like Jove and Christopher. Our dart is not one made out of the lightning-shaft, as was Lockhart's in his youth', she reflected. 'Not, however, that Maga sings small, though her present representative may be modest', she wrote, indicating that these were different times. She referred to contributions that now came 'from other distant regions as far as British empire extends, from many a manly pen, such as Maga, with a sound and wholesome partiality for her soldiers and sailors, has always loved', an acknowledgment of the magazine's focus on military and colonial subjects and its growing colonial readership. She then added, 'She has her ladies too, but, shall we own it? perhaps loves them less.'[25] It may have been a rueful comment about her own position in the magazine's inner circle, but it flew in the face of the facts. In the 1880s and 1890s the magazine became a nursery for younger women writers, many of whom went on to become important novelists and reviewers. David Finkelstein has written of a network of women novelists who were recruited to *Blackwood's* at the turn of the century, including Beatrice Harraden, Katherine Cecil Thurston, Maud Diver, Margaret Todd (Graham Travers), Somerville and Ross.[26] The full list of *Blackwood's* female contributors was impressive in both number and quality.

The opening of Oliphant's first 'Old Saloon' article was a rehearsal for a much bigger project. William Blackwood III had sound instincts when it came to capitalising on the firm's and the magazine's distinguished past and celebrating its place in the nation's cultural history.

This, I suggest, is the third of his achievements. In Margaret Oliphant he had an able lieutenant; indeed, some of the impetus came from her. Oliphant bought into the Blackwood ethos in 1851 at the age of 23, when she was introduced to Major William Blackwood through David Macbeth Moir, the 'Delta' of the magazine's early days, and at the same time met the aging John Wilson. She read up on the magazine's history when writing her *Literary History of England* (1882) and asked for copies of the early numbers when preparing her 'Old Saloon' series.

She was the obvious choice to write the firm's history, a project first envisaged by John Blackwood. Oliphant was by no means an impartial or disinterested historian, which is what makes her two-volume *Annals of a Publishing House* (1897) unique.[27] It is in some ways a record of her own relationship with the House of Blackwood, a response to the memories that came flooding back when she read through the boxes of uncatalogued but initially sifted letters and documents that were sent to her from the George Street office. Her grief over the death of her only remaining child in 1894 delayed the start of the project until 1895. Its eventual publication followed closely on the heels of her own death in June 1897, which in turn coincided with the celebrations to mark Victoria's Diamond Jubilee the same month.

William Blackwood III used these unforeseen but enabling circumstances to advantage. He wrote a preface to the *Annals* in which he paid fulsome tribute to Oliphant's long service to Blackwood and Sons. She was given an impressive send-off in the magazine that included a generous obituary partly written by Blackwood himself, an article on 'Mrs Oliphant as a Novelist' (September 1897) and a review of the *Annals* (December 1897) entitled 'Maga and her Publishers'. A year later, in February 1899, there was a double issue of the magazine to celebrate its 1000th number, containing a spoof *Noctes*. It was as though William Blackwood had deliberately seized on the conjunction of the publication of the *Annals*, the Queen's Diamond Jubilee, Oliphant's death and the 1000th number to recall and celebrate past glories, to pay tribute to the firm's and the magazine's resilience in the face of unprecedented change and to indulge in some collective self-congratulation. There was a sense of looking backward, with nostalgia and some pride, but not much sense of looking forward. Although it was generally agreed that the spoof *Noctes* fell flat – it wasn't all that funny – the 1000th number contained considerable strengths:

part I of Conrad's *Heart of Darkness*, a 'Looker-on' by Frederick Greenwood (a resurrection of the title of Oliphant's last series for the magazine) and articles by G. W. Steevens, Alexander Innes Shand and Charles Whibley. The century may have been coming to a close, but the magazine would carry on until 1980.

Conclusion

Most of the Victorian magazines that challenged *Blackwood's* in the 1860s had either ceased publication by the turn of the century or would soon do so, with the exception of the *Cornhill*, which continued until 1975. The full history of *Blackwood's Magazine* in the twentieth century remains to be written, along with the history of other titles that managed to reinvent themselves as twentieth-century publications.[28]

These long-lived publications pose particular problems for students of periodicals. The editors of the *Wellesley Index* begin their introduction to *Fraser's Magazine* with the comment: '*Fraser's Magazine* could scarcely have been published for fifty years under the control of a variety of editors and proprietors, in a period of radical change, and have remained the same periodical.'[29] This is even more true of *Blackwood's*, which had a run of over a century and a half. One crucial difference between the two magazines was the factor alluded to earlier: *Fraser's* changed its proprietor in 1847, and with it its style, ethos, political affiliation and many of its contributors. Moreover, unlike *Blackwood's*, it had never been the house magazine of any of its publishers.

Blackwood's was published by William Blackwood and Sons throughout its long history. For most of the nineteenth century, it was edited by members of the Blackwood family, the editorship passing from its founder to two of his sons, and then to his grandson. As has been emphasised, the aim of successive editors was to use the magazine to showcase Blackwood authors and Blackwood books. In looking at *Blackwood's* from the mid-1830s through to the turn of the twentieth century, it becomes clear that the magazine gradually adapted to the conditions of a highly competitive Victorian marketplace. The legacy of its early years was never far from the minds of successive editors, but they now had to appeal to a rapidly expanding and less homogeneous readership and to engage with authors who were conscious of the sums they could command from newer publications.

The Blackwood 'family', or inner circle, a concept which all editors nurtured, was markedly different from the coterie that conducted Maga in its early years. As is borne out in other chapters in this volume, in the magazine's first decade authorial identity was carefully guarded, secrecy was the norm and pseudonyms were strategically deployed. The identity of the editor, too, was conveniently unclear. The literary world of 1817 through 1830 was much smaller than the one in which William Blackwood I's successors had to position the magazine. Edinburgh at mid-century was less remote than it appeared in 1817. Alexander and Robert Blackwood's decision to open a London office in 1840 was an acknowledgement of a significant change in the publishing world; periodical publishing in particular had become more metropolitan in focus. 'Edinburgh' was officially dropped from the magazine's title in 1905. In practice, it had disappeared much earlier.

How then should the study of *Blackwood's Magazine* in the nineteenth century be approached? There are credible arguments for dividing its history into editorial regimes, beginning with William Blackwood I, and moving through to the end of William Blackwood III's term in 1912, by which time the Blackwood family's exclusive hold on its management had ended. The magazine's history could also be divided according to literary periods and emerging periodical genres, beginning as a Romantic literary magazine, followed by a transition to a magazine of the 1830s, in competition not only with *Fraser's* but with the less abrasive and non-political *Bentley's Miscellany*, the *New Monthly Magazine* and the radical *Tait's Edinburgh Magazine*. In the middle decades of the century, as has been demonstrated, it struggled to hold its own against newer and more popular house magazines, especially the shilling monthlies, whose readers included middle-class families and large numbers of women. In response, *Blackwood's* targeted readers in Britain's colonies while taking care to retain its traditional audience. At the end of the century, it held its nerve as other monthly magazines failed and a new generation of professional writers was attracted by the literary pages of newspapers.[30]

The one segment of *Blackwood's* long history which was incontrovertibly discrete, it would seem, was the first, when it was a Romantic-era literary magazine. Whether that period ended in 1826,

1830 or 1834 is less important than the fact that, at the end of this first phase of its history, Blackwood's changed from a miscellany written by a small and cohesive group of writers for a self-selecting, mainly masculine, audience – a publication which others strove to imitate and which set the agenda for its peers – into a much less cohesive house magazine, which retained the features of a miscellany, but which, although anonymity was preserved, was multi-vocal and adapted itself variously to a wider national audience and later a colonial one. The mature Blackwood's achieved a reputation for solidity and reliability. What it lost was one for innovation, wit and surprise.

Notes

1. Oliphant, 'Macaulay', p. 127.
2. Sala, 'The Cant', p. 47.
3. Latané, 'William Maginn', pp. 227–38. As suggested by its chronological range, the editors of the six-volume collection *Blackwood's Magazine, 1817–25, Selections from Maga's Infancy* regard the first nine years as a key period in the magazine's history (see Mason [gen. ed.], *Blackwood's Magazine*).
4. Oliphant, *Annals*, vol. 1, p. 198.
5. The duty on advertisements was abolished in 1853, the stamp duty on newspapers in 1855 and the duty on paper in 1861.
6. Brake, 'Maga', pp. 184–211; see pp. 187–8.
7. See headnote to 'Macaulay' in Shattock (ed.), *Essays on Life-Writing*, in Shattock and Jay (eds), *Selected Works of Margaret Oliphant*, vol. 13, pp. 49–50.
8. See headnote to 'The Anti-Marriage League' in Sanders et al. (eds), *Literary Criticism*, in Shattock and Jay (eds), *Selected Works of Margaret Oliphant*, vol. 5, pp. 457–9.
9. Oliphant, 'Life and Letters of George Eliot', pp. 540–1. See Sanders et al., *Literary Criticism*, p. 449.
10. Haight, *George Eliot Letters*, vol. 7, p. 221.
11. Haight, *George Eliot*, chapters 8–10.
12. Sutherland, *Victorian Novelists*, pp. 164–5.
13. Sutherland, *Victorian Fiction*, pp. 378, 472.
14. Sutherland, *Victorian Novelists*, p. 161. The novel was published by Chapman and Hall.
15. See Oliphant, *Annals*, vol. 2, chapters 21–24, for the political contacts of Maga under John Blackwood's editorship.

16. See Houghton, *Wellesley Index*, vol. 2, pp. 303–19, and Thrall, *Rebellious Fraser's*.
17. Houghton, *Wellesley Index*, p. 310.
18. Blackwood perfected a system of bringing novels out in three-, two- and one-volume formats at carefully judged intervals, the price reducing with each new format. See Shattock (ed.), *Essays on Life-Writing*, in Shattock and Jay (eds), *Selected Works of Margaret Oliphant*, vol. 13, p. 24.
19. Haight, *George Eliot Letters*, vol. 4, p. 35.
20. Sutherland, *Victorian Novelists*, p. 5, names Blackwood and Sons as one of seven leading publishers of fiction from the 1840s onward.
21. See Shattock, 'The Culture of Criticism', pp. 84–7.
22. Oliphant, 'New Books 23', p. 91; Sanders, *Literary Criticism*, in Shattock and Jay, vol. 3, p. 193.
23. Oliphant, *Annals*, vol. 2, p. 71.
24. William Blackwood III, Letter to Langford, 26 December 1880.
25. Oliphant, 'The Old Saloon', p. 127; Sanders et al., *Literary Criticism*, in Shattock and Jay, vol. 5, p. 8.
26. Finkelstein, 'Blackwood Female', pp. 17–37.
27. Oliphant's two volumes of *Annals of a Publishing House* appeared in 1897. A third volume, focusing on John Blackwood's editorship, was published a year later by his daughter, Mary [Mrs Gerald] Porter.
28. As well as *Blackwood's* and the *Cornhill*, these include the *Fortnightly*, *Contemporary* and *National* reviews, which continued into the second half of the twentieth century.
29. Houghton, *Wellesley Index*, p. 303.
30. See Besant, *The Pen and the Book*, p. 237 *et seq*.

Bibliography

Editors' Note on Attributions and Abbreviations

While anonymous publication remained the norm at most Romantic-era periodicals, scholars have subsequently identified the authors of many unsigned articles published in *Blackwood's* and other leading magazines and reviews. Strout's *A Bibliography of Articles in Blackwood's Magazine, 1817–1825* (1959), which remains indispensable for attributing unsigned essays, reviews, poems and tales from the magazine's first eighteen volumes, is the primary source for attributions below from *Blackwood's*. Attributions for articles published after 1825, either in *Blackwood's* or elsewhere, are principally from the *Wellesley Index to Victorian Periodicals*.

This bibliography uses brackets to indicate originally anonymous authors who have since been firmly identified (e.g., [Wilson, John]). A question mark is added for attributions that remain tentative (e.g., [Hogg, James?]). Sources for which the author remains unknown are alphabetised by article title under 'Anon.' To avoid repetition, *Blackwood's Edinburgh Magazine* is abbreviated as *BEM* and the National Library of Scotland, which archives most surviving correspondence related to the magazine, as NLS.

Ackerknecht, Erwin H., 'Anticontagionism between 1821 and 1867', *International Journal of Epidemiology* 38 (2009), pp. 7–21.
A Constant Reader (pseud.), 'Libel Law', *The Examiner* (7 September 1834), pp. 562–3.
Addison, Joseph, '*Spectator*, No.1' (1710–11), vol. 1 of *The Spectator*, 2 vols (London: Andrew Miller, 1800), pp. 5–7.
Alexander, J. H., '*Blackwood's*: Magazine as Romantic Form', *The Wordsworth Circle* 15: 2 (1984), pp. 57–68.

— (ed.), *The Tavern Sages: Selections from the* Noctes Ambrosianae (Aberdeen: Association for Scottish Literary Studies, 1992).
Allain, Jean (ed.), *The Legal Understanding of Slavery: From the Historical to the Contemporary* (Oxford: Oxford University Press, 2012).
Allington, Daniel, Sarah Brouillette, and David Golumbia, 'Neoliberal Tools (and Archives): A Political History of Digital Humanities', *Los Angeles Review of Books*,1 May 2016, https://lareviewofbooks.org/article/neoliberal-tools-archives-political-history-digital-humanities (last accessed 29 August 2019).
Altick, Richard, *The English Common Reader: A Social History of the Mass Reading Public, 1800–1900* (Chicago: University of Chicago Press, 1957).
Anon., 'Animadversions on "A Dissertation on Geology"', *Imperial Magazine* 2: 12 (February 1820), cols 18–22.
—, 'Answer to a Query on Burying in Churches', *Imperial Magazine* 3: 27 (May 1821), cols 414–16.
—, 'Colonel David Stewart's Sketches of the Highland Regiments', *BEM* 9 (April 1822), pp. 394–5.
—, 'A Curious Old Song', *BEM* 2 (October 1817), pp. 89–90.
—, 'An Extract from a Paper Concerning the Customs of the New-Zealanders', *Imperial Magazine* 3: 27 (May 1821), cols 413–14.
—, 'Bad Effects of Contracted Burying Grounds', *Imperial Magazine* 1: 5 (June 1819), cols 452–6.
—, 'Hint to the Ladies', *BEM* 2 (January 1818), pp. 377–8.
—, 'Interesting Particulars Respecting New Zealand. – By an Eyewitness', *Imperial Magazine* 3: 24 (February 1821), cols 130–3.
—, 'Introduction', *Farmer's Magazine* 1 (1800), pp. 1–30.
—, 'The King's Visit', *Scotsman* 3 (August 1822), p. 244.
—, 'Literary and Scientific Intelligence', *BEM* 2 (October 1817), pp. 97–8.
—, 'Literary and Scientific Intelligence', *BEM* 4 (October 1818), pp. 99–103.
—, 'Literary and Scientific Intelligence', *BEM* 7 (September 1820), pp. 688–93.
—, 'Lord Selkirk on Emigration', *Edinburgh Review* 7 (1805), pp. 185–202.
—, 'Memoir of the Late Francis Horner, Esq. M.P', *Edinburgh Monthly Magazine* 1 (April 1817), pp. 3–8.
—, 'Obituary', *The Gentleman's Magazine* NS 14 (July 1840), pp. 90–111.
—, 'Observations on "The Stayed Man"', *Imperial Magazine* 3 (September 1821), cols 843–4.
—, 'On the Study of Language, as Essential to the Successful Cultivation of Literature', *BEM* 5 (April 1819), pp. 55–9.
—, 'Register. – British Chronicle', *Edinburgh Monthly Magazine* 1 (August 1817), p. 543–9.
—, 'Remarks on Col. Stewart's Sketches of the Highlanders', *New Monthly Magazine* 9 (April 1823), pp. 169–71.

—, 'Report of the Select Committee Appointed to Inquire into the Wages of Labour. 1825', *Quarterly Review* 33 (March 1826), pp. 429–55.
—, Review of *An Inquiry into the Causes and Effects of Emigration from the Highlands and Western Islands of Scotland* by Alexander Irvine, *Edinburgh Review* 1 (October 1802), pp. 61–3.
—, Review of Duchess of Angouleme's Journal, *Edinburgh Monthly Magazine* 1 (May 1817), pp. 172–5.
—, Review of *Sunny Memories from Foreign Lands* by Harriet Beecher Stowe, *BEM* 76 (September 1854), pp. 301–17.
—, Review of *The Law of Libel* by Thomas Ludlow Holt, *Edinburgh Review* 27 (September 1816), pp. 102–44.
—, Review of *The Traveller's Oracle* by William Kitchiner, *London Magazine* 9 (October 1827), pp. 181–93.
—, Review of *The Traveller's Oracle* by William Kitchiner, *New Monthly Magazine* 20 (September 1827), pp. 300–4.
—, 'Ricardo and the Edinburgh Review', *BEM* 4 (October 1818), pp. 58–62.
—, 'Shocking Instance of Cannibalism, in New Zealand', *Imperial Magazine* 3: 23 (January 1821), cols 27–8.
—, 'Singular Piece of History', *Imperial Magazine* 2: 12 (February 1820), cols 62–5.
—, 'Starkie on the Law of Slander, Libel, Scandalum Magnatum, and False Rumours', *The Quarterly Review* 35: 70 (March 1827), pp. 566–609.
—, 'Strictures on an Article in No. LVI of the Edinburgh Review', *BEM* 2 (October 1817), pp. 41–4, 90–6.
—, 'Transactions of the Highland Society Vol. II', *Edinburgh Review* 4 (April 1804), pp. 63–75.
—, 'Works Preparing for Publication', *BEM* 5 (September 1819), pp. 740–2.
Aspinall, Arthur and E. Anthony Smith, *English Historical Documents 1783–1832* (London: Eyre and Spottiswoode, 1971).
Austin, J. L., *How to Do Things with Words: The William James Lectures Delivered at Harvard University in 1955* (Oxford: Clarendon Press, 1962).
[Bacon, Francis], 'The Confessions of a Cantab', *BEM* 16 (October 1824), pp. 459–67.
Bakhtin, Mikhail Mikhaîlovich, *The Dialogic Imagination*, ed. Michael Holquist, trans. Caryl Emerson and Michael Holquist (Austin: University of Texas Press, 1981).
Ballardini, Giuseppe, *Prato Fiorito di Varii Essempi. Diviso in Cinque Libri* (Venice, 1608).
Baumgartner, Barbara, 'The Body as Evidence: Resistance, Collaboration, and Appropriation in "The History of Mary Prince"', *Callaloo* 24: 1 (Winter 2001), pp. 253–75.

Benedict, Barbara, *Making the Modern Reader: Cultural Mediation in Early Modern Literary Anthologies* (Princeton: Princeton University Press, 1996).
Besant, Walter, *The Pen and the Book* (London: Thomas Burleigh, 1899).
Blackie, John, 'Defamation', in Kenneth Reid and Reinhard Zimmermann (eds), *A History of Private Law in Scotland*, Vol. 2: *Obligations* (Oxford: Oxford University Press, 2000), pp. 633–708.
Blackwood, Robert (for William Blackwood), Letter to James MacQueen, 12 May 1834, NLS MS 30005.
Blackstone, Sir William, *Commentaries on the Laws of England*, with notes and additions by Edward Christian, vol. 4, 12th edn (London: T. Cadell, 1795).
Blackwood, William, Letter to Baldwin, Cradock and Joy, 23 July 1817, NLS MS 30001.
—, Letter to Caroline Bowles, 2 November 1821, NLS MS 30305.
—, Letter to Caroline Bowles, 22 December 1821, NLS MS 30305.
—, Letter to Caroline Bowles, 28 January 1822, NLS MS 30305.
—, Letter to Caroline Bowles, 22 February 1822, NLS MS 30305.
—, Letter to Caroline Bowles, 25 June 1822, NLS MS 30306.
—, Letter to James MacQueen, 20 November 1817, NLS MS 30001.
—, Letter to James MacQueen, 25 July 1826, NLS MS 9818.
—, Letter to James MacQueen, 21 November 1831, NLS MS 30004.
—, Letter to James MacQueen, 23 February 1832, NLS MS 30004.
—, Letter to John Murray, March 1817, NLS MS 30001.
—, Letter to R. F. St Barbe, 22 December 1821, NLS MS 30305.
—, Letter to R. F. St Barbe, 20 February 1822, NLS MS 30305.
—, Letter to Thomas Pringle, 23 June 1817, NLS MS 30001.
—, Letter to Thomas Pringle, 28 June 1817, NLS MS 30001.
—, Letter to Thomas Pringle, 1 July 1817, NLS MS 4002 (Blackwood 1817).
Blackwood, William III, Letter to Joseph Munt Langford, 26 December 1880, NLS MS 4402.
Blain, Virginia, *Caroline Bowles Southey, 1786–1854: The Making of a Woman Writer* (Aldershot: Ashgate, 1998).
—, 'Southey, Caroline Anne Bowles', *Oxford Dictionary of National Biography* (Oxford: Oxford University Press, 2004).
Bleackley, Horace, 'Tete-a-tete Portraits in "The Town and Country Magazine"', *Notes and Queries* 4, 10th series (July–December 1905), pp. 241–2, 342–4, 462–4, 522–3.
Bond, Donald F., 'Introduction', in Donald F. Bond (ed.), *The Spectator*, Vol. 1 (Oxford: Clarendon Press, 1965), pp. lxix-lxxiii.
Borff, Charles, 'Extract of a Letter Lately Received from the Rev. Charles Borff, Missionary at the Island of Hueine, in the South Seas', *Imperial Magazine* 2: 12 (February 1820), cols 59–61.

Borthwick, John, *A Treatise on the Law of Libel and Slander, as Applied, in Scotland, in Criminal Prosecutions, and in Actions of Damages* (Edinburgh: Tait, 1826).
[Bowles, Caroline], 'Gentlemanly Expostulation, or a Hard Hit at the Secretary', *BEM* 17 (March 1825), p. 352.
[—], 'Letter from a Washerwoman', *BEM* 13 (February 1823), pp. 232–8.
—, Letter to William Blackwood, 30 August 1821, NLS MS 4007.
—, Letter to William Blackwood, 9 March 1822, NLS MS 4009.
—, Letter to William Blackwood, 4 June 1822, NLS MS 4009.
—, Letter to William Blackwood, 1 February 1823, NLS MS 4011.
[—], 'The Smuggler', *BEM* 10 (December 1821), pp. 630–41.
[—], 'Thoughts on Letter-Writing', *BEM* 11 (March 1822), pp. 301–4.
[—], 'To the Author of "The Shepherd's Calendar"', *BEM* 15 (June 1824), pp. 655–8.
Brake, Laurel, 'Maga, the Shilling Monthlies, and the New Journalism', in Finkelstein (ed.), *Print Culture*, pp. 184–211.
Brake, Laurel and Marysa Demoor (gen. eds), *Dictionary of Nineteenth-Century Journalism in Great Britain and Ireland* (Gent, Belgium: Academia Press; London: The British Library, 2009).
Brennan, Timothy, 'The Digital-Humanities Bust', *The Chronicle of Higher Education*, 15 October 2017, https://www.chronicle.com/article/The-Digital-Humanities-Bust/241424 (last accessed 29 August 2019).
Bridge, Tom and Colin Cooper English, *Dr. William Kitchiner, Regency Eccentric – Author of the 'Cook's Oracle'* (Lewes: Southover Press, 1992).
Broglio, Ron, *Beasts of Burden: Biopolitics, Labor, and Animal Life in British Romanticism* (Albany: State University of New York Press, 2017).
Brown, Rhona, '"Guid black prent": Robert Burns and the Contemporary Scottish and American Periodical Press', in Sharon Alker, Leith Davis and Holly Faith Nelson (eds), *Robert Burns and Transatlantic Culture* (Burlington, VT: Ashgate, 2012), pp. 71–83.
Budge, Gavin, 'Transatlantic Irritability: Brunonian Sociology, America and Mass Culture in the Nineteenth Century', in Megan J. Coyer and David E. Shuttleton (eds), *Scottish Medicine and Literary Culture, 1726–1832* (Amsterdam and New York: Rodopi, 2014), pp. 267–92.
Bullard, Rebecca, 'Introduction: Reconsidering Secret History', in Rebecca Bullard and Rachel Carnell (eds), *The Secret History*, pp. 1–14.
Bullard, Rebecca and Rachel Carnell (eds), *The Secret History in Literature: 1660–1820* (Cambridge: Cambridge University Press, 2017).
[Bulwer-Lytton, Edward], Review of *Romance and Reality* by Letitia Elizabeth Landon, *New Monthly Magazine* 32 (December 1831), pp. 545–51.
Burgess, Miranda, 'Secret History in the Romantic Period', in Rebecca Bullard and Rachel Carnell (eds), *The Secret History*, pp. 188–201.

Byron, Lord, *English Bards and Scotch Reviewers*, in Jerome J. McGann (ed.), *The Complete Poetical Works*, vol. 1 (Oxford: Clarendon Press, 1980), pp. 227–64.

—, *Lord Byron's Letters and Journals*, ed. Leslie A. Marchand, 13 vols (London: Murray, 1973–94).

Cadell, Thomas, Letter to William Blackwood, 19 November 1831, NLS MS 4029.

Calloway, Colin, *White People, Indians, and Highlanders: Tribal Peoples and Colonial Encounters in Scotland and America* (Oxford: Oxford University Press, 2008).

Cantor, Geoffrey and Sally Shuttleworth, 'Introduction', in Geoffrey Cantor and Sally Shuttleworth (eds), *Science Serialized: Representations of the Sciences in Nineteenth-Century Periodicals* (Cambridge, MA and London: MIT Press, 2004), pp. 1–16.

'Caroline Southey', *Athenaeum*, 5 August 1854, pp. 969–70.

Christie, William, '*Blackwood's Edinburgh Magazine* in the Scientific Culture of Early Nineteenth-Century Edinburgh', in Robert Morrison and Daniel S. Roberts (eds), *Romanticism and Blackwood's*, pp. 125–36.

—, *The* Edinburgh Review *in the Literary Culture of Romantic Britain: Mammoth and Megalonyx* (London: Pickering & Chatto, 2009).

Coleridge, Samuel Taylor, *Biographia Literaria*, ed. James Engell and W. Jackson Bate (Princeton: Princeton University Press, 1983).

—, *Collected Letters of Samuel Taylor Coleridge*, ed. Earl Leslie Griggs, vol. 4 (Oxford: Clarendon Press, 1959).

—, *Lay Sermons*, ed. R. J. White, vol. 6 of *The Collected Works of Samuel Taylor Coleridge* (London: Routledge & Kegan Paul, 1972).

—, *Poetical Works: Part I*, ed. J. C. C. Mays, vol. 16 of *The Collected Works of Samuel Taylor Coleridge* (Princeton: Princeton University Press, 2001).

Connell, Philip, *Romanticism, Economics and the Question of 'Culture'* (Oxford: Oxford University Press, 2001).

Constable, Thomas, 'Archibald Constable and His Friends', *Harper's New Monthly Magazine* 48 (March 1874), pp. 501–12.

Cox, Jeffrey N., *Poetry and Politics in the Cockney School* (Cambridge: Cambridge University Press, 1998).

Coyer, Megan, *Literature and Medicine in the Nineteenth-Century Periodical Press:* Blackwood's Edinburgh Magazine, *1817–1858* (Edinburgh: Edinburgh University Press, 2017).

—, 'Medical Discourse and Ideology in the *Edinburgh Review*: A Chaldean Exemplar', in Alex Benchimol, Rhona Brown and David Shuttleton (eds), *Before Blackwood's: Scottish Journalism in the Age of Enlightenment* (London: Pickering & Chatto, 2015), pp. 103–16.

Crandall, Joshua, '"The Great measur'd by the Less": The Ethnological Turn in Eighteenth-Century Pastoral', *English Literary History* 81 (2014), pp. 955–82.

Crawford, Rachel, *Poetry, Enclosure, and the Vernacular Landscape, 1700–1830* (Cambridge: Cambridge University Press, 2002).

Cronin, Richard, 'John Wilson and Regency Authorship', in Robert Morrison and Daniel S. Roberts (eds), *Romanticism and Blackwood's*, pp. 203–14.

—, *Paper Pellets: British Literary Culture After Waterloo* (Oxford: Oxford University Press, 2010).

Da, Nan Z., 'The Computational Case against Computational Literary Studies', *Critical Inquiry* 45 (Spring 2019), pp. 601–39.

[D'Angouleme, Marie–Therese], *Private Memoirs* (London: John Murray, 1817).

Dart, Gregory, *Metropolitan Art and Literature, 1810–1840: Cockney Adventures* (Cambridge: Cambridge University Press, 2012).

Davies, William, Letter to William Blackwood, 6 April 1819, NLS MS 4004.

Davis, Angela, 'Reflections on the Black Woman's Role in the Community of Slaves', *The Black Scholar* 3: 4 (1971), pp. 2–15.

Dawson, Gowan, Richard Noakes and Jonathan R. Topham, 'Introduction', in Geoffrey Cantor et al. (eds), *Science in the Nineteenth-Century Periodical, Reading the Magazine of Nature* (Cambridge and New York: Cambridge University Press, 2004), pp. 1–37.

Deans, Alex, 'Pastoral Optimism at Improvement's Frontier: James Hogg's Highland Journeys', in Alex Benchimol and Gerard Lee McKeever (eds), *Cultures of Improvement in Scottish Romanticism, 1707–1840* (London: Routledge, 2018), pp. 132–51.

De Groot, H. B., 'Hogg and the Highlands', in Ian Duncan and Douglas Mack (eds), *The Edinburgh Companion to James Hogg* (Edinburgh: Edinburgh University Press, 2012), pp. 46–54.

De La Vars, Lauren Pringle, 'Caroline Anne Bowles Southey', *Dictionary of Literary Biography: British Romantic Novelists, 1789–1832*, vol. 116 (Detroit, MI: Gale, 1992), pp. 332–42.

Demata, Massimiliano and Duncan Wu (eds), *British Romanticism and the* Edinburgh Review: *Bicentenary Essays* (Basingstoke: Palgrave Macmillan, 2002).

[De Quincey, Thomas], 'Confessions of an English Opium-Eater', *London Magazine* 4 (September and October 1821), pp. 293–312 and 353–79.

—, *The Works of Thomas De Quincey*, Vol. 3: *Articles and Translations from the London Magazine, Blackwood's Magazine and Others, 1821–1824*, ed. Frederick Burwick (London: Pickering & Chatto, 2000).

—, *The Works of Thomas De Quincey*, Vol. 10: *Articles from Tait's Edinburgh Magazine, 1834–8*, ed. Alina Clej (London: Pickering & Chatto, 2003).

Derrida, Jacques, *Dissemination*, trans. Barbara Johnson (Chicago: University of Chicago, 1981).
—, *Of Grammatology* [1967], trans. Gayatri Chakravorty Spivak (Baltimore: Johns Hopkins University Press, 2016).
Devine, T. M., *The Scottish Clearances: A History of the Dispossessed* (London: Allen Lane, 2018).
Distad, N. Merrill, 'The Origins and History of *Victorian Periodicals Review*', *Victorian Periodicals Review* 18 (Fall 1985), pp. 86–98.
Dodson, Charles Brooks, 'The Imperial Magazine', in Alvin Sullivan (ed.), *British Literary Magazines: The Romantic Age, 1789–1836* (New York: Greenwood, 1983), pp. 185–9.
Douglas, Thomas, Earl of Selkirk, *Observations on the Present State of the Highlands of Scotland; with a View of the Causes and Probable Consequences of Emigration* (London, 1805).
Dowden, Edward (ed.), *The Correspondence of Robert Southey with Caroline Bowles* (Dublin: Hodges, 1881).
Dumas, Paul E., 'The *Edinburgh Review*, the *Quarterly Review*, and the Contributions of the Periodicals to the Slavery Debates', *Slavery and Abolition* 38 (2017), pp. 559–76.
Duncan, Ian, '*Blackwood's* and Romantic Nationalism', in Finkelstein (ed.), *Print Culture*, pp. 70–89.
—, *Scott's Shadow: The Novel in Romantic Edinburgh* (Princeton: Princeton University Press, 2007).
Duncan Jr, Andrew, 'Report on the Present State of Fever in Edinburgh', *Edinburgh Magazine and Literary Miscellany* (November 1817), pp. 347–51.
Dziennik, Matthew, *The Fatal Land: War, Empire, and the Highland Soldier in British North America* (New Haven, CT: Yale University Press, 2016).
—, 'Through an Imperial Prism: Land, Liberty, and Highland Loyalism in the War of American Independence', *Journal of British Studies* 50 (April 2011), pp. 332–58.
Easley, Alexis, Andrew King and John Morton (eds), *Researching the Nineteenth-Century Periodical Press: Case Studies* (New York: Routledge, 2018).
Empson, William, *Some Versions of Pastoral* (New York: New Directions, 1974).
Fang, Karen, *Romantic Writing and the Empire of Signs: Periodical Culture and Post-Napoleonic Authorship* (Charlottesville: University of Virginia Press, 2010).
Feldman, Paula C., 'The Poet and the Profits: Felicia Hemans and the Literary Marketplace', in Isobel Armstrong and Virginia Blain (eds), *Women's Poetry, Late Romantic to Late Victorian: Gender and Genre, 1830–1900* (New York: Palgrave Macmillan, 1999), pp. 71–101.

Ferguson, Adam, *An Essay on the History of Civil Society* (London: Cadell, 1793).

Finkelstein, David, 'The Blackwood Female Literary Network, 1880–1910', in William Baker (ed.), *Studies in Victorian and Modern Literature: A Tribute to John Sutherland* (Madison, NJ: Fairleigh Dickinson University Press, 2015), pp. 17–37.

—, *The House of Blackwood: Author–Publisher Relations in the Victorian Era* (University Park: Pennsylvania State University Press, 2002).

—, 'Periodicals in Scotland', in Andrew King et al. (eds), *Routledge Handbook*, pp. 185–93.

— (ed.), *Print Culture and the Blackwood Tradition 1805–1930* (Toronto: University of Toronto Press, 2006).

—, 'Selling *Blackwood's Magazine*, 1817–1834', in Robert Morrison and Daniel S. Roberts (eds), *Romanticism and Blackwood's*, pp. 69–86.

Flynn, Philip, 'Beginning *Blackwood's*: The Right Mix of *Dulce* and *Utile*', in Robert Morrison and Daniel S. Roberts (eds), *Romanticism and Blackwood's*, pp. 23–34.

—, 'Beginning *Blackwood's*: The Right Mix of *Dulce* and *Utile*', *Victorian Periodicals Reviews* 39 (2006), pp. 136–57.

Franklin-Brown, Mary, *Reading the World: Encyclopedic Writing in the Scholastic Age* (Chicago: University of Chicago Press, 2012).

[Fraser-Taylor, Patrick], 'Remarks on "Lacunar Strevelinense" (Stirling Heads)', *BEM* 2 (November 1817), pp. 205–10.

Freud, Sigmund, 'The Uncanny' ('*Das Unheimliche*', 1919), in James Strachey (ed.), *The Standard Edition of the Complete Psychological Works of Sigmund Freud*, vol. 17 (London: Hogarth Press, 1955).

Fulford, Tim, *Romantic Indians: Native Americans, British Literature, and Transatlantic Culture 1756–1830* (Oxford: Oxford University Press, 2006).

Fyfe, Paul, 'Technologies of Serendipity', *Victorian Periodicals Review* 48: 2 (2015), pp. 261–6.

Gallagher, Catherine, 'The Rise of Fictionality', in Franco Moretti (ed.), *The Novel*, Vol. 1: *History, Geography and Culture* (Princeton: Princeton University Press, 2006), pp. 336–63.

[Galt, John], 'The Steam-Boat, No. VII', *BEM* 10 (September 1821), pp. 166–71.

General Index to Blackwood's Edinburgh Magazine, *Volumes I to L* (Edinburgh: Blackwood, 1855).

Gibbon, Charles, *The Life of George Combe, Author of 'The Constitution of Man'*, vol. 1 (London: Macmillan, 1878).

Gigante, Denise (ed.), *The Great Age of the English Essay: An Anthology* (New Haven, CT: Yale University Press, 2008).

Gillies, Robert Pierce, *Memoirs of a Literary Veteran*, 3 vols (London: Richard Bentley, 1851).
Gittings, Robert (ed.), *Letters of John Keats: A Selection* (Oxford: Oxford University Press, 1970).
Gooch, Richard, *Facetiae Cantabrigienses*, 3rd edn (London: William Cole, 1836), pp. 1–20.
Gooch, Robert, Letter to William Blackwood, 18 November 1825, NLS MS 4014.
—, Letter to William Blackwood, 2 January 1826, NLS MS 4017.
—, 'Plague, a Contagious Disease', *Quarterly Review* 33 (December 1825), pp. 218–57.
Goodman, Kevis, *Georgic Modernity and British Romanticism: Poetry and the Mediation of History* (Cambridge: Cambridge University Press, 2004).
Grafton, Anthony, *Worlds Made of Words: Scholarship and Community in the Modern West* (Cambridge, MA: Harvard University Press, 2009).
Graham, Walter, *English Literary Periodicals* (London: T. Nelson, 1930).
[Grattan, Thomas], 'The Confessions of an English Glutton', *BEM* 13 (January 1823), pp. 86–93.
Habermas, Jürgen, *The Structural Transformation of the Public Sphere: An Inquiry into a Category of Bourgeois Society* [1962], trans. Thomas Burger and Frederick Lawrence (Cambridge, MA: MIT Press, 1989).
Haight, Gordon S., *George Eliot: A Biography* (Oxford: Clarendon Press, 1968).
— (ed.), *The George Eliot Letters*, 9 vols (New Haven, CT: Yale University Press, 1954–78).
[Hamilton, Thomas], 'To the Publisher', *BEM* 2 (March 1818), n.p.
Hamlin, Christopher, 'Good and Intimate Filth', in William A. Cohen and Ryan Johnson (eds), *Filth: Dirt, Disgust, and Modern Life* (Minneapolis: University of Minnesota Press, 2005), pp. 3–29.
Hasler, Antony, 'Reading the Land: James Hogg and the Highlands', *Studies in Hogg and His World* 4 (1993), pp. 57–82.
Hayden, John O., *The Romantic Reviewers: 1802–1824* (London: Routledge & Kegan Paul, 1969).
[Hazlitt, William], 'The Periodical Press', *Edinburgh Review* 38 (May 1823), pp. 349–78.
[—], Review of *The Excursion* by William Wordsworth, *Examiner*, 21 August 1814, pp. 541–2; 28 August 1814, pp. 555–8; and 2 October 1814, pp. 636–8.
— (ed.), *The Round Table: A Collection of Essays on Literature, Men, and Manners*, vol. 2 (Edinburgh: Constable, 1817).
[Hemans, Felicia], 'Casabianca', *Monthly Magazine* 2 (August 1826), p. 164.

Hempton, David, *Methodism: Empire of the Spirit* (New Haven, CT: Yale University Press, 2005).

Higgins, David, 'From Gluttony to Justified Sinning: Confessional Writing in *Blackwood's* and the *London Magazine*', in Robert Morrison and Daniel S. Roberts (eds), *Romanticism and Blackwood's*, pp. 47–56.

—, *Romantic Genius and the Literary Magazine: Biography, Celebrity, Politics* (New York: Routledge, 2005).

Hogg, James, *The Mountain Bard*, ed. Suzanne Gilbert (Edinburgh: Edinburgh University Press, 2007).

—, *Tales and Sketches, by the Ettrick Shepherd*, 6 vols (Glasgow: Blackie, 1837).

[—], 'Noctes Bengerianae', *Edinburgh Literary Journal* 7 (1828), pp. 87–90.

[—], 'Noctes Bengerianae', *Edinburgh Literary Journal* 19 (1829), pp. 258–60.

—, *The Poetical Works of James Hogg*, 4 vols (Edinburgh: Constable, 1822).

—, 'The Pongos', in James Hogg, *Altrive Tales*, vol. 1 (London: James Cochrane, 1832), pp. 143–63.

[—], 'A Scots Mummy', *BEM* 14 (August 1823), pp. 188–90.

—, *The Shepherd's Calendar*, ed. Douglas Mack (Edinburgh: Edinburgh University Press, 1995).

—, *The Shepherd's Calendar*, vol. 2 (Edinburgh: William Blackwood, 1829).

—, *The Shepherd's Guide* (Edinburgh: Constable, 1807).

[—], 'The Shepherd's Noctes, and the Reason Why They Do Not Appear in Fraser's Magazine', *Fraser's Magazine* 8 (1833), pp. 49–54.

[—], 'A Singular Letter from Southern Africa', *BEM* 26 (November 1829), pp. 809–16.

—, *The Spy: A Periodical Paper of Literary Amusement and Instruction, 1810–11*, ed. Gillian Hughes (Edinburgh: Edinburgh University Press, 2000).

[—], 'A Strange Secret', *BEM* 23 (June 1828), pp. 822–6.

[Hogg, James, John Gibson Lockhart and John Wilson], 'Translation from an Ancient Chaldee Manuscript', *BEM* 2 (October 1817), pp. 89–96. [retracted after the first printing].

Homespun, Zachariah (pseud.), 'Law of Libel', *Examiner*, 7 January 1827, pp. 2–3.

Houghton, Walter E., *The Wellesley Index to Victorian Periodicals 1824–1900*, vol. 2 (Toronto: University of Toronto Press, 1972).

Hughes, Gillian, *James Hogg: A Life* (Edinburgh: Edinburgh University Press, 2007).

Hughes, Linda K., 'SIDEWAYS!: Navigating the Material(ity) of Print Culture', *Victorian Periodicals Review* 47 (Spring 2014), pp. 1–30.

Hume, David, 'Of Superstition and Enthusiasm' [1742], in Eugene F. Miller (ed.), *Essays, Moral, Political, and Literary* (Indianapolis: Liberty Fund, 1985).
Hunt, Leigh, *The Autobiography of Leigh Hunt*, 2 vols [1850] (New York: AMS Press, 1965).
—, 'No. XXXIX. A Day by the Fire', in Hazlitt (ed.), *The Round Table*, pp. 122–33.
—, 'No. XLI. The Subject Continued', in Hazlitt (ed.), *The Round Table*, pp. 148–62.
—, 'No. XLIV. On Washerwomen', in Hazlitt (ed.), *The Round Table*, pp. 177–88.
[—], 'Preface', *The Liberal: Verse and Prose from the South* 1 (London: 1822), pp. v–xii.
[—], Review of *Poems* by John Keats, *Examiner*, 1 June 1817, p. 345; 6 July 1817, pp. 428–9; and 13 July 1817, pp. 443–4.
Hutchinson, Sara. *The Letters of Sara Hutchinson from 1800 to 1835*, ed. Kathleen Coburn (Toronto: University of Toronto Press, 1954).
Jarrells, Anthony, 'Provincializing Enlightenment: Edinburgh Historicism and the Blackwoodian Regional Tale', *Studies in Romanticism* 48 (2009), pp. 257–77.
— (ed.), *Selected Prose*, vol. 2 of Mason (gen. ed.), *Blackwood's Magazine, 1817–25*.
—, 'Tales of the Colonies: *Blackwood's*, Provincialism, and British Interests Abroad', in Robert Morrison and Daniel S. Roberts (eds), *Romanticism and Blackwood's*, pp. 267–77.
[Jeffrey, Francis], 'Grahame's *British Georgics*', *Edinburgh Review* 16 (April 1810), pp. 213–23.
[Jeffrey, Francis and Andrew Duncan, Jr], 'Willan and Others on Vaccination', *Edinburgh Review* 9 (October 1806), pp. 32–66.
Jerdan, William, *Men I Have Known* (London: Routledge, 1862).
Johnstone, Christian Isobel, *The Cook and Housewife's Manual* (Edinburgh, 1826).
Jones, Leonidas, 'The Scott–Christie Duel', *Texas Studies in Literature and Language* 12 (1971), pp. 605–29.
Jonsson, Frederik Albritton, *Enlightenment's Frontier: The Scottish Highlands and the Origins of Environmentalism* (New Haven, CT: Yale University Press, 2013).
[Keats, John], 'On a Grecian Urn', *Annals of the Fine Arts* 4: 15 (1820), pp. 638–9.
Kermode, Frank, *English Pastoral Poetry from the Beginnings to Marvell* (London: Harrap, 1952).

Killick, Tim, '*Blackwood's* and the Boundary of the Short Story', in Robert Morrison and Daniel S. Roberts (eds), *Romanticism and Blackwood's*, pp. 163–74.
King, Andrew, Alexis Easley and John Morton (eds), *The Routledge Handbook to Nineteenth-Century Periodicals* (New York: Routledge, 2016).
Kitchiner, William, Letter to Archibald Constable, 26 March 1822, NLS MS 330.
Klancher, Jon, 'Configuring Romanticism and Print History: A Retrospect', *European Romantic Review* 23: 3 (2012), pp. 373–79.
—, *The Making of English Reading Audiences, 1790–1832* (Madison: University of Wisconsin Press, 1987).
—, 'What Happened to the Periodical?', *Studies in Romanticism*, special issue 'Romanticism in a New Key: Essays in Honor of Jerome McGann' (forthcoming 2020).
Lamb, Charles, 'The Wife's Trial; Or, The Intruding Widow', *BEM* 24 (December 1828), pp. 765–81.
—, *The Works of Charles and Mary Lamb*, vol. 2, ed. E. V. Lucas (New York: AMS Press, 1968).
Lambert, David, 'The "Glasgow King of Billingsgate": James MacQueen and an Atlantic Proslavery Network', *Slavery and Abolition* 29 (September 2008), pp. 389–413.
Lang, Andrew, *The Life and Letters of John Gibson Lockhart* (London: John C. Nimmo, 1897).
Laqueur, Thomas, *The Work of the Dead: A Cultural History of Mortal Remains* (Princeton: Princeton University Press, 2015).
Latané, David E., 'William Maginn and the *Blackwood's* "Preface" of 1826', in Robert Morrison and Daniel S. Roberts (eds), *Romanticism and Blackwood's*, pp. 227–38.
Latham, Sean and Robert Scholes, 'The Rise of Periodical Studies', *PMLA* 121: 2 (2006), pp. 517–31.
Lawrence, Lindsy, '"Afford[ing] me a Place": Recovering Women Poets in *Blackwood's Edinburgh Magazine*, 1827–35', in Alexis Easley, Clare Gill and Beth Rodgers (eds), *Women, Periodicals, and Print Culture in Britain, 1830s–1900s: The Victorian Period* (Edinburgh: Edinburgh University Press, 2019), pp. 399–412.
Leary, Patrick, 'Googling the Victorians', *Journal of Victorian Culture* 10 (January 2005), pp. 72–86.
Leask, Nigel, *Robert Burns and Pastoral: Poetry and Improvement in Late Eighteenth-Century Scotland* (Oxford: Oxford University Press, 2010).
Lendrum, Chris, '"Periodical Performance": The Editor Figure in Early Nineteenth-Century Literary Magazines', PhD Dissertation (University of Ottawa, 2010).

Lessenich, Rolf, '"Noctes Ambrosianae" (1822–35): A Comic Symposium of the Romantic Period', in Marion Gymnich and Norbert Lennartz (eds), *The Pleasures and Horrors of Eating: The Cultural History of Eating in Anglophone Literature* (Göttingen: Bonn University Press, 2010), pp. 187–203.

Levinson, Marjorie, *Keats's Life of Allegory: The Origins of a Style* (New York: Blackwell, 1988).

[Lockhart, John Gibson?], 'The Leg of Mutton School of Prose. No. I. The Cook's Oracle', BEM 10 (December 1821), pp. 563–9.

[—], 'Letter from Z. to Mr. Leigh Hunt', BEM 2 (January 1818), pp. 414–17.

[—], 'Letter from Z. to Leigh Hunt, King of the Cockneys', BEM 3 (May 1818), pp. 196–201.

—, *Memoirs of the Life of Sir Walter Scott*, 5 vols (Boston: Houghton Mifflin, 1901).

—, *Memoirs of the Life of Sir Walter Scott*, 7 vols (Edinburgh: Robert Cadell, 1837–8).

[—], 'New Series of the Curiosities of Literature', BEM 13 (February 1823), pp. 166–75.

[—], 'Noctes Ambrosianae, No. I', BEM 11 (March 1822), pp. 369–76, *359–71. [mispaginated after p. 376]

[—], 'Noctes Ambrosianae, No. XIV', BEM 15 (April 1824), pp. 369–90.

[—], 'Noctes Ambrosianae, No. XV', BEM 15 (June 1824), pp. 706–24.

[—], 'Noctes Ambrosianae, No. XLVI', BEM 26 (September 1829), pp. 389–404.

[—], 'Noctes Ambrosianae, No. LI', BEM 28 (August 1830), pp. 383–436.

[—], 'Notices to Correspondents', BEM 2 (March 1818), n.p.

[—], 'Observations on *The Revolt of Islam*', BEM 4 (January 1819), pp. 475–86.

[—], 'Odoherty on Don Juan, Cantos IX, X, XI', BEM 14 (September 1823), pp. 282–93.

[—], 'On the Cockney School of Poetry. No. I', BEM 2 (October 1817), pp. 38–41.

[—], 'On the Cockney School of Poetry, No. II', BEM 2 (November 1817), pp. 194–201.

[—], 'On the Cockney School of Poetry, No. III', BEM 3 (July 1818), pp. 453–6.

[— ?], 'Remarks on Dr Watt's Bibliotheca Britannica', BEM 5 (August 1819), pp. 553–6.

[— ?], 'Remarks on Mr Mitford's View of the Constitution of Macedonia, Contained in the New Volume of His History of Greece', BEM 5 (July 1819), pp. 443–51.

[—], 'Remarks on Schlegel's History of Literature', BEM 3 (August 1818), pp. 497–511.

[—], Review of *The Diary of Joseph Burridge*, *BEM* 14 (December 1823), pp. 702–4.
[Lockhart, John Gibson and John Wilson], 'The Last Day of the Tent', *BEM* 5 (September 1819), pp. 720–36.
[—], 'The Tent', *BEM* 5 (September 1819), pp. 627–8.
[—], 'The True and Authentic Account of the Twelfth of August, 1819', *BEM* 5 (August 1819), pp. 597–613.
[Lockhart, John Gibson, John Wilson and J. H. Merivale], 'Some Account of the Life and Writings of Ensign and Adjutant Odoherty', *BEM* 3 (December 1818), pp. 320–8.
Lodge, Sara, 'Sally Brown (1822) and Bridget Jones (1825): Where They Came From and What They Say about Thomas Hood', *Charles Lamb Bulletin*, 107 (July 1999), pp. 98–109.
Low, Dennis, *The Literary Protégées of the Lake Poets* (Aldershot: Ashgate, 2006).
Macbeth, Gilbert, *John Gibson Lockhart: A Critical Study* (Urbana: University of Illinois Press, 1935).
Mack, Douglas, 'Introduction', in James Hogg, *The Shepherd's Calendar* [1829] (Edinburgh: Edinburgh University Press, 1995), pp. xi–xx.
Mackenzie, R. Shelton, 'History of *Blackwood's Magazine*', in John Wilson, *Noctes Ambrosianae*, vol. 1, 4th edn (New York: Redfield, 1857), pp. v–xviii.
Mackenzie, Scott, 'Confessions of a Gentrified Sinner: Secrets in Scott and Hogg', *Studies in Romanticism* 41 (2002), pp. 3–32.
—, 'Pastoral Against Pastoral Modernity: Voices of Shepherds and Sheep in James Hogg's Scotland', *European Romantic Review* 26 (September 2015), pp. 527–49.
Mackillop, Andrew, *'More Fruitful than the Soil': Army, Empire, and the Scottish Highlands 1715–1815* (East Linton: Tuckwell Press, 2000).
Macnish, Robert, Letter to D. M. Moir, 4 February 1835, NLS Acc. 9856.
MacQueen, James, 'The British Colonies – Anti-Colonists', *BEM* 29 (February 1831), pp. 186–213.
—, 'The Colonial Empire of Great Britain. Letter to Earl Grey, First Lord of the Treasury', *BEM* 30 (November 1831), pp. 744–64.
—, 'The River Niger – Termination in the Sea', *BEM* 30 (July 1831), pp. 130–6.
—, *The West India Colonies; The Calumnies and Misrepresentations Circulated Against Them* (London: Longman and Hurst, 1825).
MacQueen, James, Letter to William Blackwood, 3 February 1831, NLS MS 4029.
—, Letter to William Blackwood, 6 February 1831, NLS MS 4030.

—, Letter to William Blackwood, 29 May 1831, NLS MS 4030.
—, Letter to William Blackwood, 22 November 1831, NLS MS 4029.
—, Letter to William Blackwood, 20 December 1831, NLS MS 4029.
—, Letter to William Blackwood, 29 November 1833, NLS MS 4306.
—, Letter to William Blackwood, 12 December 1833, NLS MS 4036.
Madison-MacFadyen, Margo, 'Mary Prince, Grand Turk, and Antigua', *Slavery and Abolition: A Journal of Slave and Post-Slave Studies* 34 (2012), pp. 653–62.
[Maginn, William], 'Humbugs of the Age, No. 1 – The Opium Eater', *John Bull Magazine* 1 (1824), p. 21.
[—], 'Hymn to Christopher North, Esq', *BEM* 9 (April 1821), pp. 60–4.
[—], 'Noctes Ambrosianae, No. IV', *BEM* 12 (July 1822), pp. 100–14.
[—?], 'Noctes Ambrosianae, No. VI', *BEM* 12 (September 1822), pp. 369–91.
[—,] 'Noctes Ambrosianae, No. X', *BEM* 14 (July 1823), pp. 100–6.
—, *The Odoherty Papers by the Late William Maginn*, ed. R. Shelton Mackenzie, 2 vols (New York: Redfield, 1855).
Makdisi, Saree, *Romantic Imperialism: Universal Empire and the Culture of Modernity* (Cambridge: Cambridge University Press, 1998).
Marchand, Leslie, *Byron: A Portrait* (New York: Alfred A. Knopf, 1970).
Mason, Nicholas (gen. ed.), *Blackwood's Magazine, 1817–25: Selections from Maga's Infancy*, 6 vols (London: Pickering & Chatto, 2006).
—, *Literary Advertising and the Shaping of British Romanticism* (Baltimore: Johns Hopkins University Press, 2013).
— (ed.), *Selected Verse*, vol. 1 of Mason (gen. ed.), *Blackwood's Magazine, 1817–25*.
McConnell, Anita, 'Kitchiner, William (1778–1827)', *Oxford Dictionary of National Biography* (Oxford: Oxford University Press, 2004).
McCracken-Flesher, Caroline, *Possible Scotlands: Walter Scott and the Story of Tomorrow* (Oxford: Oxford University Press, 2005).
McCreery, Cindy, 'Keeping Up with the Bon Ton: The Tête-à-Tête Series in the *Town and Country Magazine*', in Hannah Barker and Elain Chalus (eds), *Gender in Eighteenth-Century England: Roles, Representations and Responsibilities* (London: Longman, 1997), pp. 207–29.
McNeil, Kenneth, *Scotland, Britain, Empire: Writing the Highlands 1760–1860* (Columbus: Ohio State University Press, 2007).
Mee, Jon. 'The Buzz about the *Bee*: Policing the Conversation of Culture in the 1790s', in Alex Benchimol, Rhona Brown and David Shuttleton (eds), *Before* Blackwood's: *Scottish Journalism in the Age of Enlightenment* (London: Pickering & Chatto, 2015), pp. 63–74.
[Merivale, J. H.], 'Catholic Legends', *BEM* 5 (April 1819), pp. 52–5.
[—?], 'A European National Tribunal', *BEM* 6 (October 1819), pp. 45–6.

[—], 'Extracts from the "Prato Fiorito," on the Vice of Dancing', *BEM* 6 (October 1819), pp. 43–5.

[— ?], 'Louis XVIII and the French Royalists', *BEM* 6 (October 1819), pp. 42–3.

Millar, John, *The Origin of the Distinction of Ranks or, An Inquiry into the Circumstances Which Give Rise to Influence and Authority in the Different Members of Society*, 3rd edn (London: Murray, 1779).

Miller, J. Hillis, *Speech Acts in Literature* (Stanford: Stanford University Press, 2002).

Miller, Lucasta, 'The Brontës and the Periodicals of the 1820s and 1830s', in Diane Long Hoeveler and Deborah Denenholz Morse (eds), *A Companion to the Brontës* (Chichester: Wiley, 2016), pp. 283–301.

Milne, J. M., 'The Politics of *Blackwood's*, 1817–1846: A Study of Political, Economic and Social Articles in *Blackwood's Edinburgh Magazine* and of Selected Contributors', PhD Dissertation (Newcastle University, 1984).

Mitchell, Eleanor Drake, 'The Tête-à-Têtes in the *Town and Country Magazine* (1769–1793)', *Interpretations* 9 (1977), pp. 12–21.

Moir, D. M., Letter to William Blackwood, 20 November [1825?], NLS MS 4015.

—, Letter to William Blackwood, 26 January 1826, NLS MS 4018.

—, Letter to William Blackwood, April 1829, NLS MS 4025.

Mole, Tom, '*Blackwood's* "Personalities"', in Robert Morrison and Daniel S. Roberts (eds), *Romanticism and Blackwood's*, pp. 89–99.

— (ed.), *Selected Criticism, 1817–19*, vol. 5 of Mason (gen. ed.), *Blackwood's Magazine, 1817–25*.

—, '"We Solemnly Proscribe this Poem": Performative Utterances in the Romantic Periodicals', *European Romantic Review* 24: 3 (2013), pp. 353–62.

Moretti, Franco, *Distant Reading* (New York: Verso, 2013).

—, *Graphs, Maps, Trees: Abstract Models for Literary History* (New York: Verso, 2007).

Morrison, Robert, '"Abuse Wickedness, but Acknowledge Wit": *Blackwood's* and the Shelley Circle', *Victorian Periodicals Review* 34 (July 2001), pp. 147–64.

— (ed.), special issue on '*Blackwood's Edinburgh Magazine, 1817–2017*', *Romanticism* 23 (2017).

Morrison, Robert and Chris Baldick (eds), *Tales of Terror from* Blackwood's Magazine (Oxford and New York: Oxford University Press, 1995).

Morrison, Robert and Daniel Sanjiv Roberts, '"A character so various, and yet so indisputably its own": A Passage to *Blackwood's Edinburgh Magazine*', in Robert Morrison and Daniel S. Roberts (eds), *Romanticism and Blackwood's*, pp. 1–19.

— (eds), *Romanticism and Blackwood's Magazine: 'An Unprecedented Phenomenon'* (New York: Palgrave Macmillan, 2013).
Morton, Timothy, 'Introduction', in Timothy Morton (ed.), *Radical Food: The Cultural Politics of Eating and Drinking 1790–1820*, vol. 1 (London and New York: Routledge, 2000), pp. 1–32.
—, *The Poetics of Spice: Romantic Consumerism and the Exotic* (Cambridge: Cambridge University Press, 2006).
Murphy, Peter T., 'Impersonation and Authorship in Romantic Britain', *ELH* 59: 3 (1992), pp. 625–49.
Murray, Brian M., 'The Authorship of Some Unidentified or Disputed Articles in *Blackwood's Magazine*', *Studies in Scottish Literature* 4: 3 (1965), pp. 144–54.
Mussell, James, 'Beyond the "Great Index": Digital Resources and Actual Copies', in Joanne Shattock (ed.), *Journalism and the Periodical Press in Nineteenth-Century Britain* (Cambridge: Cambridge University Press, 2017), pp. 17–30.
—, 'Digitization', in Andrew King et al. (eds), *Routledge Handbook*, pp. 17–28.
—, *The Nineteenth-Century Press in the Digital Age* (New York: Palgrave Macmillan, 2012), pp. 44–67.
[Napier, Macvey], *Hypocrisy Unveiled, and Calumny Detected: In a Review of* Blackwood's Magazine (Edinburgh: Pillans, 1818).
Newbon, Pete, *The Boy-Man, Masculinity and Immaturity in the Long Nineteenth Century* (New York: Palgrave Macmillan, 2019).
Newlyn, Lucy, *Reading, Writing, and Romanticism: The Anxiety of Reception* (Oxford: Oxford University Press, 2000).
Niles, Lisa, '"May the married be single, and the single happy": *Blackwood's*, the *Maga* for the Single Man', in Kim Wheatley (ed.), *Romantic Periodicals and Print Culture* (London: Frank Cass, 2003), pp. 102–21.
Obeyesekere, Gananath, *Cannibal Talk: The Man-Eating Myth and Human Sacrifice in the South Seas* (Oakland: University of California Press, 2005).
Oliphant, Margaret, *Annals of a Publishing House. William Blackwood and His Sons, Their Magazine and Friends*, 2 vols (Edinburgh: Blackwood, 1897).
[—], 'In Maga's Library: The Old Saloon', *BEM* 141 (January 1887), pp. 126–53.
[—], 'The Life and Letters of George Eliot', *Edinburgh Review* 161 (April 1885), pp. 514–53.
[—], 'Macaulay', *BEM* 80 (August 1856), p. 127.
[—], 'New Books 23', *BEM* 126 (July 1879), p. 91.
Olson, Kristina M., *Courtesy Lost: Dante, Boccaccio, and the Literature of History* (Ontario: University of Toronto Press, 2014).

[Orlebar, Eleanor E.], 'Robert Southey's Second Wife', *Cornhill Magazine* 30 (August 1874), pp. 217–29.

Palmegiano, E. M., *Health and British Magazines in the Nineteenth Century* (Lanham, MD: Scarecrow Press, 1998).

Parker, Mark, *Literary Magazines and British Romanticism* (Cambridge: Cambridge University Press, 2000).

— (ed.), *Noctes Ambrosianae, 1822–3*, vol. 3 of Mason (gen. ed.), *Blackwood's Magazine, 1817–25*.

— (ed.), *Noctes Ambrosianae, 1824–5*, vol. 4 of Mason (gen. ed.), *Blackwood's Magazine, 1817–25*.

—, 'Repurposing and the Literary Magazine', *Studies in Romanticism* 56: 4 (2017), pp. 479–97.

Parsons, Nicola, 'Secret History and the Periodical', in Rebecca Bullard and Rachel Carnell (eds), *The Secret History*, pp. 147–59.

Perkins, Pam, '"She has her ladies too": Women and Scottish Periodical Culture in *Blackwood's* Early Years', *Romanticism* 23 (October 2017), pp. 253–61.

Peterson, Linda H., 'Nineteenth-Century Women Poets and Periodical Spaces: Letitia Landon and Felicia Hemans', *Victorian Periodicals Review* 49 (2016), pp. 396–414.

Pittock, Murray, *Celtic Identity and the British Image* (Manchester: Manchester University Press, 1999).

Poovey, Mary, 'Writing about Finance in Victorian England: Disclosure and Secrecy in the Culture of Investment', *Victorian Studies* 45 (2002), pp. 17–41.

Porter, Roy, 'Lay Medical Knowledge in the Eighteenth Century: The Evidence of the *Gentleman's Magazine*', *Medical History* 29 (1985), pp. 138–68.

Powell, Manushag N., 'New Directions in Eighteenth-Century Periodical Studies', *Literature Compass* 8/5 (2011), pp. 240–57.

Prince, Mary, *The History of Mary Prince* [1831], ed. Sara Salih (Harmondsworth: Penguin, 2000).

Pringle, Thomas, 'Supplement to the History of Mary Prince', in *The History of Mary Prince, A West Indian Slave* (London: Westley and Davis, 1831), pp. 24–40.

—, *The Poetical Works of Thomas Pringle* (London: Moxon, 1838).

Pringle, Thomas, Letter to Walter Scott, 1821, NLS MS 3892.67–8.

—, 'Letters from South Africa. No. I. – Slavery', *New Monthly Magazine* 17 (November 1826), pp. 481–8.

—, *Narrative of A Residence in South Africa* (London: Edward Moxon, 1835).

Pringle, Thomas, Letter to William Blackwood, 2 July 1817, NLS MS 4002.

—, Letter to William Blackwood, 2 July 1817, NLS MS 4002.

—, Letter to William Blackwood, 8 November 1833, NLS MS 30969.

—, Letter to Walter Scott, NLS MS 3892.

Rabb, Melinda, *Satire and Secrecy in English Literature from 1650 to 1750* (New York: Palgrave Macmillan, 2007).

Reiman, Donald H. (ed.), *The Romantics Reviewed: Contemporary Reviews of British Romantic Writers*, 9 vols (New York: Garland Publications, 1972).

Rejack, Brian, '*Blackwood's Magazine* and the "Schooling" of Taste', *European Romantic Review* 24: 6 (2013), pp. 723–42.

Richards, Eric, *The Highland Clearances: People, Landlords, and Rural Turmoil* (Edinburgh: Birlinn, 2016).

—, *Patrick Sellar and the Highland Clearances: Homicide, Eviction and the Price of Progress* (Edinburgh: Polygon, 1999).

Richardson, Thomas (ed.), *Contributions to Blackwood's Magazine*, Vol. 1: *1817–1828* (Edinburgh: Edinburgh University Press, 2008).

Roberts, Daniel Sanjiv, 'Mediating Indian Literature in the Age of Empire: *Blackwood's* and Orientalism', in Robert Morrison and Daniel S. Roberts (eds), *Romanticism and Blackwood's*, pp. 255–65.

Roberts, Jessica, 'Radical Contagion and Healthy Literature in *Blackwood's Edinburgh Magazine*', *Literature and Medicine* 34: 2 (Fall 2016), pp. 418–39.

Roe, Nicholas, *John Keats and the Culture of Dissent* (Oxford: Clarendon Press, 1997).

Rosenthal, Jesse, 'The Untrusted Medium: Open Networks, Secret Writing, and *Little Dorrit*', *Victorian Studies* 59 (2017), pp. 288–313.

Sala, G. A., 'The Cant of Modern Criticism', *Belgravia* 4 (November 1867), p. 47.

Schiller, F., 'Haslam of "Bedlam", Kitchiner of the "Oracles": Two Doctors under Mad King George III and Their Friendship', *Medical History* 28: 2 (1984), pp. 189–201.

Schlegel, Friedrich, *Lectures on the History of Literature, Ancient and Modern*, trans. John Gibson Lockhart, 2 vols (Edinburgh: Blackwood, 1818).

Schoenfield, Mark, *British Periodicals and Romantic Identity: The 'Literary Lower Empire'* (New York: Palgrave Macmillan, 2009).

—, 'Butchering James Hogg: Romantic Identity in the Magazine Market', in Mary Favret and Nicola Watson (eds), *At the Limits of Romanticism: Essays in Cultural, Feminist, and Materialist Criticism* (Bloomington: Indiana University Press, 1994), pp. 207–24.

—, 'Periodical Auto-Biography: Theories and Representations', *Wordsworth Circle* 46: 2 (2015), pp. 93–102.

—, 'The Taste for Violence in *Blackwood's Magazine*', in Robert Morrison and Daniel S. Roberts (eds), *Romanticism and Blackwood's*, pp. 187–200.

Scholes, Robert and Clifford Wulfman, *Modernism in the Magazines: An Introduction* (New Haven, CT: Yale University Press, 2010).
Scott, Patrick, 'Victorian Religious Periodicals: Fragments that Remain', in Derek Baker (ed.), *The Materials, Sources, and Methods of Ecclesiastical History* (Oxford: Blackwell, 1975), pp. 325–39.
Scott, Walter, *Hints Addressed to the Inhabitants of Edinburgh . . . in Prospect of His Majesty's Visit, by an Old Citizen* (Edinburgh: Bell and Bradfute, 1822).
[—], Review of *Emma* by Jane Austen, *Quarterly Review* 14 (October 1815), pp. 188–201.
[—], Review of *Frankenstein* by Mary Shelley, *BEM* 2 (March 1818), pp. 613–20.
[Scott, Walter and Thomas Pringle], 'Notices concerning the Scottish Gypsies', *Edinburgh Monthly Magazine* 1 (April 1817), pp. 43–58.
Shattock, Joanne, 'The Culture of Criticism', in Joanne Shattock (ed.), *The Cambridge Companion to English Literature 1830–1914* (Cambridge: Cambridge University Press, 2010), pp. 84–7.
—, headnote to 'Macaulay', in Joanne Shattock and Elisabeth Jay (eds), *Selected Works*, vol. 13, pp. 49–50.
—, 'The Sense of Place and *Blackwood's (Edinburgh) Magazine*', *Victorian Periodicals Review* 49 (2016), pp. 431–42.
Shattock, Joanne and Elisabeth Jay (eds), *Selected Works of Margaret Oliphant*, 25 vols, (London: Pickering & Chatto and Routledge, 2011–16).
Shuttleworth, Sally, *Charlotte Brontë and Victorian Psychology* (Cambridge: Cambridge University Press, 1996).
Siskin, Clifford, *The Work of Writing: Literature and Social Change in Britain 1700–1830* (Baltimore: Johns Hopkins University Press, 1998).
Smiles, Samuel, *A Publisher and His Friends: Memoir and Correspondence of the Late John Murray*, 2 vols (London: John Murray, 1891).
Smith, Adam, 'Lectures on Jurisprudence', in R. L. Meek, D. D. Raphael and P. G. Stein (eds) *The Glasgow Edition of the Works and Correspondence of Adam Smith*, vol. 5 (Oxford: Clarendon Press, 1978).
Smith, Sydney, *The Works of the Rev. Sydney Smith*, vol. 1 (London: Longman, Orme, Brown and Green, 1839).
Southey, Robert, *The Collected Letters of Robert Southey*, general eds Lynda Pratt, Tim Fulford and Ian Packer (Romantic Circles, 2016), https://romantic-circles.org/editions/southey_letters (last accessed 28 February 2020).
Starke, Mr, 'Vox Populi', *BEM* 13 (January 1823), pp. 125–8.
Stauffer, Andrew, 'My *Old Sweethearts:* On Digitization and the Future of the Print Record', in Matthew K. Gold and Lauren F. Klein (eds), *Debates in the Digital Humanities 2016* (Minneapolis: University of Minnesota Press, 2016), pp. 218–29.

[St Barbe, R. F.], 'Another Ladleful from the Devil's Punch Bowl', BEM 11 (February 1822), pp. 159–60.
—, Letter to William Blackwood, 26 November 1821, NLS MS 4007.
[—], Review of *A Widow's Tale and Other Poems* by Caroline Bowles, BEM 11 (March 1822), pp. 286–90.
Stewart, Col. David, *Sketches of the Character, Manners, and Present State of the Highlanders of Scotland*, 3rd edn (Edinburgh: Constable, 1822).
Stewart, David, 'Blackwoodian Allusion and the Culture of Miscellaneity', in Robert Morrison and Daniel S. Roberts (eds), *Romanticism and Blackwood's*, pp. 113–23.
—, *Romantic Magazines and Metropolitan Literary Culture* (New York: Palgrave Macmillan, 2011).
—, '"WE ARE ABSOLUTELY COINING MONEY": Commerce, Literature and the Magazine Style of the 1810s and '20s', *Nineteenth-Century Contexts* 30 (2008), pp. 21–36.
Strachan, John, 'Fighting Sports and Late Georgian Periodical Culture', in Simon P. Hull (ed.), *British Periodical Text, 1797–1835: A Collection of Essays* (Tirril: Humanities-Ebooks, 2008), pp. 143–69.
—, 'John Wilson and Sport', in Robert Morrison and Daniel S. Roberts (eds), *Romanticism and Blackwood's,* pp. 215–25.
— (ed.), with Nicholas Mason, Tom Mole and Charles Snodgrass, *Selected Criticism, 1820–25*, vol. 6 of Mason (gen. ed.), *Blackwood's Magazine, 1817–25*.
Strout, Alan Lang, *A Bibliography of Articles in Blackwood's Magazine, 1817–1825* (Lubbock: Texas Technological College Library, 1959).
Sullivan, Alvin (ed.), 'Preface', in *British Literary Magazines: The Romantic Age, 1789–1836* (Westport, CT: Greenwood, 1983), pp. vii–xi.
Sutherland, John, *The Longman Companion to Victorian Fiction*, 2nd edn (Harlow: Pearson Longman, 2009).
—, *Victorian Novelists & Publishers* (London: Athlone Press, 1976).
Sweet, Nanora, 'All Work and All Play: Felicia Hemans's Edinburgh *Noctes*', in Robert Morrison and Daniel S. Roberts (eds), *Romanticism and Blackwood's*, pp. 239–51.
Swift, Jonathan, *Journal to Stella*, ed. Harold Williams, 2 vols (Oxford: Clarendon Press, 1948).
Taves, Ann, *Fits, Trances, and Visions: Experiencing Religion and Explaining Experience from Wesley to James* (Princeton: Princeton University Press, 2000).
Thomas, Sue, 'Pringle v. Cadell and Wood v. Pringle: The Libel Cases over *The History of Mary Prince*', *Journal of Commonwealth Literature* 40 (2005), pp. 113–35.

Thompson, E. P., *The Making of the English Working Class* (New York: Viking, 1964).

[Thomson, Henry], 'Letter from a Contributor in Love', *BEM* 14 (October 1823), pp. 471–3.

Thrall, Miriam M. H., *Rebellious Fraser's* (New York: Columbia University Press, 1934).

Todorova, Kremena, '"I Will Say the Truth to the English People": *The History of Mary Prince* and the Meaning of English History', *Texas Studies in Literature and Language* 43: 3 (Fall 2001), pp. 285–302.

Tredrey, F. D., *The House of Blackwood, 1804–1954: The History of a Publishing Firm* (Edinburgh: Blackwood, 1954).

Trumpener, Katie, *Bardic Nationalism: The Romantic Novel and the British Empire* (Princeton: Princeton University Press, 1997).

Tytler of Woodhouselee, Lord Alexander Fraser (ed.), *The Decisions of the Court of Session: From Its First Institution to the Present Time*, vol. 4 (Edinburgh: William Creech, 1797).

[Utterson, E.?], 'Singular Anecdote', *BEM* 4 (December 1818), pp. 330–2.

Van-Ess, Willem Lodewyk, *The Life of Napoleon Buonaparte*, vol. 2 (London: M. Jones, 1809).

Vary, Mr, 'Essays of Cranioscopy, Craniology, Etc.', *BEM* 10 (August 1821), pp. 73–82.

Venn, John (ed.), *Alumni Cantabrigienses: A Biographical List of All Known Students, Graduates and Holders of Office at the University of Cambridge, from the Earliest Times to 1900*, 2 vols [1940] (Cambridge: Cambridge University Press, 2011).

Vigne, Randolph, *Thomas Pringle: South African Pioneer, Poet and Abolitionist* (Woodbridge: James Currey, 2012).

[Wainewright, Thomas], 'Sentimentalities on the Fine Arts by Janus Weathercock, Esq.', *London Magazine* 1: 3 (1820), pp. 285–9.

Wallace, Jennifer, *Shelley and Greece: Rethinking Romantic Hellenism* (New York: Palgrave Macmillan, 1997).

Ward, William S., *Index and Finding List of Serials Published in the British Isles, 1789–1832* (Lexington: University of Kentucky Press, 1953).

Wardle, Ralph M., 'The Authorship of the *Noctes Ambrosianae*', *Modern Philology* 42 (August 1944), pp. 9–17.

Watts, Alaric, Letter to William Blackwood, 8 March 1823, NLS MS 4011.

Westover, Paul, 'At Home in the Churchyard: Graves, Localism, and Literary Heritage in the Prose Pastoral', in Evan Gottlieb and Juliet Shields (eds), *Representing Place in British Literature and Culture, 1660–1830: From Local to Global* (Farnham: Ashgate, 2013), pp. 65–81.

Wheatley, Kim, *Romantic Feuds: Transcending the 'Age of Personality'* (Burlington, VT: Ashgate, 2013).

— (ed.), *Romantic Periodicals and Print Culture* (London: Frank Cass, 2003).

Whyte, Iain, *Scotland and the Abolition of Black Slavery, 1756–1838* (Edinburgh: Edinburgh University Press, 2006).

Williams, Raymond, *The Long Revolution* [1961] (Ontario: Broadview Press, 2001).

[Wilson, John], 'Burns and the Ettrick Shepherd', *BEM* 4 (February 1819), pp. 521–9.

[—], 'Clark on Climate', *BEM* 28 (August 1830), pp. 372–81.

[—], 'Essays on the Lake School of Poetry, No. III – Mr Coleridge', *BEM* 6 (October 1819), pp. 3–12.

[—], 'Hazlitt Cross-Questioned', *BEM* 3 (August 1818), pp. 550–2.

[—], 'Health and Longevity', *BEM* 23 (January 1828), pp. 96–111.

[—], 'An Hour's Tete-a-Tete with the Public', *BEM* 8 (October 1820), pp. 78–105.

[—], 'Is the Edinburgh Review a Religious and Patriotic Work?', *BEM* 4 (November 1818), pp. 228–32.

[—], 'The King', *BEM* 12 (September 1822), pp. 253–67.

[—], 'Letters from the Lakes', *BEM* 4 (January 1819), pp. 396–404.

[—], 'Letter to Lord Byron', *BEM* 9 (July 1821), pp. 421–6.

—, *Lights and Shadows of Scottish Life* (Edinburgh: Blackwood, 1822).

[—], 'Noctes Ambrosianae, No. II', *BEM* 11 (April 1822), pp. 475–89.

[—], 'Noctes Ambrosianae, No. V', *BEM* 12 (September 1822), pp. 369–91.

[—], 'Noctes Ambrosianae, No. XXI', *BEM* 18 (September 1825), pp. 378–92.

[—], 'Noctes Ambrosianae, No. XXII', *BEM* 18 (October 1825), pp. 500–8.

[—], 'Noctes Ambrosianae, No. XLVIII', *BEM* 27 (April 1830), pp. 659–94.

[—], 'Noctes Ambrosianae, No. LI', *BEM* 28 (August 1830), pp. 383–436.

[—], 'Observations on Coleridge's Biographia Literaria', *BEM* 2 (October 1817), pp. 3–18.

[—], 'Old North and Young North, or Christopher in Edinburgh, and Christopher in London', *BEM* 23 (June 1828), pp. 803–21.

[—?], 'On the State of Religion in the Highlands of Scotland', *BEM* 5 (May 1819), pp. 136–47.

[—], 'Pilgrimage to the Kirk of Shotts', *BEM* 6 (September 1819), pp. 671–80.

—, *The Recreations of Christopher North*, 3 vols (Edinburgh and London: William Blackwood and Sons, 1842).

—, 'Remarks on the Scenery of the Highlands', in John M. Leighton, *Swan's Views of the Lakes of Scotland*, 2nd edn (Glasgow: Swan, 1837), pp. i–lii.

[—], Review of *Letter to Lord Byron*, *BEM* 9 (July 1821), pp. 421–7.

[—], 'Salmonia', *BEM* 24 (August 1828), pp. 248–72.

[—], 'Streams', *BEM* 19 (April 1826), pp. 375–403.

[—], 'The Traveller's Oracle', *BEM* 22 (October 1827), pp. 445–64.
[Wilson, John, John Galt, David Robinson and William Maginn], 'Preface', *BEM* 19 (January 1826), pp. i–xxx.
Wolfe, Thomas, *You Can't Go Home Again* (New York: Harper, 1940).
Womack, Peter, *Romance and Improvement and Romance: Constructing the Myth of the Highlands* (London: Macmillan, 1988).
Woodward, Sir Llewellyn, *The Age of Reform, 1815–1870,* 2nd edn (Oxford: Clarendon Press, 1962).
Wordsworth, William, *Lyrical Ballads, and Other Poems, 1797–1800,* ed. James Butler and Karen Green (Ithaca, NY: Cornell University Press, 1992).
—, 'Preface', in *Lyrical Ballads, with Pastoral and Other Poems*, 3rd edn, vol. 1 (London: Longman, 1802), pp. i–lxiv.
Wu, Duncan, *William Hazlitt: The First Modern Man* (Oxford: Oxford University Press, 2010).

Index

abolitionism, 183–4, 187–93, 198–201
Addison, Joseph, 117, 134n
Adventurer, The, 117
advertisements, 18, 21, 23, 32n, 130, 235–6
Alexander, J. H., 50, 89
Alison, Archibald, 230, 236
All the Year Round, 228
American Antiquarian Society Historical Periodicals, 19, 21
Anti-Jacobin Review, 5
Anti-Slavery Reporter, 190
Argosy, 234
Auckinleck, Lord, 192–3
Auerbach, Eric, 22
Austin, J. L., 61–2, 63, 77–80, 82–3, 90, 93
authorship, modes of
 anonymity, 41–2, 85, 99, 118, 128, 169–70, 180n, 230, 234, 236, 242, 244
 collaboration, 98–9
 identity theft, 77, 88–92
 pseudonymity, 77–8, 99, 128, 170; see also *Blackwood's Edinburgh Magazine*, personae in
 signed, 238
Aytoun, W. E., 230, 236

Bakhtin, Mikhail, 99
Baldwin, Robert, 64, 196
Ballardini, Giuseppe, 208–15

Barrett, Elizabeth, 230
Baumgartner, Barbara, 184, 188
Beacon, The, 129, 135n
Bedham, Charles, 34
Belgravia, 234
Benedict, Barbara, 208
Bentley's Miscellany, 241
binding of serials, 18, 23–4, 29
Black Dwarf, 68
Blackmore, R. D., 233
Blackstone, William, 61, 62–3
Blackwood, Alexander, 230
Blackwood, John, 228–37, 239
Blackwood, Major William, 236–7, 239
Blackwood, William, 7–9, 12n, 34, 58–60, 64, 69, 80, 100, 109, 114n, 122, 128–9, 161–3, 165, 167–75, 183, 190, 196–8, 199–200, 224n, 228–9, 230, 231, 241
Blackwood, William III, 237–9, 241
Blackwood's Edinburgh Magazine
 anti-abolitionism, 183–4, 190–2
 appeals to secrecy, intimacy and exposure, 116–31
 Conservative/Tory agendas, 8–9, 39–40, 45–6, 60, 65, 80–1, 90–1, 93, 99, 104, 122, 141, 155, 161–2, 168, 169, 176, 184, 186, 196, 198–9, 208, 212–14, 229, 231, 234, 235

Blackwood's Edinburgh (cont.)
  counter-Enlightenment agenda, 99–100, 101–4
  dialogism, 42–3, 98–9, 105–6, 112–13, 220, 223
  legalistic style, 59, 68–70
  libellous rhetoric, 71–3
  'Maga' nickname, 9
  masculine ethos, 69, 141, 161–5
  medical/scientific discourse, 33–6, 38–51, 127–8
  nationalism, 100–1, 103–5, 107, 111, 139, 141, 150, 153, 155, 185–7, 212–15
  organ for Blackwood and Sons, 235–6, 240–1
  originality and influence, 9, 33, 34, 35, 40, 164, 227–8, 229, 236, 241–2
  origins and early history, 7–10, 12–13n
  pastoralist discourse on Highlands, 138–9, 141–8, 151–5
  polarised responses to, 2, 9–10, 59, 69
  post-Romantic evolution, 227–42
  promotion of foreign literature, 6, 10, 99–100
  Protestant/anti-Catholic agenda, 208, 210–15, 223
  self-mythologising, 9, 48, 106, 114n, 123–5
  women contributors, 162–5, 172–8, 230, 231, 232–3, 238
Blackwood's Edinburgh Magazine, personae in
  Bob Buller of Brazennose, 152, 158
  Christopher North, 5, 45, 47–50, 53n, 84–5, 87, 88, 89, 90, 92, 117, 123–5, 128, 132n, 137–8, 143, 147, 148, 152, 175, 177, 186, 227, 236
  Ebony, 122, 148
  Morgan Odoherty, 45, 132n, 146, 148, 152, 164, 227
  Patience Lilywhite, 175–7
  Philip Kempferhausen, 168
  strategic uses of, 76–93, 121
  The Ettrick Shepherd, 88–92, 130, 137, 142–3, 145, 186
  The Opium Eater, 85–7, 88, 92, 94n
  Timothy Tickler, 47, 59, 90, 137, 146, 147, 227
  Z., 8, 68–70, 72, 109–13
Blackwood's Edinburgh Magazine, works in
  attacks on 'Cockney School', 8, 59, 64, 68–70, 72, 105–13, 114n, 135n, 173–8
  commentary on 'Lake Poets', 2, 8, 9, 70, 72, 105, 121, 141, 168
  confessions, 126–31
  fiction, 169, 172–3, 230–4
  Noctes Ambrosianae, 9, 42, 45, 46, 47, 59, 72, 80–92, 98–9, 119, 133n, 137–8, 146–8, 152, 164, 173, 186, 228, 236–7, 239
  non-fiction essays, 40, 172–3
  poetry, 168–70, 173, 177
  prose pastoral, 142–3, 148–9
  satires, 8–9, 45, 99, 105–13, 122, 130, 173–8, 197–8
  tales of terror, 40–1
  'The Tent' issue, 128–9, 158, 164
  translated extracts, 208–15
  'Translation of an Ancient Chaldee Manuscript', 8–9, 59, 72, 89, 105–6, 114n, 121–3, 131, 132n, 133n, 197–8, 210
Blain, Virginia, 162
Borthwick, John, 63
Bowles, Caroline, 161–2, 165–78, 180n, 230
Bowles, William Lisle, 175

Braddon, Elizabeth, 229
Brake, Lauren, 228, 234–5
Bray, Anna Elizabeth, 230
Bridge, Tom, 44
British Critic, 163
British Periodicals (ProQuest), 18–19, 20, 21–2, 25, 26, 27, 37, 43, 45
Broglio, Ron, 149
Brougham, Henry, 59, 63
Brown, Rhona, 185
Buckingham, James Silk, 131
Budge, Gavin, 50
Bullard, Rebecca, 118
Bulwer-Lytton, Edward, 170, 230, 231, 234, 236
Burgess, Miranda, 119
Burke, Edmund, 22, 39, 102, 104
Burns, Robert, 142, 144, 185
Burton, John Hill, 234
Busk, Mary Margaret, 230
Byron, Lord George Gordon, 1, 2, 57–8, 83–4, 89, 92, 109

C19: The Nineteenth Century Index, 21
Cadell, Thomas, 60, 64, 199–200
Calcutta Journal, 131
Cantor, Geoffrey, 35
Carnell, Rachel, 118
Chambers's Edinburgh Journal, 143
Christie, Jonathan, 76, 135n
Christie, William, 3
Cleghorn, James, 8, 12n, 68, 98, 116, 196–7
Clive, Caroline, 230
Cobbett, William, 4
Coleridge, Samuel Taylor, 2, 8, 59–60, 70, 72, 75n, 94n, 102, 104–6, 121, 161, 180n
Collins, William Lucas, 230

Connell, Philip, 39
Conrad, Joseph, 238, 240
Constable, Archibald, 35, 44, 122, 139, 140, 143, 149, 152, 163, 197
Contemporary Review, 228, 235
Cooper, Colin, 44
Cornhill Magazine, 177–8, 228, 232–4, 240
Cox, Jeffrey, 110
Coyer, Megan, 3, 58
Croker, John Wilson, 3, 162
Croly, George, 161, 230
Cronin, Richard, 3, 47, 58, 82
Cruikshank, George, 25

Dallas, E. S., 234
Dalyell, John, 59
Dart, Gregory, 175–6
Davies, William, 59–60, 64
Davis, Angela, 191
Davy, Sir Humphry, 46–8
De Man, Paul, 78
De Quincey, Thomas, 85–7, 92, 94n, 126, 161, 173, 230
Deans, Alex, 143
Delane, J. T., 231
Derrida, Jacques, 78, 131
Dibdin, Thomas Frognall, 26
Dickens, Charles, 228, 231
Dictionary of Nineteenth-Century Journalism, 5
digital databases
  browsing, 22–6, 29–30, 50
  'distant reading', 6–7, 12n, 26, 28
  organisation by article vs volume, 19, 21, 23–6
  quantitative modelling and 'data mining', 6, 28, 42
  searching, 6–7, 17–22, 26–8, 36–42, 50–1
Dodd, Charles Edward, 66–8

Index

Dodson, Charles Brooks, 216
Doubleday, Thomas, 161
Douglas, John, 69
Drew, Samuel, 216
Duncan, Ian, 35, 141

Early English Books Online, 24
Edinburgh Literary Journal, 91
Edinburgh Magazine and Literary Miscellany, 33, 35, 196
Edinburgh Medical and Surgical Journal, 39
Edinburgh Monthly Magazine see *Blackwood's Edinburgh Magazine*: origins and early history
Edinburgh Review, 1, 3, 8, 9, 33, 35, 57, 59, 63, 65, 97, 106, 107, 109, 114n, 134n, 139–40, 141, 144, 154, 163, 164, 165, 185, 196, 225n
Eighteenth-Century Collections Online (ECCO), 17, 19, 20, 24, 27
Eighteenth Century Journals, 20, 27, 28
Eliot, George, 231, 232–3, 236, 237
Empson, William, 141
Examiner, The, 2, 5, 60, 63, 72, 131, 163

Fang, Karen, 3
Farmer's Magazine, 139, 140
Ferguson, Adam, 145–6
Finkelstein, David, 126, 134n, 227, 232, 238
Flynn, Philip, 122, 207
Fortnightly, The, 228, 234–5
Foss, Edward, 200
Franklin-Brown, Mary, 209, 223
Fraser's Magazine, 3, 17, 77, 91, 131, 228, 235, 240, 241

Friend, The, 2
Fyfe, Paul, 51

Galt, John, 161, 211
Gentleman's Magazine, 23, 84
George IV, 147–8, 150, 186–7
Gifford, William, 5
Gillies, R. P., 122
Glasgow Courier, 190, 193, 199
Gooch, Robert, 34, 37, 38–40
Google Books, 8, 17, 19, 20, 25, 27, 28, 30, 52n
Gore, Catherine, 230
Grafton, Anthony, 18
Graham, Thomas John, 47–50
Graham, Walter, 19
Grant, Anne, 165

Habermas, Jürgen, 19
Hamilton, Thomas, 161
Hardman, Frederick, 230
HathiTrust Digital Library, 19, 20, 21, 24, 25, 27, 28, 52n
Hayden, John O., 3
Hazlitt, William, 2, 4, 22, 59, 68–9, 77, 92, 97, 109, 116, 127, 132n, 135n, 173
Hemans, Felicia, 1, 162, 165, 169, 180n
Hempton, David, 217
Higgins, David, 3, 126
History of Women's Periodical Culture in Britain, 5
Hogg, James, 2, 8–9, 12n, 69, 77, 87, 88–92, 98, 118, 119–20, 128, 129–31, 135–6n, 137, 142–4, 146, 148–9, 156n, 161, 167, 173, 195–6, 197
Holt, Thomas Ludlow, 65
Hood, Thomas, 177
Household Words, 228
Howison, John, 40

Hughes, Gillian, 195–6
Hughes, Linda, 42
Hughes, Thomas, 233
Hunt, John, 5, 60, 64
Hunt, Leigh, 1, 2–3, 4, 8, 59, 60, 68–70, 72, 84, 97–8, 106–12, 114n, 115n, 127, 131, 135n, 173–7

Imperial Magazine, 208, 215–23

Jarrells, Anthony, 149
Jefferies, George, 57
Jeffrey, Francis, 3, 9, 57, 59, 109, 128, 135n, 141
Jerdan, William, 5, 44
Jerrold, Douglas, 230
Jockers, Matthew, 6
John Bull Magazine, 86
Johnstone, Christian Isobel, 185–6
Journalism and the Periodical Press in Nineteenth-Century Britain, 5

Kant, Immanuel, 102
Keats, John, 1, 2, 9, 97–8, 110, 127
Kermode, Frank, 141
Killick, Tim, 40
Kitchiner, William, 36, 42–51
Klancher, Jon, 3, 33–4, 61, 117
Knight, Joseph, 192, 193

La Belle Assemblée, 25
Lady's Magazine, 20, 25, 31–2n, 163
Lady's Monthly Museum, 25
Laidlaw, William, 51n, 148
Lamb, Charles, 4, 77, 81, 116, 173
Lambert, David, 190
Landon, Letitia, 1, 5, 169–70
Langford, Joseph, 237
Laqueur, Thomas, 220

Latané, David, 48, 227
Latham, Seth, 23
Lawrence, Hannah, 230
Lawrence, Lindsy, 165
Leary, Patrick, 37
Lessenich, Rolf, 47–8
Lever, Charles, 233
Levinson, Marjorie, 110
Lewes, George Henry, 230, 232, 234
libel law, 60–5, 199–200
Liberal, The, 2, 174
Literary Gazette, 5, 44, 169–70, 203n
literary periodicals, eighteenth-century, 4, 84, 117, 119, 123
literary periodicals, general
  print vs digital collections, 17–31
  problems of remediation, 23, 25, 28, 37
  rhetoric of intimacy in, 117–19, 123–31
  tools for searching, 20–1, 28, 33, 36–8
  units of study, 18, 20, 24–5, 29–30
literary periodicals, Romantic
  distinctiveness of, 20, 29, 33–4, 48
  extracted content in, 207–23
  golden age for genre, 1–2, 8–9
  leading scholarship on, 3, 17–20, 31n, 33–4
  medical and scientific discourse in, 33–51
  methods for researching, 17–31, 33–42
  miscellanies vs specialised serials, 26, 35, 40–1, 235, 242
  need for sustained attention to, 4–7, 29, 228–9
  performativity in, 78–83
  political and ideological biases of, 38–40, 97, 163

literary periodicals, Romantic (*cont.*)
  scholarly neglect of, 2–5
  women contributors to, 164–5,
    168–78, 230
literary periodicals, Victorian, 4,
    227–42
literary studies in the twenty-first
    century, 6–7
Lockhart, John Gibson, 5, 8–9, 59,
    68–70, 72, 76, 88, 89, 92,
    98–113, 115n, 128, 132n,
    135n, 146, 161, 164, 170,
    172, 185, 187, 195, 197, 238
Lodge, Sara, 177
London Magazine, 43, 76, 77, 81–2,
    85–6, 97, 126, 131, 135n, 228
London Society, 234
London Spy, 117

Mack, Douglas, 88
Mackenzie, R. Shelton, 122
Mackenzie, Scott, 128–9
Mackillop, Andrew, 150
Maclean, Charles, 39
Macmichael, William, 38
Macmillan's Magazine, 228,
    232–4
McNeil, Kenneth, 150
Macnish, Robert, 40, 47
Macpherson, James, 146, 148
MacQueen, James, 183, 190–5,
    197, 198–201
Madison-MacFadyen, Margo, 191
Maginn, William, 69, 86, 89, 91,
    98, 99, 113n, 148, 161, 170,
    172, 174, 230
Menippean satire, 99, 105–13
Merivale, J. H., 164, 208–15, 219,
    224n
Millar, John, 146
Miller, Lucasta, 164
Modernists Journals Project, 30

Moir, David Macbeth ('Delta'), 34,
    41–2, 47, 58, 161, 180n, 230,
    236, 239
Moir, George, 230, 236
Mole, Tom, 121
Moore, Thomas, 109, 110
Moretti, Franco, 6, 12n
Morrison, Robert, 12, 20
Morton, Timothy, 90
Murphy, Peter, 76
Murray, John, 2, 64, 164, 166–8,
    197
Mussell, James, 24, 38

Napier, Macvey, 9, 163–4, 179n
National Review, 235
Neaves, Charles, 230, 236
New Monthly Magazine, 3, 43,
    151, 194, 241
Newlyn, Lucy, 2
Niles, Lisa, 164–5
Nineteenth Century, 228, 235

Obeysekere, Gananath, 222
Oliphant, Lawrence, 233
Oliphant, Margaret, 64, 161–2,
    164–5, 179n, 196, 228, 229–30,
    231, 233, 237, 238–40
Onslow, Arthur, 210–11

Palmegiano, E. M., 36
Parker, Mark, 3, 26, 33–4, 42, 76–7
Parsons, Nicola, 119, 123
Perkins, Pam, 165
Phillips, Samuel, 230
Piper, Andrew, 6
*Poole's Index to Periodical
    Literature*, 20, 36
Poovey, Mary, 125–6
Price, Bonany, 234
Prince, Mary, 183–5, 187–95, 197,
    198–201

Pringle, Thomas, 8, 12n, 68, 98, 116, 119, 129, 183–4, 188–201
prose non-fiction, 6

Quarterly Review, 1, 3, 5, 8, 38, 39, 65–8, 69, 70, 71, 76, 101, 118, 128, 134, 163, 167, 185, 208

Rabb, Melinda, 131
Rambler, The, 4, 117
Ramsay, Stephen, 6
Reade, Charles, 233
Reiman, Donald H., 3
Rejack, Brian, 45
Research Society for Victorian Periodicals, 4
reviews (in periodicals)
  authority and influence of, 2–3, 57–8
  legalistic style, 58, 65–73
  milestones in, 1–2, 9
  regulatory intent, 60, 66, 72–3, 207
Roberts, Daniel Sanjiv, 20
Roberts, Jessica, 39–40
Robinson, Mary, 1
Roe, Nicholas, 110
Rosenthal, Jesse, 131
Routledge Handbook to Nineteenth-Century British Periodicals, 4–5, 32n

St Barbe, R. F., 171
St James's Magazine, 234
Saint Paul's, 234
Sala, G. A., 229, 234
Schlegel, Friedrich, 87, 100–9, 111–13, 113n
Schoenfeld, Mark, 3, 26–8, 75n, 88, 207, 209, 218
Scholes, Robert, 23

Science in the Nineteenth-Century Periodical, 33, 37
Scotland, history and culture
  attitudes toward slavery, 192–3, 200–1
  Enlightenment, 139–40, 145
  Highland Clearances, 137–9, 140–1, 143, 144–5, 148–50, 152, 154–5, 155n, 185
  legal statutes and history, 59, 63–4
  nationalism and identity, 88–9, 101, 105–6, 141, 145–6, 155, 184–7
  notions of home in, 184–7
  rural culture and economics, 137–40, 149, 185
Scots Magazine, 33, 133n, 140, 143, 146, 196
Scotsman, The, 186
Scott, John, 76, 135n
Scott, Patrick, 216
Scott, Sir Walter, 1, 59, 88, 105–8, 111, 119, 125, 128–9, 135n, 143, 145, 150, 151, 185–7, 195
Scourge, The, 25
Scribner's Journal, 30
Sellar, Peter, 151
Shattock, Joanne, 141
Shelley, Percy Bysshe, 2, 47, 70, 83–4, 173–7
Shuttleworth, Sally, 34, 35
Siskin, Clifford, 139
Smith, George, 232–3, 235
Smith, Sydney, 60
Smith, Thomas Southwood, 39
Smith, William Henry, 230
South African Commercial Advertiser, 206
Southey, Caroline Bowles *see* Bowles, Caroline

Southey, Robert, 1, 2, 34, 162, 166–8, 170–2, 174–5, 176, 178
Spectator, The, 4, 32, 117, 132n, 134n, 163
Spy, The, 2, 88–9, 118
Starkie, Thomas, 65
Stauffer, Andrew, 24
Steele, Richard, 117
Stewart, Col. David, 150–4
Stewart, David, 3, 50, 84–5, 124, 165, 207, 215
Strickland, Susanna, 184
Strout, Alan Lang, 36, 41, 135n, 173–4
Sullivan, Alvin, 1
Sutherland, Marquis and Marquise of, 151, 152
Sweet, Nanora, 169
Swift, Jonathan, 163

Tait's Edinburgh Magazine, 86, 185, 241
Tatler, The, 4, 117
Temple Bar, 234
Thackeray, William Makepeace, 231, 233
Thompson, E. P., 19
Tinsley's Magazine, 234
Todorova, Kremena, 185
Town and Country Magazine, 123

Trollope, Anthony, 233–4, 236
Trumpener, Katie, 154

Underwood, Ted, 6

Victoria Magazine, 234
Victorian Periodicals Review, 4
Vigne, Randolph, 184, 196
Voyant Tools, 28

Ward, William, 21
Warren, Samuel, 40–1, 230, 236
Watchman, The, 2
Watts, Alaric, 177
Wellesley Index of Victorian Periodicals, 4, 20–1, 36, 41, 50–1, 235, 240
Westminster Review, 39
Westover, Paul, 142
Wheatley, Kim, 3, 76, 121
Whyte, Iain, 193
Williams, Raymond, 19
Wilson, John, 5, 8–9, 36–7, 42–51, 59, 69, 70, 72, 86, 88, 89, 91, 92, 98–9, 105–6, 107, 123, 124, 128, 142–5, 148–9, 153, 154, 161, 164, 167–8, 170, 172, 191, 195, 197, 230, 236–7, 239
Wooler, T. J., 68
Wordsworth, William, 2, 3, 9, 102, 109, 110, 141, 148, 167

EU representative:
Easy Access System Europe
Mustamäe tee 50, 10621 Tallinn, Estonia
Gpsr.requests@easproject.com

www.ingramcontent.com/pod-product-compliance
Lightning Source LLC
Chambersburg PA
CBHW071830230426
43672CB00013B/2800